A MIRROR TO POWER

A MIRROR TO POWER

NOTES ON A FRACTURED DECADE

M.J. Akbar

HarperCollins *Publishers* India

First published India by
HarperCollins *Publishers* in 2015
An imprint of HarperCollins Publishers
HarperCollins *Publishers* India, Cyber City, Building 10-A, Gurugram, Haryana-122002, India
www.harpercollins.co.in

2

P-ISBN: 9789350296837
E-ISBN: 9789350296844

Typeset 12/15 Adobe Garamond by
SÜRYA

Printed and bound at
Manipal Technologies Limited, Manipal

MIX
Paper | Supporting responsible forestry
FSC® C043100

This book is produced from independently certified FSC™ paper
to ensure responsible forest management.

HarperCollins *Publishers*, Macken House, 39/40 Mayor Street Upper, Dublin 1, D01 C9W8, Ireland

For
Nikki & Mark Nordenberg
and
Sonia & Gopal S.J.B. Rana

CONTENTS

INTRODUCTION

Journalists do a serious job. Should they take themselves equally seriously? There is, one appreciates, the relentless pressure to pose as a hero, not least before a mirror. But those who set out to save the world probably need a health warning: the world may have less need of them than they imagine. It is salutary to laugh at yourself if your day job includes the licence to laugh at others.

This provokes a thought. Who, in that pantheon of popular Indian filmstars, a great denominator of public approval, would be the ideal symbol of journalism? Raj Kapoor seems to lead the possibilities. He was half-saviour, half-joker. He was terribly handsome, though his trousers didn't fit. He swooned over the motherland, but danced a devilish waltz. He was too grand a presence, and could rarely resist a lecture. Pontification is for pontiffs, not hacks. The other epic name, Dilip Kumar, cried too much. Too tragic. Too noble. Dev Anand could be a better fit. He lived on Real Street rather than Poet's Tavern. But while writing a story you need to shoot straight, and Dev Sahab tended to wave his gun in every direction but that of the villain, which rather misses the point.

May one suggest a modest character from the Sixties? Joy Mukherjee. He became a surprise (and perhaps surprised) hit between 1960, when *Love in Simla* was released, and 1968, when *Love aur Mohabbat* flopped. He burst into fame as suddenly as he burnt out. But while he was at the top it was such wholesome fun. He had a square jaw, high forehead, wide nostrils, a spread smile, and wore T-shirts made of synthetic Banlon which clung to his undulating, baby-fat body. He never ventured into high drama, but was transparently sincere in whatever he did. 1960 was perhaps the greatest year in the history of popular cinema, but no one would have offered Joy the lead in *Mughal-e-Azam* or *Jis Desh Mein Ganga Behti Hai*, which were also released that year. The first movie rescued the past and the second saved the future; Joy lived happily in the present. You got what you saw in film after film, an amiable chap who won the girl by the last reel after struggles with snowflakes, without much strain on his IQ or ours. When his persistent fans learnt, after he faded, that his first son was named Boy Mukherjee, it seemed perfectly logical. For all we knew, a second son might have been christened Toy Mukherjee.

Journalists must answer an existentialist question at the very beginning of their careers: should they pursue their mission with a long face or a short one? My own recommendation is unambiguous: be like your copy, and keep it short. A smile always restores a face to its best size. Keep smiling. If nothing else, it disconcerts those you have to confront.

A long face also encourages the worst crime in the profession: sermons. Good journalists should evade the temptation of piety, stop believing they are agents of either God or king, and let loose their primary instinct, which is flirtation with the audacious.

Any collection of columns such as this book is an invitation to dance on a pedestal. It's merry for a bit, and then you can fall with a thud, severely injuring your ego. There is never sufficient space on a pedestal for posturing.

Let me refer you to that ultimate paragon of literary honour and social morality, P.G. Wodehouse. When he wrote an introduction to his first omnibus edition of tales about the immortal butler Jeeves, Wodehouse confessed to 'a slight feeling of chestiness, just the faint beginning of that offensive conceit against which we authors have to guard carefully. I mean to say, an omnibus book . . . Well, dash it, you can't say it doesn't mark an epoch in a fellow's career and put him just a bit above the common herd.'

Such potential conceit, he argues, could only be justified by the public good. And so he listed the many ways in which the Jeeves omnibus might serve the masses. It would, he pointed out, make an excellent paperweight. If you were on vacation, you could rip off a page at a time and use it as shaving paper. You might want to place the heavy book on your chest, jerk it up and down, and obviate the need for any further physical exercise. Finally, schoolboys could always use it as a weapon in any inter-study brawl.

I do not know how to say this without sounding like a puffed-up bullfrog, but I might be one up on The Master.

Some four decades ago I got my first proper job in journalism, thanks to the incomparable Khushwant Singh, then editor of *The Illustrated Weekly of India*, and his wonderful deputy, Fatma Zakaria. They made me read proofs, of course, as is the fate of residents on the lowest rung of the ladder, but they also encouraged me to write, which was the preserve of those on the highest. The *Weekly* sold a humungous 400,000 copies, at a time when the rest of India's English magazines could not together sell 100,000. I was 20, and floating.

I started to soar when in just a few weeks my first cover story was published. There is nothing quite so heady as seeing, for the first time, your name on the cover of a household publication. I was walking on air as I neared the entrance of the imperial Mumbai offices of the Times of India Group when I noticed a homeless mother on the pavement wipe her baby's bottom, literally, with my first cover story.

I challenge Wodehouse to top that on the scale of services to humanity. Journalism may do little to clear a politician's head, but if it can help clean a baby's bottom it is worth every word.

Journalism may be the spark that adds life to democracy, but it is never wise for a journalist to become too worthy for his own good.

Politics naturally dominates the discourse of our craft. Journalism may not quite be the first draft of history, but it is a pretty good log-book of the many ships that sail on time. Life is a spectrum, and there is more colour to it than just the few shades of politics. As this collection indicates, cricket and cinema offer as much opportunity to enjoy the genius of talent. These columns wander between the critical, the analytical and the wistful. If the former put you to sleep, try the latter. This selection owes much to the diligence of my colleague Joyeeta Basu and the intense scrutiny of my editor at HarperCollins, Krishan Chopra, so you know who to blame if you think you've wasted your money by buying this book.

I dare not suggest that this compilation is meant to be instructive, but if it does offer some fleeting pleasure, then the soul of one journalist shall sing one of many memorable songs from the films of Joy Mukherjee.

A FUNDAMENTAL SHIFT

When you are in power, you never hear the volcano rumbling in the belly of the mountain, although fires are licking at the mouth of the crater.

EYELESS IN INDIA

One cannot be a superpower on an empty stomach

26 November 2006

If I was, God forbid, chief censor of world media there is one four-letter word that I would ban completely: doom. Doomsday is dull; it is the end of all action. Doomsday is the ultimate reaction. Why, then, worry, since you can do nothing about it? Stick to sunshine instead of sniffling through gloom.

But there are limits to optimism, and they have been crossed by those who have concluded that India is a superpower. A curious and crazy mania of self-congratulation has overtaken some of us Indians.

That needs some elaboration. First: who is 'us'? I suppose every reader of an English newspaper would belong to 'us'. At the top of this category are the silver-spooners. In addition, 'we' or 'us' are those who have crept, slithered, slimed or worked our way out of the misery index.

Poverty is only one of the lines dividing Indians. Poverty converts so easily into a line of non-resistance. The truly impoverished do not have the strength to resist, or they would wreak havoc of a kind you might not deem suitable for a mere doomsday.

Adjacent to the poverty line is the anger line. These are Indians who have escaped from destitution, and exercise their right to anger. For them democracy is not a matter of a vote every five years; they test its flexibility as often as they can, and with a gun if they can find one. Call them Naxalites, Maoists, whatever: they don't care. They have no interest in categories. They argue that Indian democracy's methods of healing are to offer a Band-Aid when the disease is cancer. They have been told that the honey of economic growth will trickle down to them eventually. Try offering the mirage of a trickle to a man dying of thirst.

Their leaders cling on to the hatred line. It is a thin but potent demarcation. They channel anger towards violence. It is not a moral line, for those who hate also know how to negotiate.

Above hatred is the envy line, that huge mass of Indians who are almost there, seething through small towns and villages, anxious to join the long queues of upward mobility. Envy is a good spur for aspiration, as anyone in mass marketing, or indeed banking, will confirm. This is the target group of future consumers which wants the growth rate at 10 per cent and possibly higher. Envy is good for the economy. May it always flourish.

And on top of it all sit the exalted 'us': a mix of the smug, the complacent, the rich and the wealthy which now believes that it has arrived, and is totally convinced that because it has arrived India has also reached her destination. This is the hyper India class. This is the fairy-tale 'middle class', the subject of international attention, which hates looking below, except occasionally, to find servants. This class has invented a new morality. It believes that the less fortunate deserve their misfortune. The new lines are not, however, rigid. You can buy your way across the divide with a colour television set; and there are no questions asked once you reach the Maruti 800.

The new middle class has created its own deities. Mother India now carries, in her ten invulnerable arms, a nuclear weapon, a share market index printout, a mobile phone, a cricket ball, a ticket from a low-cost airline, a job offer from an outsourcing company, a colour television set, patched jeans, an iPod full of superbly arranged dancing music from Bollywood and an English dictionary. The high priests of Rich India are politicians and businessmen, two terms that encompass a wide variety of types.

It is not as if impoverished India lives in another geography. You can see poverty in the slums of Delhi, the stench of Mumbai, the peeling decay of inner Kolkata, in the thousands of street orphans and beggars that are a constant reminder of failure. We, all of 'us', are Eyeless in Delhi. Who has time for the hungry at our doorstep?

I am not a Utopian who believes that prosperity must march in step with equity; economic growth will come in stages, and there will be inexplicable disparity as we seek a better future. But what is it with the successful Indian that makes him so criminally indifferent to the truth of our poverty?

We have certainly moved away from a hopeless past. India might become a superpower; India should become a superpower. But we are not there yet. We cannot call ourselves any kind of power as long as half of India still goes to sleep on a stomach that is only half full.

ABOVE THE ANGER OF BHOPAL, THE SILENCE OF DELHI

Waking up our conscience to a continuing tragedy

13 June 2010

Can you hear the silence above the rising anger over the betrayal of Bhopal? The three most powerful people in India, Prime Minister Manmohan Singh, Mrs Sonia Gandhi and Prime Minister-in-waiting Rahul Gandhi have not said a word through a week of national outrage after a first-tier judicial verdict on a mass murder 26 years ago.

True, silence is also a statement, but one besieged by questions. Perhaps they have much to be silent about. The Congress party is not used to so much silence at the top. Unsurprisingly, its second-tier players made a mess when confronted by the pressure of public opinion. Sycophancy is not necessarily synonymous with clarity. By the end of the week, Congress activists could only pray that the quiet would speak up, and the loud-mouthed shut up.

Lip service is not the sort of service that always fetches you a complimentary tip. Jairam Ramesh, who loves his voice almost as much as his hair, thought he would help out by announcing that his proposed Green Tribunal would be located in Bhopal. It only served to remind us that on his only trip to Bhopal as environment minister,

Ramesh had sneered at the anguish of the victims with a remark so utterly glib and insensitive that it fails comprehension. Ramesh said, triumphantly, 'I held the toxic waste in my hand. I am still alive and not coughing. It's 25 years after the gas tragedy. Let us move ahead.'

How fortunate for the nation that Ramesh was not sleeping in a slum on that night in December 1984 when methyl isocyanate seeped out of the Carbide plant, killing nearly 20,000 and maiming over a 100,000 more, before its eerie poison exhausted itself. Perhaps we should be thankful that Ramesh was not a foetus killed in unknown wombs; or that he had not reached the age of 26 with twisted limbs and dark, angry eyes while a mother covered her son with a protective shawl in a helpless gesture of love. How fortunate that Jairam Ramesh never met Raghu Rai, the great and compassionate photographer who has done more for the helpless in Bhopal through his epic pictures than the Government of India, or indeed the Government of the United States.

But let us touch the toxic soil with a smile and move on!

Bhopal is a saga of contemptuous indifference in which anyone who aided American corporate interests over the anguish of Indians was rewarded. The stain of shame began with Warren Anderson's arranged escape in a government plane. It was only the beginning of the story. The CBI chargesheet in 1987 sought a ten-year jail sentence against Anderson for culpable homicide, 'not amounting to murder'. Chief Justice A.H. Ahmadi watered this down; it is ironical that a Muslim Chief Justice should have been used to compromise a case in which most of the victims were impoverished Muslims. Ahmadi was given handsome post-retirement benefits. Anderson was never unduly troubled by the thought of returning to face trial despite an extradition treaty between India and the US. His bond was only Rs 25,000, exactly the same amount that the guilty have been required to pay per victim after 26 years.

Token crumbs have been thrown periodically before victims. The latest is a reconstituted Group of Ministers, headed by P. Chidambaram. Guess who was head of the previous GoM? Arjun Singh. And what is Chidambaram's claim to fame? As finance minister he lobbied, along with Kamal Nath, Montek Singh Ahluwalia and Ronen Sen, on behalf of Dow Chemical, promising India's Prime Minister rich rewards in the shape of American investment if Dow was forgiven. Why did Dow really want to return? To reclaim Carbide land in India, since it had bought Carbide but disclaimed Bhopal's liabilities. Dow had kept aside over $2 billion for asbestos-victim compensation for Americans in another case, but had no money for Indians.

Why should it? Indians had no money for Indians. Jairam Ramesh, of course, is a member of the new GoM as well. Congress spokesman Abhishek Singhvi was a lawyer for Dow, and sent his missives on Congress letterheads.

There is so much to be silent about.

The heroism of volunteers who have fought a powerful, sneering bipartisan system on behalf of victims, for no reward other than the calm of a conscience, is beyond words. Am I dreaming, or will there come a moment when every Indian conscience is touched by Bhopal?

THE PROFIT AND LOSS OF SILENCE

Is our democracy, as Pranab Mukherjee said, too noisy?

12 December 2010

It is entirely appropriate that the man in charge of India's volume control, Pranab Mukherjee, should have uttered what is unarguably the comment of the year: our democracy has become too noisy. Through a long career stretching from the 1960s, Pranabda (as he is fondly known) has always preferred the brain to the lung. Noise has been neither in his temperament nor in his bhadralok-Brahmin culture. His metier is ministerial; he is a fish out of water when his party is in the Opposition. He knows that government has a tremendous advantage in the parliamentary form of government, even more so than in the presidential form, but only if it understands the mechanism of power. He would be the first to appreciate that Opposition very often has no option except to play its first and last card, noise.

Noise has become a pejorative term, which is a bit unfair. Noise does not have to be necessarily loud. Oratory is beautiful noise. Music is noise touched by magic. Politics rarely rises to oratory, and never to music, but every Opposition knows that while it cannot survive if it is not heard, it must trade with the voter in intelligible noise. Rising decibel levels can be justified only if there is the logic of public interest at the core. The delicate twist that lifts Mukherjee's statement from the passé to the relevant is a descriptive qualification, 'a bit too'. Noise is essential to the system. Excess, however, grates. There is a clash of civilisations when the throat threatens to destroy the eardrum. Democracy works when all five senses are in harmony. Mukherjee's diagnosis was perfect, but his prescription was, shall we say, a bit ambiguous. He advised a bit of silence.

The virtues of silence can never be overstated. Silence breeds reflection and reflection encourages maturity. If that was Mukherjee's advice to Opposition, then it was imbued with motive. It is equally within the Opposition's rights to point out that government very often treats silence in precisely the same manner as an accused—as its first line of defence. In any criminal case, police have to give an accused the legal right of silence, so that he does not incriminate himself. Both Prakash Karat of the CPI(M) and Arun Jaitley of the BJP are asking Dr Manmohan Singh whether he rejects the idea of a Joint Parliamentary Committee (JPC) because Dr Singh fears that if he speaks he will incriminate his government in a scandal that continues to have the most astonishing reverberations as layer after surprising layer peels off. We now learn that government tapped the middlewoman Niira Radia's phones because it believed that she was 'indulging in anti-national activities'. This takes the allegations against her beyond the edge of conventional corruption, and provides further justification to the Opposition demand for a JPC to probe the most sensational scandal in two decades.

It is ironic that government was forced to state this in the Supreme Court because of a petition filed by Radia's chief financial mentor and public guardian, Ratan Tata, the industrialist who has helped Radia's company grow from nothing to Rs 300 crore in just nine years. Acting on poor legal advice, Tata went to court to blanket out information, condemning India as a banana republic along the way. No weapon has ricocheted back faster than the Ratan boomerang.

It may be relevant, therefore, to consider when Pranab Mukherjee asked for a bit of silence. He was speaking to industrialists. While it is axiomatic that there cannot be bribery without money, and where there is cash there will be businessmen, the 2G show is slowly turning into theatre where the lead role in the first act has faded before the aggressive emergence of businessmen on the stage. Ratan Tata has been dominating headlines with a persistence uncharacteristic of his class. He has been interventionist rather than reticent, often storming into the debate despite overwhelming evidence of sleaze on the part of his protégé. It was only a matter of time before another businessman decided to label this as hypocrisy, which Rajeev Chandrashekhar did, albeit more politely. Tata's response was to claim personal virtue in the name of the Prime Minister, a double-edged tribute which Dr Singh might want to ignore; and accuse an Opposition party, BJP, of association in the exercise.

This might be the moment to point out that Niira Radia's telephones were tapped by the Manmohan Singh government, not the BJP. They were leaked by those today in power, not a BJP mole. If Ratan Tata finds his name in media stories on Indian scams, it is because the present government made the Radia tapes available to the media. It is possible that the leaks had Home Minister P. Chidambaram's approval; after all, Home Secretary G.K. Pillai has, on record, promised to provide much more.

Time to understand what Pranab Mukherjee implied: silence begins at home.

AN APPEAL ON BEHALF OF THE LEARNED SOCIETY OF COMMON SENSE

One more tragedy, this time in Delhi, as a deadly terrorist blast claimed 15 lives and injured 79 people, in the high court complex

11 September 2011

Calm down, everyone. Relax. Our invaluable Home Minister P. Chidambaram has finally found the answer to terrorism. He did so on 13 July, after the Mumbai blasts.

On 13 July, Chidambaram explained that the blasts were not the 'fault of intelligence agencies'. They might have been to blame in those bad old days when the comb-loving Shivraj Patil (now condemned to life under chandeliers in some Raj Bhavan) was home minister of India. But no longer. Under Chidambaram's watch, cops get intelligence every hour, every day. Maybe under Patil they got intelligence only every second hour, and never on weekends. But that slipshod era is over. It's all clockwork now.

It isn't his fault if this magic prescription has not quite worked, and death has returned to Delhi. Nothing is ever his fault. Anyone who thinks otherwise has to be either a fool or an enemy agent, which means his enemy, not the nation's.

So why haven't the terror attacks stopped? Why doesn't this torrent of intelligence include information of planned attacks? The infallible Chidambaram has the answer. It is because terrorists work 'in a very clandestine manner'. Eureka! Of course! Those dastardly cowards! How dare they remain clandestine! The next time the Lahore-based chief of Lashkar-e-Taiba, or any extremist villain in India, gets ready with a bomb he should send a detailed letter to Chidambaram, preferably by courier since normal mail cannot be fully trusted.

And then, based on incontrovertible evidence, a potbellied policeman can trot off to the sites, defuse the bomb, hold a press conference and start a nationwide agitation for the promotion of Chidambaram to the next job on the ladder of upward mobility.

Chidambaram has been a brilliant lawyer, and no one believes that his IQ is inadequate for his present job. Why then does he make silly remarks? Does a crisis bring out the worst rather than the best in him? Do our ministers believe that the Indian voter is devoid of common sense, and that inane excuses of the clandestine sort are sufficient to ward off public rage?

The Indian is patient. He is not unreasonable in his expectations. He does not believe that there is some magic wand that will eliminate this scourge with a whoosh. But he is not a fool. The luminaries of this government, most particularly Rahul Gandhi, got evidence of what the voter thinks when he was heckled during his courtesy visit to the hospital to meet the victims of terrorism.

Sadly, even as terrorists get more brazen, police get more complacent. They know nothing will happen even if they do nothing. What has happened after the July Mumbai incidents apart from tokenism? But the knee-jerk motions continue after each outrage.

May I be permitted to publish an appeal on behalf of The Learned Society of Common Sense to our police officers? Please do not continue to indulge in that sorry hoax called a computer-generated likeness of suspects. The truth is that the police are clueless and these images are planted on the front pages of newspapers to simulate a sense of urgency in the hunt that has absolutely no relationship with reality.

If the police had a clue, the bombs would not have gone off. The justification is that the images are a composite of responses from survivors at the site of the attack. How does anyone in that unfortunate crowd know who placed the bomb? The terrorist put some distance between his weapon of destruction and himself or he would be dead too. The Delhi outrage was not the work of suicide bombers. Is there ever any eventual resemblance between these images and actual suspects, if any are discovered?

These images are more likely to be the outcome of imagination propelled by fear among the people and cynical prejudice on the part of the police. Check: these instant images of 'suspects' will almost always be adorned with a beard. This is institutionalised communalism, and not very subtle either, against Muslims. Forty-eight hours after the Delhi incident the home minister said that leads were promising but not very conclusive. As far as public sentiment is concerned, however, judgement has already been passed.

SEEN, OBSCENE AND UNSEEN

The Planning Commission has a minimalist approach to poverty

9 October 2011

Wealth is far easier to recognise than poverty. Wealth is either seen or obscene; poverty remains largely unseen. Poverty of the worst kind is hidden in those parts of India—or indeed the world—where it is outside the provenance of government, and beyond the interest of individuals and institutions who fuel the engines of modern life, like business concerns or bureaucracy or media. Those of a liberal persuasion do feel the occasional moral twinge at the passing sight of near-starvation, but poverty does not appear on any balance sheet, liberal or conservative. The cure for liberal guilt is aversion. We take our eyes off the hungry. We leave the responsibility to government.

Government is a curious mixture of personal interest and impersonal decision-making. We know from experience that the most consistent service that government provides is lip service. Lip service has been developed into a science. Statistics are the data of this science. They seem to have the legitimacy of fact, as if facts were synonymous with truth. But it is a good alibi, a perfect vehicle for the psychological postponement of a decision, since no one is really desperate for a solution. Data keeps whirring away in some dark corner of government, giving the illusion that someone is actually doing something about anything. In our case, data is the preserve of a cavernous Planning Commission, headed at the moment by an impervious 'foreign-returned' bureaucrat who confuses self-importance for governance. It would be a good idea to introduce Montek Singh Ahluwalia to India. Both he and India would benefit from greater familiarity, since Ahluwalia will remain the effective head of the Planning Commission as long as Dr Manmohan Singh is Prime Minister.

The interesting part of the story is that Ahluwalia, now even more famous as the father of the Rs 32-a-day poverty line, does not apply the criterion for measurement of poverty that nations like America and Britain observe. We take the bottom-up approach: the minimalist cost of a handful of essentials required for basic survival, in effect a computation of calories sufficient to keep you alive. The richer nations calculate poverty as a percentage of average wealth; if anyone slips a certain percentage point below that average then he or she is deemed poor, and therefore in need of help. This is why the poor in those nations never fall into a starvation net, or are forced into a subsistence existence.

The argument offered for changing the parameters seems plausible. A rich nation, ipso facto, has the ability to raise the poverty line because of its economic surpluses. How about a different perspective? Rich nations are rich precisely because they have changed their definition of poverty. What makes a nation rich? The creation and appropriation of wealth by a thin community at the ozone layer of society, which then uses its power to prevent dissemination of this wealth downwards to the extent it can? Or the creation of what might be called a more general, and therefore generous, wealth that ensures a better life to the hundreds of millions at the lowest economic levels?

There is a harsher Indian response, a violent theory barely disguised in smug accusation, that the poor deserve what they get, that they are responsible for their own fate. When logic confirms that this is absurd, that the poor are victims, that poverty cannot be dismissed as a self-perpetuating punishment, we resort to silly fallacies like destiny, the ultimate argument for complacency. We have got away with this in the past because the hopeless were also helpless, bereft of the ability to challenge the injustice that was killing them, in slow, tortured stages. It is one of the great achievements of democracy that such devastating inequity is not sustainable. Political rights are a means to economic empowerment, or they are nothing.

Feudalism and colonialism could get away with long periods of brutality, of which famine was an extreme symptom. But the best of emperors and viceroys knew that empire ebbs when the poor are driven to death by economic apartheid. An American museum edition of *Jahangirnama* in my library is liberally illustrated with wonderful reproductions of Mughal miniatures. Among the heroic scenes there is one very unflattering portrait of Jahangir, given pride of place on a full page. The emperor has drawn his bow, not while on a hunt, or in battle, but in order to kill an ugly hag. This is hardly an image that the lord of India would want to preserve for the future. It puzzled me until I read the caption inscribed around the picture. The hag represented poverty, and the emperor was killing poverty.

Diwali is around the corner. Maybe we should raise a collection and send this edition of *Jahangirnama* to each member of the Planning Commission as a Diwali gift.

HOW ABOUT 51 PER CENT FDI IN PARLIAMENT?

Mobile phones are the spice of life at Cabinet meetings

4 December 2011

It is time for the father of economic reforms to initiate political reforms. Step 1: Dr Manmohan Singh should abandon the oath of secrecy which Cabinet ministers take. Step 2: Ban mobile phones during Cabinet meetings. Which of the two is more difficult? The first, since it is easier to amend the Constitution of India than change the unflinching commitment of politicians to their self-image. Populism has its demands.

The present Union Cabinet has made a total mockery of its obligation towards official secrecy. Some ministers do not even wait for the Cabinet meeting to end before they begin to regale friends and journalists with gossipy details of what transpired; they SMS. You have to be first off the block if you want to try and shape public opinion with your version of the story. In the old days, a leak was considered serious enough to constitute a scandal. The Cabinet no longer leaks; it gushes forth in monsoon torrents. If the Prime Minister is upset he has no opportunity to show it. Discipline is not on the UPA's minimum or maximum programme.

There was word-by-word commentary, embellished with intricate details of what happened when, and who said what, during the Cabinet meeting that pushed through the decision to permit 51 per cent foreign equity in multi-brand retail chains. We know precisely how Finance Minister Pranab Mukherjee snubbed his Bengal ally Dinesh Trivedi; how Trivedi stormed out and then stormed back after Kamal Nath's persuasive intervention. Jairam Ramesh's comment that the decision would cost Congress a few seats in Uttar Pradesh has been so accurately reported he might as well have issued a press release. Sharad Pawar's dismissive retort, that the Congress wasn't in good shape there in any case, got equal play in diary columns. A serious dialectical debate has ensued on whether Congress merely informed its allies, conversed with them or consulted them on Foreign Direct Investment (FDI). It is all terribly exciting. For the media, that is.

Step 3: Parliament should be converted into a virtual Parliament. There should be no need for an MP to actually go to the House; he or she can sit at home and participate through a networked screen-and-sound system. If private sector employees can turn their home into an office, thanks to the audio-visual net, why not Parliament? The savings on air tickets and housing would be enormous as MPs would not have to fly into Delhi. Collective behaviour would be instantly eliminated, thereby ending that common rush to the well which forces the Speaker to adjourn proceedings. We might even have a full session without disruption, and while that would be terrible for television, it might be good for legislation and debate. Some states have tried surreptitious reform by curtailing the length of sessions to a bare minimum. The Delhi Assembly met recently for just two days. A virtual Parliament would not need such unsavoury tactics. However, there should never be any restrictions on any MP attempting to visit Parliament for a cheap meal in the canteen. This is a fundamental right of MPs, and a cornerstone of Indian democracy. (The cornerstone of British democracy is the pub in Parliament, which is why its debates are more spirited.)

Step 4 (and last): Dr Singh must permit 51 per cent FDI in Parliament. This would immediately bring transparency and order into the Indian body politic. The purchase of Lok Sabha shares would be restricted to democracies, thereby removing any threat from China. If the Americans bought majority control of the Lok Sabha we could switch at once to a Presidential form of government, turn large parts of Rashtrapati Bhavan into respectable office space, and offer all the political drama necessary to sustain a proper media from the base of electoral primaries to a direct contest for Number 1. If the British took 51 per cent of the shares, instead, they could start three pubs in Central Hall, which would certainly improve the mood of members. If the French took charge, they could ensure fast delivery of their Rafale fighter jets to the Indian Air Force. The only possible danger in this reform is that Rome or Athens might take control, turning India into Greece or Italy, but fortunately they no longer have the money.

ST AUGUSTINE'S CHASTITY

The Manmohan Singh government has become a library of closed books—and open palms

3 June 2012

There are enough Catholic saints to fill a thick register, but only a few have become legendary. St Augustine, who lived between 354 and 430 CE, has left such an indelible mark that no anthology of quotations is complete without him. One prayer, recorded for posterity in Book 3 of Confessions, bears the burden of any immortal aphorism; it is almost always misquoted, although never misrepresented. Augustine prays to the Lord: 'Give me chastity and continence—but not yet!'

This could serve as the motto of the UPA government. Every minister wants to be chaste and honest, but only after he is out of office. When in power too many ministers install a taxi meter outside their cabins, clocking up a running account of bribes. UPA 2 has become the dark and fetid nemesis of UPA 1.

Scams are born fast. The initial arrangement is done quickly enough. It does not take long to communicate intention on both sides; brokers are efficient. If any time is lost, it is only in the haggle. The sums involved, after all, are staggering. But since both sides know that they are going to do the deal in any case, negotiations end within a reasonable time frame. What takes time is unravelling of the scam.

It can take years for the Comptroller and Auditor General (CAG) to put together a meticulous report that can withstand the scrutiny of those who are going to be exposed: bribe-givers and bribe-takers invest a lot in legal advice and PR management to save vulnerable skin. Even after exposure, the revelations may not quite catch fire instantly. The massive scam in coal blocks has been known for a while; the involvement of the minister's relatives in this loot and the corruption of his predecessor are also hardly a secret. But the real fuse was set off when Team Anna brought Prime Minister Manmohan Singh into the line of fire.

There has been much hand-wringing by the establishment, all around the lines that the PM's personal integrity is unimpeachable. Perhaps it is, although it says something that the qualifying term has shifted from certainty to 'perhaps'. But the PM cannot escape one fact. He has been the senior minister in charge of coal ever since Shibu Soren resigned. If this massive loot took place under his watch, then he has to be accountable. If he signed away the nation's resources, then he has to answer, even if others took the loot. The only response he might have, and it may even be an honest one, is that he did not read the files; but that is inadequate.

It is ironic that a Prime Minister who has often claimed, publicly, that his life is an open book should preside over a government that is a library of closed books. No government since 1947 has had such a continuous record of corruption; a venal sin now compounded by the collapse of governance. In 2009, Dr Singh had a track record he could campaign on. By 2012, this record has been so vitiated that the Congress cannot go to the people and ask for their vote. They will not give it, either. Mrs Sonia Gandhi recognises this. Her body language at even core group meetings indicates her total frustration. She knows that the time has come to change the government; because if she does not change it, the people will, and when they do so even tatters might not be visible.

The political calendar provides an opportunity. A President is due to be elected. Congress silence about its candidate has led to speculation about all sorts of hidden horses, some dark, others speckled, and a couple which are visibly lame but still insistent that they are in the race.

Mrs Gandhi can do her party a world of good by promoting Dr Singh to Rashtrapati Bhavan, and then installing a radically different government. She has a natural successor in Pranab Mukherjee. While the chattering classes insist that there is a gulf of suspicion between the two, surely they have now worked together long enough to put sentiment aside. Politics is a hard place. It needs cool decisions. Mrs Gandhi does not have options, as Dr Singh's replacement must be acceptable to allies and, more important, the people of the country. She may want to see her son Rahul Gandhi as Prime Minister, but that idea will not walk in the immediate future. Rahul Gandhi could have won his spurs in UP. He did not.

This transition to a Mukherjee can happen in mid-June. It may not, to repeat another memorable quote, this time from the Second World War leader Winston Churchill, mark the beginning of the end, but it could end the disastrous beginning of UPA 2.

THE PRICE OF A WOMB

A natural resource is a national resource, not Congress property

26 August 2012

The government headed by Dr Manmohan Singh and Mrs Sonia Gandhi has laid down its code of governance. You can sell a fertile womb at a heavy discount as long as the child is still inside. This metaphor passes the test of common parlance: our natural resources, like coal, are the gift of Mother Nature. The Supreme Court has held that a natural resource is also a national resource. It is a property of the people, and government is only a temporary caretaker. Government is duty-bound to maximise returns to the people in case of any economic exploitation of natural resources.

The CAG, or the Comptroller and Auditor General, is the government's premier audit authority. Vinod Rai, who holds the position, has had a distinguished career in government, reaching the status of a secretary in finance when P. Chidambaram was minister. Dr Manmohan Singh sponsored him for CAG precisely because of his reputation for competence and integrity; and he duly took over on 7 January 2008.

Rai sent a report on coal mines to Parliament during this monsoon session affirming that 'Delay in the introduction of the process of competitive bidding has rendered the existing process [of allotting coal blocks] beneficial to private companies. Audit has estimated financial gains to the tune of Rs 1.86 lakh crore likely to accrue to private coal block allottees.' The language is simple enough. For a substantial portion of this period (November 2006 to May 2009), the Prime Minister held the portfolio.

After some brainstorming the UPA government has formulated a response: coal has not begun to be mined from these allotments, so there has been no gain; hence the CAG report is unsustainable. This argument would be valid if the government also announced that it was cancelling these allotments, returning the money paid and auctioning the blocks. This should be very easy, since, as per the government's own statement, no mining has begun. In other words, the private sector has not made any investments in its purchase; the original price therefore should be sufficient compensation. This is the only way to ensure that Finance Minister P. Chidambaram's claim of 'no gain' means what it claims. Nor should the private companies complain. As noted, they have not begun mining. The CAG report itself states that its figure of Rs 1.86 lakh crore (about $37 billion) constitutes the gains that are 'likely to accrue'. Cancellation is the only insurance against unwarranted torrents of profit.

The other UPA argument is that some BJP-ruled states also once favoured the process of allocation over auction. So what? The blocks they allocated should be cancelled as well. The point is not a political party's deeds or misdeeds but the people's rights, and their welfare. A sum of $37 billion will buy a lot of free meals for children in districts dominated by the Maoist insurrection, even after we have deducted the percentage that will inevitably be corroded by inefficiency and corruption, and leave enough for a healthcare plan for mothers and infants.

But the catch is in the opening sentence of the quoted CAG paragraph. The loss to government was due to a 'Delay in the introduction of the process of competitive bidding'. There was a system in place, which all parties when in government used. But in 2004, after the UPA came to power, and possibly encouraged by Dr Singh's reputation for probity,

Coal Secretary P.C. Parakh recommended, in a formal note dated 16 July 2004, a change to auction on the valid grounds that this would be less open to favouritism and generate far more revenue. This view emerged from a meeting with all stakeholders, held on 28 June 2004.

One would imagine that the Cabinet would applaud. Instead the idea was blocked by officials within the Prime Minister's Office. On 11 September 2004, the PMO circulated a note asserting that there were flaws in the competitive bidding; on 1 November 2004, the PMO opposed an amendment to the Coal Mines (Nationalisation) Act, 1973. Why? There is no convincing answer. These are not the only instances. And if auction was wrong then, how has it suddenly become right after at least 57 blocks were awarded by this government to private businessmen—a list that includes some very famous names along with the usual lot of unknowns. A draft Mines and Minerals Bill incorporating auctions was finally readied in 2011, but it has still not been passed.

Diversionary tactics to confuse the truth work, up to a point. Whether the BJP should stall Parliament in order to get its message across may be a moot issue in many minds. But the forum of confrontation has shifted from Parliament to the teashops and courtyards of the country. The decisive arguments are being heard by the ultimate judge in a democracy: the voter. Judgement will be heard on election day. Mother Nature's womb belongs to the people.

GHOSTS OF THE PAST HOVER OVER GENDER JUSTICE

Two judgements, and a question of prejudice

10 February 2013

A Supreme Court judgement may be anchored in law, but it sails a long way through the minds of judges before it becomes a public pronouncement. Law and justice are both human and therefore prone to frailty and error. We respect the Supreme Court as the final authority because we trust its integrity enough to believe that even the occasional mistake is an honest one.

One means through which the legal system protects its credibility is the doctrine of 'contempt of court'. Dissent is not recommended, at least if you want to stay at home rather than in a cell. But surely their lordships will permit some space for perplexity? There must be an ante-room for discussion, particularly since a Supreme Court judgement is much more than the final word on the fate of an individual criminal. It is also the template by which all courts in the nation will shape their decisions in millions of cases in the process of judgement, or in crimes of the future.

On 5 February, newspapers reported that a bench of Justices P. Sathasivam and J.S. Khekar confirmed the death penalty on an adult who had kidnapped a seven-year-old boy and then killed him after failing to obtain ransom. The justices concluded that they saw no hope of reform in the criminal, that his perversion was inhuman, and the murder was cold and premeditated. The rationale for their decision to confirm the death penalty is inarguable.

But there was a curious codicil in the justification, which their lordships noted as aggravating circumstances. I quote: 'The parents of the deceased had four children, three daughters and one son ... Kidnapping the only male child was to induce maximum fear in the mind of his parents. Purposefully killing the sole male child has grave repercussions for the parents of the deceased ...' The bench continued, 'Agony for parents for the loss of their male child, who would have carried further the family lineage, and is expected to see them through their old age, is unfathomable.'

The implications of such thinking are astonishing. It implies clearly that the parents' agony would have been less if one of the three daughters had been similarly kidnapped and murdered, for the girl would not continue family lineage or provide for her parents in old age. The judges stressed on the 'sole male child' as being the bearer of 'the family lineage' and sustenance provider.

Which world are the judges living in?

We know the world they inhabit from another judgement, delivered just a week before, also involving an appeal against a death penalty. Justice Sathasivam was again on the bench, this time in the company of Justice F.M.I. Kalifulla. It is difficult to repeat their decision without a sense of horror at the double standards that the Supreme Court has applied. Before them was a man convicted by both the trial and high court. This savage murderer had raped his minor daughter, and been arrested after his wife complained to the police. When released on parole, he axed both his wife and daughter to death.

This abominable, barbaric rapist and killer lives, thanks to their lordships Sathasivam and Kalifulla.

One wonders: has the great ferment rising across India against rape and gender prejudice escaped the attention of the Supreme Court? Chief Justice Altamas Kabir has certainly heard the howl of anguish from women. He said that if it were possible he could have joined the protests in Delhi. Was the Chief Justice helpless while his brothers delivered such discordant pronouncements? What will trial courts and high courts do in future when a father who has raped and killed his minor daughter, and has axed his wife for being a mother, appears before them? Will they stop long short of a death sentence the next time, because of the precedent sent by Justices Sathasivam and Kalifulla? Is the life of a raped and murdered minor girl less than equal to the life of a kidnapped and murdered boy? Does a man who killed two women deserve clemency, while the man who killed one boy gets hanged?

Is this justice?

The Honourable Supreme Court has the option of silence. We cannot push our questions beyond a limited point. Is silence the only answer that the court will choose?

If the Supreme Court, and Parliament, have the courage to do so they should abandon the death penalty. Then there will be no debate when governments delay the implementation of a death verdict on Afzal Guru for years, and finally act only when the President of India indicates that his patience is over. Our prisons can teem with rapists who have also killed minor daughters and wives. But as long as the law permits this ultimate weapon called the death sentence, that sword of justice must swing without conscious or unconscious prejudice.

Gender equality is being buried in parts each day.

SINGH PREFERRED A PALACE TO A PLOUGHING FIELD

If Manmohan Singh had stepped aside in late 2009 or any time in 2010, there would have been, today, a nationwide clamour demanding his return

8 September 2013

Livy, the ancient historian, records the remarkable story of Cincinnatus, whose memory has been reduced to an academic fringe instead of being made compulsory reading for politicians. In 458 BCE, Rome was threatened by the Sabines and Aequi. Cincinnatus was ploughing his fields when summoned to public service. Appointed dictator, he defeated the invading tribes, distributed the booty among his troops, and returned to his field, where the plough was precisely where he had left it. That was unsurprising. He had been dictator for only 15 days.

Be it noted that no other dictator or ruler of Rome and its subsequent empire displayed such exemplary virtue. The idea that there is serenity and fulfilment in some pursuit other than power is alien to the powerful. Only 28 of the 130-odd emperors of Rome died from old age or illness. Most arrived by the sword, and died by it. Political nature craves the pomp of office, and is terrified by the loneliness of retirement.

The only instance of a powerful Indian minister voluntarily giving up office is that of Lal Bahadur Shastri, when he was railway minister. Six decades later, when accidents are the norm rather an exception, the principle seems quaint if not foolish. The present Parliament would run out of MPs to promote if ministers were held accountable. Jawaharlal Nehru was the only Prime Minister who contemplated retirement—at the pinnacle of his success in 1957, rather than when in the depths after the defeat in the 1962 war with China. Nehru's reasons were so human they seem extraordinary: he wanted to read, write and spend time with his family. He was easily persuaded to remain. Every political story, it is said, ends in tragedy. Nehru's came in 1962.

But surely political compulsion has not disappeared from politics. Opinion polls confirm visual and anecdotal evidence that Prime Minister Manmohan Singh has sunk from asset to liability. This is an extraordinary fall, given the levels of popularity he enjoyed in 2009. Perhaps he raised hopes too high, and there was nowhere he could go after that but down. But the facts have hardened to a point where they are unlikely to change. Narendra Modi is way ahead with 47 per cent support in the contest for PM, according to an ABP News poll; Rahul Gandhi gets only a diehard 18 per cent and Dr Singh is not really in the picture. The gap between parties is equally disturbing, if you happen to be a Congress loyalist: BJP gets 36 per cent support versus 22 per cent for Congress. Bear in mind that the BJP base is narrower, so this support will have more depth where it exists.

Our parliamentary system gives ruling parties a chance for pause and correction in such a crisis; they can change a Prime Minister without losing a government. Mrs Sheila Dikshit would have been an excellent replacement, filling both the administrative and political vacuum created by the second UPA government. Why does Congress persist with the status quo? There must be an invisible reason amenable to logic. Mrs Sonia Gandhi will not consider any successor other than Rahul Gandhi, and he is incapable, in his own mind, of stepping up to the plate.

So Congress strategy remains concentrated upon using every mechanism to try and destroy the BJP's nominee for the top job rather than doing what it can to build Rahul Gandhi as a leader who can deliver the party out of this mess. This can be counter-productive.

Confusion would be worse. If Congress leaves the question of who should be its candidate for Prime Minister unanswered, it will be vulnerable to an affliction that has traditionally been an Opposition malady. Both age and record rule out Dr Singh as a candidate for a third term. The only way to woo a sceptical electorate is to establish what Rahul Gandhi stands for, rather than fudge what he is hiding from.

In 2009 Dr Singh was a much younger man than he is today; he has aged more than a decade in less than five years. He looked positive and confident during his first press conference after re-election. He dispatched the inevitable question about Rahul Gandhi promptly. He was ready to step down, he said, whenever Rahul Gandhi wanted the job. Everyone smiled and carried on.

But if Dr Singh had stepped aside in late 2009 or any time in 2010, there would have been today a nationwide clamour demanding his return. His first five years would have been praised as a golden spell, equivalent to the 15 days during which Cincinnatus destroyed the nation's enemies and made Rome the springboard of unprecedented future glory.

But Dr Singh preferred a palace to the ploughing field.

WHY RAHUL GANDHI WAS IN A TEARING HURRY

He has aged, or middle-aged, without having matured

6 October 2013

If Mrs Sonia Gandhi were half as concerned about the future of the Congress as she is about the future of Rahul Gandhi, Congress might have been far more capable of fulfilling her dream of making him Prime Minister of India.

This paradox will be lost on those Congresspersons who have become so subservient to dynasty that nothing matters other than ritual hallelujahs before a prince who has aged, or at least middle-aged, without having matured. Rahul Gandhi's interventions are a step-up from the extra-constitutional authority formula. His preferred style is beyond anything known in democracy: press conference dictatorship. A privileged individual is more important in the current dispensation than the complex edifice of constitutional government in which any decision has to be nudged and nurtured carefully through numerous checks and balances, not the least of them being President of India.

The funniest sight at the press conference where Rahul Gandhi tore apart the little that remained of Prime Minister Manmohan Singh's credibility was Ajay Maken's face. Maken was chosen by Rahul Gandhi to head the party's communication in the crucial months before a general election. Maken had summoned media to defend the Congress government's ordinance offering reprieve to convicted politicians. You could see Maken's little heart doing a crazy dance in his mouth as his leader in this lifetime and beyond dismissed a decision taken by Mrs Sonia Gandhi, through the core committee, and Dr Singh, through the Cabinet, as complete nonsense.

It is such instances that revive the Indian's deep and abiding faith in the medicinal qualities of laughter. A political party can always win an election against mellifluous oratory. But it is impossible to win an election against jokes.

Nothing sums up the current mockery of government better than the latest joke doing the internet and conversational rounds: Dr Singh went to America, and even America's government shut down.

For three years at least this UPA government has been imploding. It is now exploding, and its fragments are scattered across the news. Each Cabinet meeting ends with the grinding sound of Congress crumbling just a little more. The Telangana decision was a crash rather than a crumble: contrast this with the smooth manner in which Jharkhand, Uttarakhand and Chhattisgarh were created. The UPA has disintegrated visibly after the ordinance flip-flop and the Telangana chaos.

The compulsion behind both decisions was not conviction, but electoral manoeuvre impelled by desperation. The flip side of the ordinance was a wish to protect party MPs like Rashid Masood and allies like Lalu Yadav; the flop side was Rahul Gandhi's attempt to establish popular credit at favourable interest rates.

A party can survive without government. A government cannot be effective without a party. That is an iron law of democracy. The party limits damage in adversity and maximises gains during prosperity. The mistake Mrs Sonia Gandhi made was to hand over party management to an heir who did not realise that it was a blood-and-sweat job, not a private sector project fuelled by computer printouts. In a state as crucial as Uttar Pradesh, therefore, the party has simply withered under a hand-picked state president, Nirmal Khatri, whose visits to Lucknow are such an occasional event that they necessitate a press release.

The decay has come at a time of radical change in the electorate. The most important demographic mobilization in UP, to continue with a persuasive example, is not going to be by Brahmins, Muslims or Dalits in the next general elections, but what might be called the New Minority: youth. Some 2.3 crore, or 17.6 per cent of the state's electorate, will vote for the first time. This is higher than the number of Brahmins or Muslims or Dalits in UP. The young are searching for the politics of addition, a surplus of hope, not the cynicism of fracture on lines of caste and creed. True, all the young will not vote alike, but then neither does any other group.

It is not the BJP which is dividing the Congress, as Mrs Gandhi claimed during her recent public meeting in Karnataka; indeed the BJP is the only thing that unites the Congress from Caucus Singh at one end to Quibble Khan at the other. The Congress is in disarray because it has lost direction.

The UPA worked well as long as its leadership was an isosceles triangle. Mrs Gandhi was pre-eminent; Dr Singh and Pranab Mukherjee were equal sides who kept government and party stable, with Mukherjee given the vital charge of perception management. When Dr Singh began to wilt, Mukherjee should have replaced him. Instead, he went into comfort zone, and the Congress into a spin. We now have a hapless Mrs Gandhi, an indifferent Prime Minister and Rahul Gandhi rushing in and out, when he feels like, through blank space on the third side.

GDP DOWN, GROSS DOMESTIC BITTERNESS UP

The quality of governance is measured by the management of change, and the UPA government hasn't shown much capability in respect of Telangana

13 October 2013

Between 1757 and 1857 the British patched together an Indian empire full of geographical odds but with one logical end: an administrative map which maximised their security and trade, rather than reflected what people wanted. Blaming the British is pointless. They ruled India for Britain's benefit, not India's.

Robert Clive is justly famous for winning Bengal, but an equally significant achievement of his time was conquest of the Andhra coastal belt, called the Northern Circars, in 1758-59. The Nizam of Hyderabad had ceded this region to the French, who promptly lost it to the British. Clive's strategic interest was to control the coast, and establish a land route between the premier British trading cities, Calcutta and Madras, strengthening the defences of both. He knew its value from experience. In 1756, when Clive set out to recapture Calcutta, seized by Siraj-ud-Daula and renamed Alinagar, his fleet was forced to sail from Madras via Ceylon and Burma to the Hooghly river in Bengal.

The Mughal map had deeper roots in local history and ethnicity, because Mughal expansion, after Akbar, sought to assimilate as much as to acquire. A regional dynasty was permitted to rule over its fief as long as it accepted the Mughal emperor as overlord. The identification between land and people in princely India was deeper, thanks to continuity and feudal tradition. When free India sought a new internal map, based on the will of the people, most disputes emerged from British India, and why would they not when Sind and Gujarat were ruled from Marathi Bombay, and half of Andhra from Tamil Madras?

The Circars were not included in the new state of Andhra Pradesh when it was formed after the end of the Nizam' rule in 1948. It required massive protests, and a fast unto death that actually ended in death to correct the absurdity of keeping Andhras out of Andhra Pradesh. But poisonous tensions embedded in that initial mistake could never be buried because they had never died. Telangana, consisting of the poorer districts of the Nizamate, soon convinced itself that its progress was being sabotaged by the economic aggression of the old Circars. By the 1970s a popular movement, also known as the 'mulki struggle', took shape, spurred by the thought that demonstrations and fasts could change a decision in a democratic polity.

Of Andhra's myriad chief ministers, spanning the scale from heroic to useless, only one man seemed to understand that if the problem was economic then the solution did not have to be political. He was Y.S. Rajasekhara Reddy, father of Jagan Reddy, and, ironically, the Congress leader who could legitimately claim to be close to Mrs Sonia Gandhi. The demand for Telangana all but evaporated over his six years as CM because he delivered development.

The casualty rate in public life rises not from murder, but suicide. In an astonishing blunder four years ago, a little after Rajasekhara died in a tragic helicopter accident, P. Chidambaram, then home minister, revived a comatose conflict by offering Telangana. Since then, everyone has suffered grievously because of this mistake, except the man who made it.

One of the great mysteries of the present UPA government has been its phenomenal indifference to public rage. It lined up a team of ministers, headed by Kapil Sibal, to sneer at Anna Hazare. Today, Andhra Pradesh is in cinders. What is the response of its top leaders? Mrs Sonia Gandhi emerges now and then to scold the BJP and returns to silence. Rahul Gandhi is deeply concerned about Jupiter velocity touched in the head by lunar sagacity. And Dr Manmohan Singh stops by in Delhi to implement some Rahul Gandhi diktat before he boards again a fast plane to somewhere far, far away. Andhra? It could be on another planet; and if Digvijay Singh has been left in charge, it probably has reached stratosphere in any case.

Political malpractice punishes the nation more than it does any ruling party. Has anyone measured the economic cost of Andhra's meltdown after Chidambaram's blunder? How much of our GDP have we lost in the last four years? And how much has gross domestic bitterness grown?

There will never be unanimity over Telangana, but the quality of governance is measured by the management of change. Far from ensuring peace, the Congress has itself splintered. Some solutions being suggested are downright stupid, like declaring Hyderabad as a common capital. Hyderabad is over 100 kilometres from the border of Seemandhra.

You cannot toss a bomb into the air, get out of the way, watch who gets hit on the street and then pick up votes from the debris.

WHY THERE IS NO AMETHI MODEL

How can you talk about something that does not exist?

26 April 2014

Have you ever wondered, amidst the manufactured debate about the Gujarat model of development, why there is never any talk of an 'Amethi model'? No mystery there. There is no development in Amethi. Congress cannot talk about something that does not exist. When your track record is regression, the only choice is pre-emptive aggression.

In the same decade when Amethi was wallowing in stagnation despite having the second most powerful person in India as its Member of Parliament, Gujarat was lifted from agricultural growth of around 2 per cent to 10 per cent. A few simple facts should suffice, without any overdose of statistics: with 5 per cent of India's population, Gujarat now soaks up 18 per cent of national investment and contributes 26 per cent towards its exports. Most important, a substantive portion of the meagre growth in employment during the arid decade between 2004 and 2014 has come from Gujarat. If Rahul Gandhi had done a quarter as much for Amethi as Modi has done for Gujarat, he could have offered a far more credible bid for leadership. Instead, his only option is silence on Amethi and diversionary tactics on Gujarat.

If anything, non-UPA parties have so much surplus ammunition that they do not quite know what to do with their reserve arsenal. In any other election, observations made by the Supreme Court on Tuesday 22 April would have made headlines. The highest court asked counsel of the Government of India, in sharp and even acerbic terms, why UPA had refused to obey a Court order to reveal names of Indians who had secret bank accounts in that convenient state known as Liechtenstein. Refusing to buy the Congress' limp excuses for delay, the Court noted, 'The direction to share the information forthwith cannot be understood as after completion of investigation by SIT. The Court said forthwith disclose . . . The language of the Court is clear. The directions are crystal clear when it said disclose forthwith . . . From July 4, 2011 till now, the revenue secretary and the joint secretary in the ministry of finance had kept our orders in cold storage.'

Such flagrant disobedience of a Supreme Court order is as astonishing as the complacent reaction to such a cover-up. Why did UPA hide these names? You can rest assured that if the list contained names of Opposition leaders this would have been lead story on Doordarshan and All India Radio for three years, and Congress spokespersons would have had a great deal to say on each day of this election campaign.

Government protected these names only because they include either those at the top of the present establishment pyramid or those within that charmed circle.

If media has missed this message, then the people have not. Now that voting machines have shut for nearly 350 Lok Sabha seats, it is quite evident that the Congress game plan for 2014 has gone belly up. Its very hinge, a total dependence on minorities, has been dislocated. Reports from Mumbai indicate that Catholic voters, for instance, refused to follow any diktat from a religious leader and went where their minds took them. A significant proportion of Muslims in the city refused to vote at all, rather than tread the traditional route to a Congress button.

The heart-warming reality is that a rising share of the electorate is voting for its stomach, for its welfare, and for the nation's economy, rather than out of fear or emotionalism. It matters less who the voter trusts than that it trusts a party for the right reasons. The young are turning out to be the most mature voters within the demographic pattern, for they have the most to lose from a lost economy. Their anger might have been sufficient to push any government out, but their rage is now laced with hope that Narendra Modi will restore the vision and horizon that has faded.

Modi will have to deliver both as Prime Minister and as Member of Parliament. In Varanasi, for instance, the tremendous enthusiasm of the people, across all traditional fissures, is based on the conviction that the massive ills within and around this ancient city, one of the great intellectual capitals of world civilisation, will be healed and the region nourished back to health. The phrase is not in use at the moment, but within five years Narendra Modi will have to create a Varanasi model of development, just as he has ensured a Gujarat model. That should become the template in 2019 against which other constituencies will be measured.

If the vote is at an all-time high for Narendra Modi on the banks of Ganga, and across the varied expanse of the Indian compass, then expectations are even higher. It has been a hard slog towards the Lok Sabha, but once he reaches that apex of democratic achievement, Narendra Modi will have to turn his energies and mind back to the India that sent him to Delhi.

A NOD IN THE WRONG DIRECTION

Why Rahul fell asleep in Parliament

13 July 2014

My sympathies are entirely with Rahul Gandhi in the Curious Case of the Sleeping Leader. The great inner chamber of the temple of Indian democracy, the Lok Sabha, can be infected with a languorous air during a hot Delhi summer afternoon. Some of the speeches do not help. Better parliamentarians than Rahul Gandhi have had to fight off a dangerous yawn during those critical hours after lunch when the body, drugged by food, and the mind, poisoned by torpor, yearns for a nap.

This used to be a consciously protected secret, in the best traditions of a cosy club, in that remote age before Speaker Somnath Chatterjee, seeking greater visible glory for MPs, permitted real time television recording of speeches. MPs welcomed the opportunity to become screen idols. What they did not fully appreciate is that cameras have no soul, and their handlers, cameramen, are wicked by nature. They wait for their brief moment, and pounce.

Perhaps Rahul Gandhi could have ordered suitable flunkeys in the information and broadcasting department to censor those startling images of him dropping off into sleep as soundly as a baby after a feed, during the debate on price rise. It is possible that the bureaucrats would not have even needed to check; they would have blanked the screen without being told, such is the culture of sycophancy in Delhi. But that was when Congress was in power. The same lot are ready to show his neck tilted somewhere close to 90 degrees when he should have been alertly leading the Congress charge on an issue at the top of the party's counteroffensive against NDA. I don't know if Rahul Gandhi has fully absorbed the meaning of defeat or not. His tragic nap in Parliament, to twist a metaphor, is his wake-up call.

It was touching to watch Parliament next morning, when Finance Minister Arun Jaitley rose to deliver his marathon Budget speech. Mrs Sonia Gandhi, like a very concerned mother, was taking no chances. She made her son sit beside her, on the front benches, where the chances of nodding off are negligible. Rahul Gandhi had spent his time during Prime Minister Narendra Modi's long reply to the debate on the President's address cleaning his mobile phone, or tinkering with it. This time he was on best behaviour. He had even come armed with pen and pad to make notes.

It would be interesting to discover what notes Rahul Gandhi actually made during Jaitley's oration, but one doubts that history will get that document for its archives. However, if Congress reactions to the Budget are any reflection, then those pages might well have been full of doodles.

Democracy is a partisan business. To that extent Congress hostility to the first NDA Budget is both predictable and understandable. But at the least Congress could have opted for a better line of fire. Its response was lazy, knee-jerk and thereby counter-productive.

Its first salvo accused NDA of merely copying UPA budgets. If that was indeed true then Congress should have praised Jaitley. Or has Congress now taken the position that Budgets produced by Dr Manmohan Singh and P. Chidambaram were a load of rubbish? Look before you leap, and think before you talk. The more likely reason for this misfire is that Congress propaganda had built up the argument that this Budget would be anti-poor. This was astonishing misjudgement given the consistency with which PM Modi has said that if government does not serve the poorest of the poor first, then it is no government at all. The best positive-discrimination welfare schemes today are being run in BJP states like Madhya Pradesh and Chhattisgarh, not Congress provinces like Maharashtra or Karnataka. The Budget exposed such propaganda as the lie it was.

The second charge was that the Budget lacked any big ticket vision. This too is a bit absurd. The Budget promised proper housing for every Indian by 2022; electricity in every home; sanctioned seed money for a hundred new satellite cities; opened up foreign direct investment in housing, defence; expanded infrastructure spending to add roads and link rivers; promised return of growth to 8 per cent or 9 per cent; and began the drive to create a clean India, with a pristine Ganga, by 2019, which is the 150th birth anniversary of Mahatma Gandhi. Is that too little for a first Budget that had to factor in an empty treasury, left desolate through reckless spending by desperate Congress governments?

Delhi's thinking is largely in the hands of those who think a power cut is a calamity, rather than those who have never seen power in their huts; those fantasising about palaces in Lutyens' Delhi dying instead of living without a roof; those who love a siesta instead of thirsting for clean water or slaving for a morsel of simple sustenance.

The promise is there in the Budget. The articulation is there. The vision exists. Now comes the tough part: the government has to deliver on a nation's dreams.

MODI SPOKE TO, AND OF, THE PEOPLE

His horizon was set by the heart, the compass magnetised by his mind

17 August 2014

Prime Ministers choose one of three options when they step up to the podium at the Red Fort on Independence Day. They speak to their governments; or mumble to themselves; or talk to the people of India. The first is easiest, since government is both narrator and narrative, and can enjoy the false comfort of self-congratulation: we did this (applause); we will do this (obligatory high-five).

The second option is a consequence of diffidence more than introspection. And if Dr Manmohan Singh made it a habit, it was possibly because introspection told him he had much to be diffident about. Dr Singh was a curious case of a Prime Minister who had to bow before a Supreme Leader in a dysfunctional relationship. He got stuck with the responsibility while Mrs Sonia Gandhi and her temperamental son Rahul Gandhi enjoyed power. The country suffered.

No prizes for guessing Prime Minister Narendra Modi's preference. He spoke to the people. His problem was not being better than the competition. That would have been too easy. His challenge was to excel himself, after the extraordinary standards he had set during a tumultuous election campaign. Now he had to establish his destination, notch priorities along the perspective and chalk out the route map of delivery, for if you soar without direction you can end up on a long flight to nowhere.

On the morning of 15 August we saw and heard the quintessential Narendra Modi. The horizon was set by his heart, the compass was magnetised by his mind. The thrust of his message was controlled by an elemental idea: India's progress is not just a government project; it is a people's project. As he put it in an eloquent metaphor: if 125 crore Indians take a single step each, then India moves ahead by 125 crore steps.

And so what in previous hands had degenerated into a bookkeeper's report to the annual general meeting of shareholders, swivelled on a fulcrum that probed, on the one hand, any malaise in national character, and repeatedly dragged our focus towards the curse and indignity of poverty, or the many crimes of gender bias. But this was realism, not pessimism. He also offered a vision that transformed the national mood with the conviction that achievement was not only possible, but within our grasp. The loudest cheers came from the young; the applause of teenage children in the audience at the Red Fort echoed the hopes of hundreds of millions in towns and cities across the land.

The exhilaration was explicable. India had found not just a Prime Minister but also a leader. Narendra Modi asked the questions that no one has raised: Why are we indulgent towards sons at the expense of daughters? Who is responsible for the utter shame of female foeticide? Do we need a law to keep our homes, our streets, our nation clean? When is the poison of caste and communal violence going to end? He challenged Indians to witness the rewards of harmony within ten years. Perhaps it is only the outsider, which is how the Prime Minister described himself, who can clearly see the plain truth of Delhi's insiders; but it needs leadership to tell the oldest elite of Indian democracy, the governing political-bureaucratic class, that its civil wars had damaged governance to a point where drastic reform was the only alternative.

An obituary notice was read out for the Planning Commission, for the very good reason that it has lost purpose. The significant failure of this body in the last decade has been its smug and arid approach to our gravest national crisis: poverty. A common sense estimate shows that in six decades of planned economy, we have reduced the number of Indians living under the poverty line by only an abysmal half per cent or so every year. This is both astonishing and unacceptable. Moreover, instead of searching for solutions through cooperation with states, the Planning Commission functioned through a series of imperial commands. It told state governments to beg before Delhi, so that they might be awarded their scrap or two. India is a federal nation, in law and practice. The Union Government does not rule directly over any geography other than a few tiny territories. Development works best through state governments. Delhi must be an enabler, not a dictator.

The world, as the Prime Minister noted, is changing. We cannot be insular; we need the creative energy of international cooperation in an era where technological innovation and state-of-the-art manufacturing are largely in the private sector. Jobs, in both industry and agriculture, are the best antidote to poverty, for they link individual welfare to national growth. India must prepare itself, as he said, to become a manufacturing hub of the world.

Prime Minister Modi knows that dreams become a reality only during waking hours. You cannot sleepwalk your way towards enchantment. He has the will to rouse the nation from inertia. The next months will show us how.

THE TIPPING POINT

The only surprising fact about most corruption stories is that anyone in authority gets surprised.

THE CULTURE OF POLITICAL CASH

Delhi recognises the colour of money, but does not always comprehend the culture of cash

4 June 2006

Delhi recognises the colour of money, but does not always comprehend the culture of cash. Delhi does not need any lessons in the colour, nuances, excesses, limitations and even the curiosities of power. Power is the legitimate coinage of Delhi. Money, in contrast, is the illegitimate child of politics.

A successful Mumbaikar is comfortable with money, and has every right to be so, because his dharma is business, and wealth creation is the proclaimed horizon of any business plan. Perhaps virtue might be an excessive word, but the wealth creator certainly does not view his obsession as immoral.

The wealth of a politician is more problematic. On the one side there is the arguable case of need. Democracy is an expensive business, and one is using both these words with care. I have no idea in which world the Election Commission lives, but in the real world the cost to the candidate in an election to Parliament is far above a crore of rupees. The more extravagant, or the more nervous, types can easily multiply that figure. Leaders with the safest of constituencies do not have the courage to take a chance and spend within the limits of a law that is totally unreal. Take a very simple fact. A Lok Sabha constituency could have up to 1,500 polling booths. A serious candidate would have at least four workers per booth. He would have to provide two meals and tea through the day. There is a huge outlay on transport on D-Day, and a buzzing network of party offices and functionaries to feed and lubricate. The budget for just the personnel management of election day can go up to Rs 20 lakh.

At the institutional level, political parties have to maintain a large and complex machinery, of which the central office is possibly the least expensive bit. No one has given any thought to the basic paradox of Indian democracy: its institutions have a massive cash flow requirement, without any revenue base. Theoretically, this circle is meant to be squared by membership fees, but that is now a joke. We do not discuss the anomaly because every political party is united by hypocrisy. Everyone knows the practical answer: black money, but nobody is ready to admit it.

SPEECHLESS

Does Dr Manmohan Singh ever listen to himself?

3 June 2007

Prime Minister Manmohan Singh gave a thoughtful speech at the annual session of the CII (Confederation of Indian Industry for all you yokels who do not know what the country's most powerful acronym stands for). He asked the captain, majors, colonels and generals of Indian business to remember that those who are not members of the CII are also Indians. The speech was overdue by about three years, but no matter. The 'also Indians' are ever grateful for the smallest mercies.

He also made the speech to the wrong group. He should have begun with an audience of one.

There is an exclusive telephone system in Delhi meant only for the Very Very VVIPs called RAX. It is an internal line for the highest of the high in government. Dr Singh should have picked up his RAX phone and called his finance minister for a cup of tea. Over tea, stressing each sentence till there was no room for misunderstanding, Dr Singh should have read this speech to Finance Minister P. Chidambaram.

Mr Chidambaram has produced three budgets. How come no one told him that Prime Minister Singh was interested in the welfare of the poor, and that he had thought out a Ten Point Charter to save the nation? Each one of the issues raised by Dr Singh could have been addressed in the national budget. None was.

Why should the CII listen to the Prime Minister when his own Cabinet could not care less?

Let's start with executive salaries, which Dr Singh condemns as 'excessive remuneration' which can lead to 'social unrest'. Let us say that the owner-chief executive of a major company pays himself around Rs 2 crore as salary for working hard, and delivering profits as chief executive. He pays the maximum-slab tax on this sum. But how much does the government pay him for being the owner? The latest issue of *India Today* informs me that in just one year, 2006-07, Dr Singh's government permitted shareholders of 1,100 companies to pocket Rs 40,000 crore in dividends. Did they pay any tax on Rs 40,000 crore? Not a rupee. Take out a calculator and do the maths.

Why preach about Rs 2 crore a year, with tax, when you have handed out an untaxed Rs 40,000 crore a year to the members of the CII?

Does Dr Singh listen to himself?

The sixth point of this Social Charter should have been Message No. 1. I had better quote the strong words used by the Prime Minister to avoid any accusation of misrepresentation. 'The operation of cartels by groups of companies to keep prices high must end . . . It is even more distressing in a country where the poor are severely affected by rising commodity prices. Cartels are a crime and go against the grain of an open economy. Even profit maximisation should be within the bounds of decency and greed!'

I hasten to point out that the exclamation is the Prime Minister's, and not an intrusive addition from the fevered brain of a mere columnist.

What do we learn from this searing paragraph?

1: Cartels exist and control prices.

2: They are willing to push up prices even of basic commodities, the bread line of the poor.

3: Cartels are a crime.

So what has Dr Singh's government, now in power for over a thousand days, done to punish this crime? Even one gesture, executive or legislative, would be worth knowing. When an ordinary thief steals, the majesty of the law imprisons him. When a criminal cartel of businessmen robs the poor of food, and exceeds the limits of decency and greed (the Prime Minister's words, not mine), all that the Prime Minister of India can do is plead self-restraint! (This time the exclamation mark is mine.)

Why preach when you are so utterly helpless?

There is a certain inevitability about Point No. 9 on Dr Singh's Social Charter, because everyone in public life tends to use this cane as a crutch. May I quote? 'Nine, fight corruption at all levels. The cancer of corruption is eating into the vitals of our body politic. For every recipient of a bribe there is a benefactor and a beneficiary.'

How true. So who is this mysterious recipient? Trust me, without a recipient, with hand outstretched and power in his eyes, no one would pay a bribe. No businessperson enjoys giving a bribe. He would rather spend the money on creature comforts. So who does he give the money to?

The politician. What has Dr Singh done to curb corruption in his government? Nothing. His personal honesty can no longer disguise the fact that money is being made at a rampant pace by many of his ministers. He knows this and is silent.

Why preach about the mote in the other's eye when there is a beam in your own?

Point No. 10 has an inevitable ring to it as well. He asks industry to 'finance socially responsible advertising'. I hope you know what 'socially responsible advertising' means. It means taking out acres of full-page ads, paid for by taxpayers' money, telling the world how wonderful the government is. With Dr Singh's picture at the top, of course.

'India has made us,' says the Prime Minister. 'We must make Bharat.' That is a good two-sentence one-liner, which rather forgets to mention that Bharat is no longer in any mood to be patronised.

HOW MUCH SLEAZE CAN YOU SPARE, BROTHER?

How did a lobbyist know of portfolio distribution?

9 May 2010

'My case is cleared, *na*?' said the politician who wanted to be telecom minister to the lobbyist for a telecom major four days before the present Union Cabinet was sworn in last summer. The middlewoman, Niira Radia, was coy and comforting in her first-name-basis response: 'Your case was cleared last night only.'

The touching aspect of this politician's piteous plea is a syllable, *na*. It has every shade of pathos, not to mention every variation of bathos, kneaded into it. The lobbyist is in command, and why shouldn't she be? She knows something that is privy to perhaps three or four people at the very highest level of the present government. She has a vested interest in telecom, and therefore a direct stake in the person who will run this department. The minister-to-be, A. Raja of the DMK, is in her debt, and he better not forget it. She does not convey how she knows the decision was taken the previous night, but she implies that she has intervened on Raja's behalf. Raja does not care whether a corporation got him this job or not. He is merely desperate to get it.

We know this today, a year later, because of some sterling journalism done by the television channel Headlines Today, which obtained transcripts and audio recordings of the taped conversation.

Raja is an intimate associate of the DMK's Karunanidhi family and Radia must now be the most famous middlewoman in the world. She is on the payroll of some of the most important corporates in contemporary India, both those with a tradition of grease and those with historic claims to probity.

Corporate warriors did not record this conversation, as a hapless Congress spokesman vainly tried to suggest in defence of an indefensible ally. It was taped by income tax authorities, who suspected Radia of tax fraud. Permission to do so was given by the home secretary. Raja's phone was on tap; Radia's was too. It was fortuitous that the six-month window of taping coincided with a general election and formation of a new government. This information has been available with the Manmohan Singh government for many months now. All it did was to harass and transfer officials, in order to protect politicians.

Partners can, in a coalition, demand their quota of Cabinet members, but the allotment of portfolios is the privilege of the Prime Minister. The DMK accepted a change in the other portfolios allotted to its ministers, but made telecom conditional to its participation in government.

Why was the DMK insistent and the PM reluctant?

Because both knew that Raja, as telecom minister in the first UPA Cabinet, was involved in a rip-off of incredible proportions. The Bofors allegations, which damaged the Congress in the 1980s, amounted to Rs 64 crore. This 2G telecom scam is said to be of the order of over Rs 60,000 crore, or a thousand times that of Bofors. If you want to understand the scale of this rip-off, think of this. Mrs Sonia Gandhi has been pressing government to provide food security for those below the poverty line. Agriculture Minister Sharad Pawar has said government does not have the resources to do so. The cost of a year's food security is far less than Rs 60,000 crore.

The unambiguous fact is that Dr Singh and Mrs Sonia Gandhi were aware of such sheer theft by DMK, but chose silence because the price of disclosure would have been collapse of this alliance. The DMK has levelled a cash pistol at the head of government, and the head has nodded to prevent its brains from being blown up.

The most important question is: how did a lobbyist know of portfolio distribution?

Radia was privy to specific details of government formation. The tapes are proof of her contacts, at one level; at another, they reveal squalid civil wars within the DMK.

Think of the perhaps hundreds of conversations between minister and middle-woman that could not be taped. How much sleaze is stored in them?

FROM RAGE TO OUTRAGE

Robber barons are too intelligent to steal from one another

1 August 2010

Is there a tipping point to corruption, that last straw, or rupee note, on the corrupt camel's back that ignites the dormant fuse of public response, and transforms rage into outrage?

Corruption is often draped in fig-leaf cynicism: everyone is corrupt, so why bother? If everyone is a thief, then theft becomes the law. There are no outlaws in a country teeming with in-laws.

Robber barons are too intelligent to steal from one another. They don't need to. That would also introduce unnecessary conflict into a cosy system. They all steal from the public. Robbery has graduated to daylight robbery.

Here are some facts printed on the front page of the *Times of India* on Saturday, 31 July. This, remember, is just one day's news, not the whole story. The Central Vigilance Commission has scrutinised only 16 Commonwealth Games projects so far, ranging from upgrades of stadiums, road construction, pavements, street lighting, etc., worth Rs 2,477.22 crore. Every quality certificate it examined was either forged or suspect. Each one. There is little point wasting space over details; they will be repetitive. Suffice to say that there has not been undiluted stink of this order for some time.

The odour is multinational, but naturally: this is the Commonwealth Games, after all. There is something called the Queen's baton relay, which means that the baton honoured with Queen Elizabeth's blessing has to reach Delhi by relay. If there is an event there must be a function, and if there is a function there must be corruption. The British authorities have provided a small glimpse into what is going on. The CWG Organising Committee sent about Rs 1.68 crore, in British pounds, to a company called AM Films UK Ltd for video equipment in a deal where there was no tendering, no procedure and no paperwork. The office address of this company shows only the presence of an AM Vehicles Hire Ltd, and on its books it says that it hired cars, makeshift toilets and barriers, not video equipment. Its director resigned, very conveniently, on 14 July.

Sports Minister M.S. Gill has admitted in Parliament that the cost of the Games increased 17.5 times since the *tamasha* began in 2003. Repeat that sentence 17 times for better effect.

Doesn't Prime Minister Manmohan Singh read newspapers? Is he going to preside over the opening ceremony of the Games in the company of those who should be on trial for loot? How long can he distance himself from the muck? There will come a time when his silence will be heard at a volume that speech could never match.

WANTED, A NOBEL PRIZE FOR HONESTY

What Indian politicians would really win is the Nobel Prize for Hypocrisy

12 September 2010

I have an excellent nominee for the first winner of the Nobel Prize for Honesty: Alexei Kudrin, finance minister of Russia. In the first week of this month he told the news agency Interfax that the best thing his countrymen could do to help the Russian economy was to smoke and drink more. These are his specific words: 'If you smoke a pack of cigarettes, that means you are giving more to help solve social problems such as boosting demographics, developing other social services and upholding birth rates . . . People should understand: Those who drink, those who smoke are doing more to help the state.'

There is an also-ran for the prize. On 10 September, Sha Zukang, Undersecretary General for Economic and Social Affairs at the UN, encouraged by a glass or four of alcohol, told Ban Ki-moon, the Secretary General, 'I know you never liked me, Mr Secretary-General—well, I never liked you, either . . .'

But the winner is Alexei Kudrin, by a long shot. He was sober.

His message is logical. Smoking gives you cancer; cancer kills you early. A dead person cannot claim state pension, which is good news. Death also shifts the age–youth ratio in favour of the young. Further, you pay higher taxes on cigarettes and drink—more money, then, to the exchequer. QED. Die to save the fatherland!

This is exactly how any finance minister driven to despair by deficits should express himself. But the rules tell him to talk like a weasel and promise more food, electricity, shelter and security even if he has to bankrupt the future in order to secure your votes today.

Dr Manmohan Singh, who had a hard time as finance minister and isn't actually on a picnic as Prime Minister, is straining at the leash. Years of being politically correct are beginning to tell. He tipped over when the Supreme Court instructed his government to feed impoverished Indians instead of letting grain rot. Dr Singh's retort was sharp; in sum, that the government was not in the business of charity. If the grain had to rot, so be it; if the impoverished wanted food they would have to go to the market. There is economic sense, apparently, in letting rats get fat.

Being a politician, Dr Manmohan Singh knows that his main responsibility is to keep the government afloat until heir-apparent Rahul Gandhi declares himself fit to rule rather than merely campaign through non-sequiturs. Dr Singh keeps sane in the waiting room thanks to a quiet sense of humour. How else can he deal with a colleague like Commerce Minister Anand Sharma who, poor chap, has declared to the Prime Minister that he has personal assets of a mere Rs 26,741? It is a shame, in these post-Gandhian times, that as important a personage as Anand Sharma should have less in his bank than it costs to buy an official suit, unless of course he buys his suits from what is stacked in his cupboard rather than in his bank account.

Given the parlous state of so many of our ministers—the indigent Subodh Kant Sahai, for instance, has personal assets of only Rs 1.4 lakh—should we suggest to Sweden that they should also offer a Nobel Prize for Poverty?

But what Indian politicians would really win, year after year, is the Nobel Prize for Hypocrisy.

NOW, FREEDOM FROM SOME INDIANS, PLEASE

Gandhi would never have let us sleep in peace as long as hunger and corruption raged across the motherland

14 August 2011

We lost the hinge of the plot on 15 August 1947 when we thought that raising the tricolour marked the end of the freedom project launched by Mahatma Gandhi in 1921. It was only the beginning of a second and equally difficult freedom struggle. The first had been against the British. The second freedom struggle is against fellow Indians.

Past and present compete for primacy as I ponder over the innumerable things we still want freedom from. There is, at the very top of the list, hunger. We do not have to search for hunger in the rural and tribal hinterlands where Maoists have mobilised masses. The Maoist gunfire is still only a growl; this hunger has not yet turned into anger. God help the indifferent fat-cat and complacent middle class the day—and night—the poor decide that those who have nothing also have nothing to lose.

The poor are not a distant reality. They sleep on the pavements of India's most spoilt and smug city, Delhi, on the plains in front of rising apartment towers whose value could buy up a small town. The street has been the only home of generations of children who still manage to smile when they are not begging. What is the upward mobility of a homeless child? The roof of a prison? Ninety per cent of the teens who end up in Tihar do not even possess a second shirt. Prison is the only home that Indian India offers them, after six and a half decades of freedom.

I do not want to sound unduly harsh. We inherited an India in 1947 in which up to four million had died in a Bengal famine. We have left famine, a consequence of British economic policies, behind. But that is scant solace to those half a billion who still live on the edge of sustenance, their hopes gone at 20, their teeth gone at 40, their lives withered not much later. This is the freedom project that must consume the whole of India's attention over the next decade.

We need freedom from corruption. If corruption was limited to powerful ministers, there would be enough space in prison for the guilty. But the caste system of corruption permeates down to the lowest levels of authority, the clerk at the passport office who milks a hundred-rupee note out of your misery; the babu in the district magistrate's office who will not hand over your legitimate due without keeping a percentage in his pocket; the constable who treats every rule as a means of self-enhancement. Every pothole that you see is a signature scar of corruption: have you wondered why our roads become a serrated battlefield after the first rains? Is Delhi the only city in the world where it rains? Why doesn't rain lacerate roads in London, Istanbul or Singapore—where, in fact, it rains every afternoon?

The liberation list is a long one. Indians want freedom from inequity, hypocrisy, sycophancy, stupidity. The sly corruption of sycophancy is perhaps the worst of these maladies, because it twists truth in order to feed the leader's ego.

Mahatma Gandhi, who made 15 August possible, did not celebrate freedom. He was not among the joyous revellers in Delhi; he was in Calcutta, saving Indians from Indians. He could not even find a celebratory phrase when BBC interviewed him at his lonely perch in Belgachia, a single-heart army against the depredations of human evil. Gandhi was a far happier man in 1920; he knew, once the people had risen, that freedom was now a question of when, not if. He could see a quarter-century ahead. Gandhi would have beamed at modern India's great accomplishments; but he would never have let us sleep in peace as long as hunger and corruption raged across the motherland.

THE WILL AND WON'T OF CORRUPTION

Whenever corruption tops the voters' agenda, the ruling party is reduced to at least half its strength in the Lok Sabha

28 April 2013

A neuroscientist of Indian origin, V.S. Ramachandran, has noted that the human brain might get lost in variations of 'free will', but can certainly be clear about a 'free won't'. Mr Ramachandran should start classes for powerful Indian politicians. Dangle a temptation before them, and 'will' shall trump 'won't'.

One sign of the march of Indian democracy is creative progress in the science of corruption. In the shoddy old days, someone took a bag stuffed with cash, a flunky counted the rupees and took it to the master's bedroom. A high dignitary like a Prime Minister would get more respect; his cash came in a proper suitcase. A bull operator on the Bombay Stock Exchange claimed in the early 1990s that he had gifted P.V. Narasimha Rao with a suitcase packed with Rs 1 crore in neat bundles. These days, of course, such a pittance would be below the dignity of even junior Cabinet ministers. You will recall that last year Beni Prasad Verma, a proud member of Dr Manmohan Singh's Cabinet, laughed when his colleague was accused of skimming Rs 70 lakh. Too small a figure to be credible, Verma chortled. Did Dr Manmohan Singh frown? Not at all. Verma is still a Cabinet minister.

Perhaps suitcases are passé, perhaps not. More sophisticated politicians use a brilliant variation. They pick up loot through a relative. And so a minister's wife gets crores in professional fees for a transaction worth possibly lakhs, if worth anything at all. How can you argue with that? Value, like beauty, lies in the eyes of the beholder. If a chit-fund businessman treats your wife's legal acumen at such worth, who are we to argue?

One great illusion of the last decade has been our belief that Dr Manmohan Singh would ensure corruption-free governance since he himself was above board. The latest exposé in the spectrum and coal mine scams proves beyond any argument that his personal reputation provided cover for massive theft by his ministers. He knew, and did nothing about it, because his own survival as PM was at stake. The CBI affidavit to the Supreme Court in the coal scam is a devastating indictment of his government. It proves that CBI and law officers lied to the Court earlier to protect the government. It admits that its affidavit was vetted by the Prime Minister's Office and the law minister, Ashwani Kumar. Kumar's claim that he was making only grammatical corrections is stupid. It assumes that the rest of us, including justices of the Supreme Court, are fools.

Mrs Indira Gandhi once dismissed corruption as an international phenomenon. She was right. It is also an old story. Witness this report, datelined Berlin, first published exactly 100 years ago, in 1913, and reproduced in the *International Herald Tribune* of 22 April 2013: 'The charges of bribery of Government officials by members of the Krupp firm have momentarily sunk into insignificance compared with new charges launched against German armament interests of fomenting international rivalries and ill-feeling. Selecting France as a fertile field for these machinations, the armament interests endeavoured to circulate false reports in the French press with a view to frightening Germany into buying large supplies of arms. The false announcement that the French army intends to double its supply of machines was evidently intended to spur the Germans on to double their own supply.'

The difference between Europe and India a century later is that Europe reveals the names of those who hold secret accounts in Swiss banks. In India we specialise in creating escape routes for the unlucky few who are discovered with their hands in the nation's treasury.

There is a saving grace. India is a democracy. When Indians get angry on an epic scale, they rise with a fury that ravages the ruling party.

Whenever corruption tops the voters' agenda, the establishment is reduced to roughly half its previous strength in the Lok Sabha. In 1974, Jayaprakash Narayan led an unprecedented stir against corruption. A desperate Mrs Gandhi was forced to declare an Emergency in 1975. In 1977 the Congress lost over 200 seats, ending up with only 150 MPs. In 1989, Bofors allegations slashed the Congress from 420 MPs to less than 200. Narasimha Rao, who had more than corruption to worry about, was similarly mauled in 1996. If the pattern persists, the Congress could drop to around 100 after the next general elections.

IDENTITY AND ELECTIONS

Around half a billion people, spread across a complex ethnic range, from every segment of wealth and poverty, vote to hold authority accountable, and their collective will is distilled into the next government: as modern miracles go, this is top of the class.

AT THE DROP OF A TEAR

The limited uses of sentimentality in winning votes

12 February 2012

Tears are a fragile weapon in public life. Sentiment can be a powerful virtue in mass mobilisation, but sentimentality never works. Genuine tears, which can only appear very rarely, can be powerful. However, tears of helplessness or regret invite scorn: the first is evidence of impotence, the second is proof of uselessness.

Law Minister Salman Khurshid committed double jeopardy when he tried to win Muslim sympathy during the current UP Assembly campaign by claiming that his leader Mrs Sonia Gandhi cried when he showed her pictures of the Batla House incident more than three years ago, in which Delhi Police shot down suspected terrorists. The dead young men were from eastern UP.

Khurshid was trying to send multiple signals simultaneously with this purported claim, not least of them being his personal proximity to the leader. It just might have worked if Mrs Sonia Gandhi had been leader of the Opposition during the Batla House encounter. Instead, this lachrymose recollection backfired spectacularly. Instead of being the answer to a dilemma that has troubled the Congress since it happened, it awakened fresh and self-defeating questions.

If Mrs Gandhi was so moved by pictures of dead young Muslims, what did she do about it? She was not a helpless politician. The home minister of India and the chief minister of Delhi belonged to her party in 2008. Why did she not take any action against them if she thought they were wrong, and the killings were an act of police excess? Was Mrs Gandhi merely shedding crocodile tears? Mrs Sonia Gandhi has successfully maintained a distance from the government on controversies like this. Khurshid's faux pas has inadvertently carried the blame to her desk. Khurshid claims he briefed her. He showed her photographs which presumably blew the police version apart, inducing tears. She cried. And then? Three years of nothing.

Mrs Gandhi clearly understood the inherent contradictions immediately, and authorised the Congress general secretary in charge of Uttar Pradesh, Digvijay Singh, to dismiss Khurshid's story as fanciful. Perhaps she was also embarrassed by an implicit stereotype to which women are subjected: women are expected to be teary. Mrs Gandhi does not see herself as a gushy person. Would any colleague of Mrs Indira Gandhi have ever suggested that she wept profusely after any incident, and Mrs Gandhi saw more havoc than perhaps any Indian leader. Mrs Sonia Gandhi has fashioned her political image in her mother-in-law's cast.

We cannot blame Khurshid for the sob-sop to voters, even if he chose to overdo it. The memory of the Batla House encounter has been troubling UP Muslims, and has clearly affected its electoral attitude. No politician touches a controversy unless compelled to. But the memory of Batla House was far more fresh during the general elections of 2009. Why was it absent from the electoral agenda then? The Congress soared from a measly 22 Assembly victories in 2007 to a stunning 22 Lok Sabha seats in 2009 largely because of Muslim support in UP. This means a virtual quadrupling of Assembly seats: you have to win over 80 Assembly segments to get 22 MPs.

UP Muslims had empathy for Mrs Sonia Gandhi, because they did not consider her complicit in the destruction of the Babri mosque. This bought her time. But they have watched with increasing dismay as the Congress government permitted Home Minister P. Chidambaram to justify the Batla House incident as legitimate without even the grace of an independent enquiry. Muslims are tired of sops dangled before an election, which then mysteriously disappear once the vote is in.

The only leader, at least in my knowledge, who used a teardrop effectively was the great Kashmiri giant Sheikh Muhammad Abdullah, when he came under sudden pressure in the last days of the 1977 Kashmir campaign. Eyes moist during his last rally in Srinagar, he reminded his people of his lifelong sacrifice and commitment. He won by a landslide. But his eyes never went moist a second time.

POWER OF LOVE, AND LOVE OF POWER

The voter does not worry about bedrooms

19 February 2012

Every good election contributes something to folklore. Uttar Pradesh is the land of lore; and the turbulence of its politicians is matched only by the sardonic wit of its voters. The culture of Awadh has many dimensions, but a principal inheritance is the nuance of language. Awadhis can turn a conversation into a duel of scalpels, interspersed with the stiletto stab that penetrates just enough to puncture an ego without hurting the flesh. Cut and thrust are an art form, not a Western duel at high noon. The sophisticate leave invisible scars; they do not kill. That would be vulgar. The poet prefers to die a thousand deaths rather than injure a feckless or faithless lover; he might be tempted to ambush a rival but he would never waylay.

Lucknow is the nerve centre of this culture, but the neural tingle stretches across the hinterland, adjusting to local need or idiosyncrasy, but ever vibrant in a dialectical manoeuvre, making its point through askance analogy rather than a confrontational joust. Life, after all, must continue when scores are settled. Ganga complements and competes with Jamuna as both enter the domain of a hundred kingdoms, and the resonance of religion, history, culture and war, lifted by human endeavour or sunk by its indolence. The two rivers bear the weight of past and future lightly, and then embrace in Allahabad, where Uttar Pradesh ends, before wandering off through the east towards the ocean.

The daughters of Awadh are not to be underestimated. There is more fertility of imagination in a raised eyebrow, the toss of a henna-hair curl, than in an anthology of anecdotes from arid elsewhere. And while humour is so often the solace of misfortune, whether the cause of ruin be the love of power or the power of love, nothing excites the genius of gentle laughter more than the innumerable frictions, and sometimes the bombastic fictions, of the troubled relationship between age and virility. It is particularly pleasing to the feminine sensibility that only men can be victims.

Virility is both the pride of man and his desolate downfall, as inevitable as the passage of time, retribution for the plumed strut of youth, evidence that in the battle of sexes women have the staying power. When along comes that rare instance when a man can claim, with credible hints, that he has defeated time, there is jealous admiration from his peers and a bit of awed jollity among women. The late artist M.F. Husain had the ability to sustain such an image, and this was sufficient, for discretion prevents a peep into the bedroom. The hero of the present hour is clearly the octogenarian politician Narayan Dutt Tewari. There has been no story as remarkable in Indian politics as the rise of a wolf in khadi clothing.

Less than two years ago Tewari was shoved out of his grace-and-favour habitation in the palatial Governor's residence in Andhra Pradesh because a caustic madam had photographed, on her mobile, women massaging parts of his body that tend to ache rather more than shoulders or neck. He was jeered all the way into retirement in the Himalayas by a middle class that gets especially vindictive when it feels it has missed out. In Dehra Dun Tewari was, and is still being, chased by a man who wants his DNA sample to confirm that Tewari is his real dad. Tewari refuses to undergo this test of paternity. The embarrassment of three Karnataka ministers who were caught, weeks ago, watching pornography on their phones while officially serving the electorate in the Assembly, is nothing compared to what Tewari must have undergone. And yet today he is a star of the Congress campaign in Uttarakhand and Uttar Pradesh. According to reports, the public response of crowds is noteworthy, and the private response impressive. Men talk in hushed admiration of the One Who Defeated the Ancient Law of Sanyas.

The Indian has never confused the morality of public life with the stresses of private behaviour. He accepted Gandhi as a Mahatma despite confessions that would have destroyed a father figure in another society. Peccadilloes might invite the occasional laugh, but the Indian leaves punishment of infidelity to God. This does not mean that sexual vice is condoned. But Indians do not enforce Victorian, or even contemporary American, codes of behaviour upon their leaders. Voters will judge Tewari at the hustings on the basis of his political arguments rather than his bedroom preferences.

It might be a sign of old age that you recover the gall that you lost in your middle age. Certainly Narayan Dutt Tewari has sufficient chutzpah to put a photographed past into the abyss of amnesia as he struts ahead to canvass for a party far older than him. He is the stuff of lore.

LIFE AFTER ANOTHER RESHUFFLE

With turbulence ahead, Rahul has only one option, the long view

28 October 2012

I would be surprised if Rahul Gandhi joined Dr Manmohan Singh's Cabinet in the next reshuffle. Barring one exception, no member of the Nehru family—now known as the Nehru–Gandhi dynasty—has served either as Chief Minister, or under some Prime Minister in Delhi.

It was far from certain in 1937 that India would be free in 1947, but Jawaharlal Nehru, the most famous leader of the United Provinces (the British name for the area now broadly Uttar Pradesh), did not ever consider the possibility of heading the first Congress government formed in the state, even as a stepping stone to post-Raj prime ministership. It was either the Delhi penthouse or nothing, no matter how long the wait or how bleak the immediate circumstance. The one exception was when Mrs Indira Gandhi became Lal Bahadur Shastri's information and broadcasting minister. She quickly tired of this middleweight portfolio. She was born to fight in a higher division.

When Mrs Sonia Gandhi could not become Prime Minister in 2004, there was no question of serving instead as home or finance minister. Conversely, if she had been sworn in, Dr Singh would have been delighted to become her finance minister. Curiously, no heir has even been a member of a parent's Cabinet. Mrs Indira Gandhi became Congress president when Jawaharlal Nehru was alive; she played a crucial political role both in the dismissal of the first Left-alliance government in Kerala as well as during the aftermath of the military defeat in the 1962 China war. But she did not serve as a minister under Nehru. Nor did Rajiv Gandhi believe that he ought to join his mother's Cabinet, if only to train for her job.

Rahul Gandhi can read the tea leaves as well as anyone else. The gossip society gets hyperactive before any reshuffle, and there are many who believe that he wants to transition towards the future through a spell as external affairs minister, considered a soft job (which it is not, incidentally). The family line, however, wanders between either PM or Leader of the Opposition. In 1977 Mrs Gandhi would have been Leader of the Opposition if she had won her seat in Rae Bareli. When she was elected from Chikmagalur in a later by-election, a nervous (or fatuous) Janata Party foolishly wasted its time trying to debar her from sitting in the Lok Sabha. Rajiv Gandhi was Leader of the Opposition in the 1989–91 Parliament. Rahul Gandhi will get both public sympathy and real-time training on the vital intricacies of our form of government, if he sits in the House on the Opposition benches after the next general elections.

Rahul Gandhi's assessment of Congress problems is relevant when he says he wants to rebuild the party. Corruption and poor governance during UPA 2 will of course take their toll when these elections are held; but this is compounded by a collapse of party infrastructure. Compare the Congress with Sharad Pawar's NCP, for instance. Even at any low ebb of its reputation, the NCP will always deliver a seat or two more than its electoral worth because of organisational strength. The Congress, on the other hand, disappears when it is defeated. It is heavyweight in power, and flyweight in Opposition.

The 'wave theory' has made the Congress complacent. This is a belief that the voter identifies the Congress with a sympathetic and stable government, rather than organisation and ideology; therefore there is no point in wasting any time upon the latter. It is hardly an accident that ideologically motivated parties, like the leftists or the BJP, have the more loyal organisations.

It is perfectly logical that Rahul, who can look forward to at least three more decades in politics, should take a long view, particularly with so much turbulence ahead. The coming storms will test not just the skills of the skipper, but also the sturdiness of the ship. At the moment the Congress is leaking like an upturned water sprinkler. Rahul Gandhi's attempts to add tar to the party's keel by improving the Youth Congress base have mostly failed, but he needs to persist till the cadre understand.

Victory and defeat are cyclical, as indeed they should be; UPA 2 is in tatters because it thought it had purchased a permanent seat in power. A party has to be ready for life after defeat. Mrs Indira Gandhi could save the Congress from 1977's desolation because of her own emotional relationship with the underprivileged, and the fact that the Congress organisation had not yet withered. Rahul Gandhi has neither of these advantages. It is going to be a hard life ahead.

THE BUSINESS OF POLITICIANS IS POLITICS

Judgement is so much easier than introspection

30 June 2013

Very curious. When Barack Obama suspended his campaign for re-election to supervise relief for victims of a terrible hurricane on the East Coast, there was applause even from his opponents. Republican strategists later suggested that this intervention provided the momentum that ensured an Obama victory. But when Narendra Modi stepped into Uttarakhand, very hurriedly followed by Rahul Gandhi, voices rose in protest and some columnists brandished a long pen to call them ambulance chasers.

Obama wanted votes. So do Modi and Rahul Gandhi. What is so terribly wrong about persuading voters that you can govern by proving you can deal with a crisis? What is so venal about politicians wanting to indulge in politics? There is a very welcome downside to this: if you leap into the fray without knowing how to jump, the negative backlash will be ferocious. Accountability is every democracy's insurance policy against incompetence.

A few marginal elements in media, slipped into stupidity. The news website for Hotmail, owned by Microsoft, framed a 'Yes or No' poll in cringe-inducing terms that bashed the whole community of Indian politicians. It offered a choice between 'Yes, it is natural for selfish politicians to take credit' and 'No. Politicians must not stoop to such low levels'.

May I suggest a similar poll about Microsoft? 'Yes. Microsoft is a multinational which would never dare to describe an American politician as selfish because he or she tried to help citizens during a natural calamity'. And: 'No. Multinationals like Microsoft must never reduce webspace media into a heckling circus with the IQ level of a garrulous judge on a reality show'.

What did we expect those in charge of governments to do? Go off on holiday while their citizens were in danger? Did some pundits carp because Modi, always a favourite lightning rod, got the idea first? Would they have queued up to applaud if some other chief minister had led the way?

Rahul Gandhi, to his credit, understood what some journalists did not, that the people's view would not be swayed by media pulpit oratory, but by the quality of relief work in affected areas. He may have even tested this proposition with a quick opinion poll, which is now almost obligatory in any serious campaign process. People are not silly. They do not blame politicians for an act of nature. But neither do they forgive governments that are unable to respond to the administrative challenge which comes in the wake of such a tragedy. If the Congress is in trouble in Uttarakhand it is because the state government was missing from action.

There is space for tension in the wide territory over which the paths of media and politics criss-cross. This is perfectly normal, and should even be encouraged. What is fascinating is the constantly evolving dynamic of this relationship.

In an innovative reversal, journalists are now beginning to lay down rules on how politicians should do their job. We are not talking corruption here, but the rather more vague 'moral ambience' of decision-making. Both politicians and journalists once set standards for themselves; they now seem intent on setting standards for each other. Judgement is so much easier than introspection.

We shall see how this plays out, particularly with an election season under way. Tensions will peak as politicians seek to rise in the estimation of voters, and journalists try to puncture them. With so much at stake, it is almost inevitable that 'facts' will sometimes be twisted for partisan ends, and that 'truth' will be manipulated to defame opponents. This is going to be a particularly tough election, because power is neither gained nor surrendered easily.

Fortunately, the supreme court of both professions is the citizen. Wherever ego might lead a journalist, or an exaggerated sense of power take a politician, the true measure of worth is determined by the court of public opinion. There is no journalism without an audience. There is no political office without a voter. This is the balance that keeps democracy sane.

f the Congress had truly believed in Telangana, it would have mpleted the process three years ago, used this time to absorb reaction d respond by showcasing the practical merits of its decision. A ecision now is mercenary: to milk the environment for what votes it an bring, and postpone ensuing problems. The timing is determined not by advantage to the people but by thoughts of benefit to the party.

But politics is not a parlour game, even when the parlour is as charming as the one in a spacious Delhi bungalow. All that Telangana has managed to achieve so far is to split the Congress, spur rage on the Andhra street, and provide more fodder to separatist banners. The dispute over Telangana has generated a quarrel over Hyderabad. The second can become as chronic as the first. What was intended as a win–win situation could become a lose–lose scenario for Congress.

Likewise, nothing stopped UPA from passing food security legislation in the first six months of its second term, rather than the last six months, except fear that implementation would expose the inadequacies of the project.

A promise is only as good as the worth of its trust. In 1971, Mrs Indira Gandhi was not enveloped by the odour of corruption, including within her own family. The poor believed that she would usher in an Indian version of socialism that would end their misery. No one laughed at Mrs Indira Gandhi, or indeed her defence minister, except at his own peril. Today, there are reasons for scepticism. The Congress has been in power for three of the four decades since 1971, in sustained spells rather than the sporadic bursts of V.P. Singh, Chandrashekhar, Deve Gowda or Inder Gujral. Indira Gandhi's promise is still a dream.

Every election is another gate towards the future, not a back door to the past. We must solve inherited problems, of course, the most important of which is surely poverty. But this needs an economic programme that takes change forward in quantum leaps, not throwaway sops. In 2009, UPA won handsome endorsement because voters believed that if it got five more years, it would create a new India. Five years have passed. We are staring instead at a very old India.

The dark side of today's political satire is the evil of corruption.

THE VOTING PATTERNS OF HUMOU

Laughter is judgement. The life of UPA is over

11 August 2013

Humour is a mortal enemy of politicians. A joke might not destroy reputation quite as effectively as a corruption scandal, but it deflates credibility. Through his long career Defence Minister A.K. Antony has been wise enough never to get tempted by a wisecrack; wit is not his forte. He might therefore be a little bewildered by the artillery fire of jokes after his disastrous mismanagement of the border incident in which five Indian soldiers lost their lives. Such humour has a memory. The voter will remember 'Pakistan has two deadly weapons: AK-47 and A.K. Antony'.

If it is any consolation to Antony, jokes about Prime Minister Manmohan Singh and Mrs Sonia Gandhi are far more harsh. As we leapfrog our way towards another general election, the Congress might discover that its biggest problem is ridicule.

It does not matter now when the next general election is held. We a in the last chapter of a drama that has gone on too long. The life of t government is over; dreaming of resurrection on a deathbed is a w of time. For most of this term, policy was lost in a swamp. N decisions are designed to serve as slogans.

There is a school within the ruling establishment selling the theory that corruption as an election issue has been deflected. This is delusion. The voter is not going to be finessed by the argument that all politicians are corrupt, and so theft of the present lot should be condoned. A jury can punish only the person in the dock, and the present government is on trial in the next electoral court.

Jokes are both evidence and argument in this trial; the voter is lawyer and judge. But there is some good news for those in custody. The maximum sentence is just five years in wilderness. The next five years will pass as quickly as the last five.

MODI HAS LAID SIEGE TO DELHI

Sardar Patel did not end princely raj in 1947 so that we could create one in 2014

3 November 2013

During a week when we pondered over the iron man of India, Sardar Patel, and remembered the iron lady, Mrs Indira Gandhi, a question kept flitting through my mind. Did the great Sardar dismantle the princely order of the British Raj only so that it might be replaced by a princely order of an Indian Raj?

Both Patel and Mrs Gandhi were undiluted nationalists, but the Sardar was not encumbered by any ism other than nationalism. Mrs Gandhi selected a limp form of socialism as her security blanket when the electoral temperature dropped for the Congress in 1969. Her weak-pink socialism provided the temporary warmth of false comfort. A highlight of her programme was the abolition of commitments made by Sardar Patel in 1947 to princes who surrendered their treaty rights with the British to join the Union of India.

And then, when the political weather turned icy in the wintry Emergency of 1975 and 1976, Mrs Gandhi turned her own party into a princely order, by opting for dynasty. The Nehru–Gandhis once belonged to the Congress; the Congress now belongs to the family.

The idea of dynasty, however, had such rare power that it went viral and infected other strains of Indian socialism, particularly the Ram Manohar Lohia school, which once took its ideology a little more seriously than it took God. The most lurid examples of reverse takeover are parties led by Mulayam Singh Yadav and Lalu Yadav. Their sperm-antics have had significant consequences, not just for them but also for the larger politics of north India. As the credibility of socialists gets punctured repeatedly in the north, the non-Congress space is being filled by BJP. Socialists lost the game early in Madhya Pradesh and Rajasthan; they could now be marginalised in UP and Bihar.

In theory, democracy provides an egalitarian opportunity base for merit to flourish and mediocrity to wither. A dynastic dispensation imposes entitlement on democracy. If pushed, dynasty seeks relevance through sentimental history. Rahul Gandhi wants legitimacy for his personal ambitions in the assassinations of his grandmother Mrs Indira Gandhi and father Rajiv. If the sacrifice of ancestors was sufficient to propel anyone to power, then surely the articulate Gopal Gandhi, great-grandson of the one Gandhi who was a Mahatma, deserves a look-in.

Those who milk a sentimental past are missing the bigger point: young India's attention is locked into the future. Confidence in economic growth has snapped. Rising prices and falling incomes are the visible sides of an economy dropping south. While their parents feel helpless, the young are beginning to feel hopeless. They want to believe in India, which is why they are so deeply incensed by the betrayal evident in the careless indifference of the UPA government. Their anger across the country is palpable to everyone except occupants of gilded cages in the Delhi zoo.

Narendra Modi is the flavour of this season not because he is building a statue of Sardar Patel, but because he is the outsider who has laid siege to Delhi. He is voice and beneficiary of this rage. Whenever Delhi's sniffy elite responds with contempt—as when a Cabinet minister dismisses Modi as a mere chaiwallah—it only increases the multitude behind Modi. After all, there are more Indians earning their livelihood through tea and labour than sons of an elite that has passed its sell-by date. Modi has walked into the void of governance created by UPA.

The best one can say about the spat over Patel and Jawaharlal Nehru is that, for a change, the debate is on a civilised subject. But not a single vote will be cast in 2014 about who would have been a better Prime Minister in 1947. The vote will be about who can be the best Prime Minister for 2014. Modi is lucky. He is facing a double vacuum. Dr Manmohan Singh has faded out, and Rahul Gandhi is unable to creep in.

It is perfectly reasonable for a political party on the dipping end of public support to raise its drowning spirits by clutching at a straw. Hence the floater that Modi has peaked too early; elections are still six months away. The objective answer lies in the Diwali depression visible in the shops. A recent survey showed that 57 per cent respondents believed this is the worst Diwali in a decade. As for the next six months, 77 per cent thought the economy would remain as bad or get worse. Such a trend might ease, but will not disappear. India is not a happy nation. That should make any ruling party deeply unhappy.

DEMOCRACY IS KARMA COME TO LIFE

Curiosity never killed the cat. If the cat died it was because it jumped to conclusions

17 November 2013

Which sensible person can ever ignore the irresistible charm of a useless fact? Formal Western dinner table seating, in which a woman is placed between two men, emerged during the Crusades on the very sound principle that the presence of a lady was essential to ensure good manners among men. No Latin poet was born in Rome. Puerto Ricans cure a hangover by rubbing a lemon under their arms, while Casanova had an equally useful need for them, which, alas, cannot be mentioned in a family newspaper. The Russian tennis star Mariana Sharapova had an on-court grunt during Wimbledon in 2005 that was measured at 101.2 decibels, which is louder than a macho motorcycle.

Does such knowledge, which I picked up at random from travel reading, serve any purpose? This question is hopelessly puritan. The charm of knowledge lies in its catholic breadth. How do we know what we need to know unless we know what we do not know?

Every scientist must be as curious as a philosopher. 'Low' curiosity, of which I have provided some splendid examples, is as engaging as 'high' curiosity. I bet you really do want to know what precisely Casanova did with lemons.

Curiosity, in my measured view, never killed any cat. If the cat died it was only because it jumped to conclusions. Enquiry into the unknown is the start of any adventure. Nothing venture, nothing gain. It is true that for every Columbus who lost his way towards a glorious new world, there are dozens who ended up at the bottom of an ocean. So what? Failure is only an incentive for the next generation. That's progress.

If old Christopher Columbus had a fault, it was that he opened up the way for the transfer of Europe's diseases to a people who had never known anything as fatal as smallpox, or pox. Discovery becomes a curse when it fuels aggression and exploitation, both of which give full expression to man's infinite capacity for cruelty. Who knows what the many missions, including India's, will find on Mars, but it would be terrible folly if we sought to convert Mars into another Earth. If we ever find Martians, we will discover a derogatory word for them, and then launch a genocide to steal their minerals. Private American companies have already begun offering investors a speculative piece of Mars.

The value of curiosity lies in tidbits. There is no race more inquisitive than the Indian, which is why no train or bus journey on the subcontinent is ever silent. Conversation is the stimulant of the masses. Communication with a stranger is a sign of good behaviour, quite unlike Britain, for instance, where it would be considered intrusive.

Indians never learn the truth about India from media, much as media might like to believe otherwise. They know that truth, in any case, is much larger than fact, and they learn about politics and power from one another, through chat between strangers in a train compartment, or on a bus seat, which they then circulate through the teashop or the office. A stranger has no vested interest. India had social media long before technology blinked its way into our palms. Every Indian face is a book. Every Indian voice is a twitter.

Indians, therefore, do not make up their minds only in anticipation of a poll. They enjoy opinion for the sake of opinion, and as a tool of empowerment. They judge the powerful with thorough due diligence.

They take their time, for they have plenty of it. But once they have made up their mind, they do not change it easily, or ever, until judgement day, which is the day of elections.

They love the structure of democracy, with its marvellous bookends: free speech holding up one side of space, and free will closing the other. They know that the day of judgement is a fundamental right; it can be neither deferred nor aborted. They do not need torchlit processions every week, or rallies in a maidan. There will come a day on which their volcanic rage can explode, and be replaced by fresh investment in hope.

Democracy is karma come to life. For one day the Indian voter becomes god of his world. What more could he want? Politicians' nerves get shot while waiting for election results. Media gets frantic. Government bites its nails. But a voter is never curious about the result. There is no reason to be. The voter knows the result long before an election.

THE THREE MISTAKES OF CONGRESS

Chidambaram believes he is a better leader than Rahul Gandhi

23 February 2014

Every good drama needs a few sub-plots whirling through the mainframe. The most captivating within our current political theatre is surely the joust that P. Chidambaram has begun with Narendra Modi. On surface level, it is not much more than a claim for primacy between a politician who inherited wealth, English and Harvard as a birthright, and the outsider who learnt life's lessons in a teashop. But no story-within-a-story is worth the price of admission if it is limited to the obvious.

We can never be sure what transpires within the recesses of the mind, let alone the heart. But one wonders if Chidambaram is also signalling, with his jibes and jabs, to his own party that he would have done a far better job than Rahul Gandhi if he had been made Congress candidate for prime minister.

If Chidambaram does believe this, he is right. He, and indeed at least three other Congress leaders, would have ensured that Congress did not fade away mid-journey. Others have internalised the angst of legitimate ambition denied; Chidambaram has gone vocal. Nothing is more compelling evidence than his extraordinary statement that he is 'not unhappy' at Jayalalithaa's desire to release Rajiv Gandhi's assassins. Chidambaram was among those for whom Rajiv's tragic death was a personal, in addition to being a national, loss. He has suddenly put some distance from emotional bonds with the ruling Nehru-Gandhi family.

There were at least three occasions on which Congress could have signalled that the family was only part of the Congress rather than the whole of it. The first was the Presidential election of 2012. If Dr. Manmohan Singh had been shifted upstairs to Rashtrapati Bhavan and Pranab Mukherjee made PM, Congress would have been in play in the general election of 2014. Mukherjee was the opponent that BJP feared most. He had experience, articulation, party commitment and would have been able to retain as well as bring in allies.

The second person on BJP's worry list was Meira Kumar. She would have energised the traditional Congress base by restoring its lost links with the Dalit voter. Her pedigree is classy and classic; her father Jagjivan Ram, a veteran of the freedom movement, and defence minister during the Bangladesh war, always believed that he was best suited to become PM. Both Congress and opposition denied him this office. Meira Kumar has history in her profile. Her personal temperament would also have been a major asset, for she is accommodating rather than confrontational; any personal attack on her would have boomeranged. No one in Congress dared mention her name.

Congress had a final opportunity after December's Assembly election results, when it had become obvious even to diehard loyalists that Rahul Gandhi was the weakest link in the Congress leadership chain. With Sheila Dikshit having lost Delhi, Meira Kumar and Chidambaram were the only credible claimants still standing. But Mrs. Sonia Gandhi put the fate of Congress in the trust of genes instead of ability.

Congress is consequently facing not one but two potential calamities. Its leaders, like England's King Canute, sit on the shore and order the Modi wave to recede; and the waters remain disobedient. The second is an internal earthquake within the party as a generation gloomily contemplates what will be, in effect, its last election. This is, broadly, the age-group of Mrs. Sonia Gandhi, plus or minus a few years on either side. Even if a few of them return to the House, they will not return to power. Rahul Gandhi will reshape Congress in his own style. This is as it should be.

He has already begun to blood a fresh set of people in his own age bandwidth for the tough years ahead. Digvijay Singh might want to believe that he will continue as mentor, but soon enough it is Digvijay's son who will step out and step up. The same could be said of Chidambaram's son, of course, but a son's future is scant consolation for a father whose political hormones are still in search of ambition's destination.

Age is relative. What options do Congress leaders who were young in 2013 but will become old in 2014 have? A split will be both predictable and desultory. The sensible choice is to fade into the sunset, but it is the rare politician who is tired enough to retire. But as they stare at the perhaps empty years ahead, they might reflect on a couplet by the great Persian philosopher-poet Hafez: 'Boast not of knowledge, for at the time of death/Aristotle and beggar walk side by side.'

We either move together or we barely move at all. It was an incisive efinition of inclusive growth. At a time when Modi could have been ɔrgiven for being emotional, he was practical, clearly focused and etermined to pursue an economic vision. This fit a pattern. In a eech on 15 August last year, he said that the religion of anyone in ıblic service was the Constitution of India.

A compilation of his views by Siddharth Mazumdar, released a few eks ago, opens with this sentence: 'The essence of secularism is that religions are equal before the law.' It asserted that sarva darma nbhav was the philosophical magnet that united India from an cient age.

But how do such principles accord with the fact of the Gujarat riots, ich is a constant theme in all attacks on him? I raised questions at time of the riots as much as any other journalist did. Paradoxically, e questions were answered over ten years by the UPA government re has never been, since independence, such intense scrutiny, or absolute determination to trace guilt to a Chief Minister, as Modi d from institutions loyal to the UPA government over two full s.

ery relevant instrument of state was assigned the task of finding thing, anything that could trace guilt to Modi. They could not. e Supreme Court, which is above politics and parties, and which r invaluable, independent guardian of the law and Constitution, rtook its own enquiries. Its first findings are in, and we know that nswer is exoneration. Moreover, there has been judicial ntability to an unprecedented degree in Gujarat. We are still g for justice in a hundred previous riots.

suspects that only some politicians have a vested interest in the uring an election when Indians want to vote for their future. The want a government that gives them jobs; parents want turn into n the plate, into schools for their children, and into ahorizon of

n Modi talks of building a hundred new cities, they can see jobs portunity rise with every floor of a new township. One significant or of the public anger lies in a statistic: employment has grown,

WHY I JOINED THE BJP

We either move together or we barely move

Anyone who speaks in public, whether master orator c
shuffler, comes to a platform after some preparation. Tl
no one can quite prepare for is a crisis; and there is n
an individual than a threat to one's life. At that mom
more likely to emerge from a heart than the head.

The bombs that began to burst at Narendra Mo
were aimed at the crowds, of course, but also a
response was to ask a powerful question to both H
that went to the crux of the principal challenge be
included its solution as well. He asked these two g
choose: they could either fight each other, or
confront that shaming curse called poverty.

This placed everything in context and priority:
country as an absolute fundamental necessity. Tl
to rescue an economy that has been sent to hos
before it sinks to a deathbed. The primary purpo
is to lift the poorest from their awful misery;
achieved only when every Indian, across differe
works hand in hand.

on an average, at only 2 per cent in the past decade. If the rate was higher in the first five years of UPA, when the economy was faring better, then one assumes it must have sunk to less than 2 per cent in the second UPA term. A nation that was soaring on achievement and hope has sunk into depression.

We need a national recovery mission. Only someone who has delivered can offer a credible promise of leading such a critical mission. For those on the wrong side of 30 or 40, five years is just another passage in life. For those who are 20, five years is the difference between aspiration and despair. If a young person does not find a job in these five years, he or she begins to lose that vital energy which comes from self-confidence. If the young do not power the economy then the economy will be stuck in the quagmire of idle waste. There is only one way forward. And there is, among the visible choices, only one person best suited to lift the nation out of a septic swamp. You know his name as well as I do.

EINSTEIN, BISWAJIT AND INDIAN ELECTIONS

It is tough to challenge the rising tide

29 March 2014

If Albert Einstein could not pass his college entrance examination at the first attempt, then there is surely hope for us lesser mortals.

Biswajit Deb Chatterjee, the Hindi film star from Bengal, who warbled his way across the Seventies with songs like Humdum mere, maan bhi jaao, kahna mere pyaar ka, and now, at the impressive age of 78, has become Mamata Banerjee's candidate for New Delhi, is unlikely to pass his first entrance test for the Lok Sabha either. But his future reputation could also rest on an impressive theory. Biswajit's subject is a political science rather than nuclear science, but genius is genius, no matter where deployed.

Just two weeks before polling day, Biswajit told the Hindustan Times that he knew nothing about his opponents, had not even entered his constituency, and could not be bothered about the problems and demands of voters. 'I am now socialising . . .' he said. He did add that he could soon step out. He promised to resolve all local problems once elected. He was confident of victory. Why? Because his leader Mamata Banerjee's fame and popularity was not restricted to Bengal; it had reached Delhi.

Biswajit may have got his practicals wrong, but give a thought to his Sanguine Wave Theory, by which a campaign travels at the speed of light, and energy is irrelevant to outcome. If there is a wave, he will be swept in; if there isn't, he will be swept out: E (Election)=MC (Minimum Concern) Squared.

More politicians believe in this theory than would care to admit publicly. They have evidence. Who knew the names of most Aam Aadmi Party MLAs in Delhi before they were elected? Politics is a human business, and human beings are magnets for controversy. Candidates absorb the minor storms that rise and fall in the course of daily events, convinced that they will eventually be subsumed by larger issues before the electorate.

An election becomes truly tough for any candidate who challenges a tide. For instance, Biswajit's rival for the people's affection in New Delhi, Ajay Maken of Congress, is distancing himself, as discreetly as possible, from the black hole of corruption that is swallowing his party. His radio advertisement, after affirming that he helped city professionals, ends with the charming claim that he has a 'Bedaagh naam', or spotless reputation.

This, however, is not the only advertisement within hearing range of voters. Congress should probably worry more about ad spots from neutral sources like radio stations, urging citizens to go to the ballot stalls, if they want to end corruption. The fancy price for toilet paper bought during the Commonwealth Games years ago is still good enough for a laugh. There is a pretty effective ad in which children are asked what has been happening in our country. The rich are getting richer, they say, and the poor poorer. And what have our leaders been doing? Nothing, claim the kids in three sing-along Hindi syllables ('Kuch nahin!'). So Ajay Maken has to explain why he did nothing, and indeed defended a soiled regime.

Every issue remains relevant for a voter, but every election also slowly rearranges issues on a graded scale of importance depending on what the election is all about. The drain outside your door logically rises to the top of the agenda in a municipal poll; water and electricity demand huge attention when the vote is for a government in a city-state (literally) like Delhi. But a general election sharpens the focus on national issues. Corruption and rising prices are a nationwide phenomenon. And most voters from Ladakh to Kanyakumari want a stable government in Delhi.

The reaction to such concerns cannot be uniform, or every constituency would deliver the same result. Local sentiment, or sectional hopes and fears, affect results as well. India is a fascinating mix, and the strength of our democracy is that there is space for every viewpoint in the great halls of Parliament. There have been Parliaments so fractured by differences that governance became dysfunctional. But that process has been reversed, step by step, and the idea of stability is acquiring critical mass once more.

So is our hero, Biswajit, right? Can any candidate afford to be indifferent to municipal problems? As that ageless cliché goes, yes and no. As accountability becomes a legitimate weapon in the armoury of the electorate, the MP has acquired a schizophrenic responsibility. He might be elected for macro reasons, but once he gets the tag he is held responsible for micro ones as well. That is what makes incumbency a double hazard, if you are on the wrong side of the swelling tide.

MPs are targeted not only for what has gone wrong in Delhi but also for the mess at the doorstep.

The second entrance examination, in politics, is so much tougher than the first one.

A VOTE FOR JOBS

Why the young are voting for change

12 April 2014

Where did it all begin to go wrong for the UPA government? The precise point, if there is ever such a thing in the rolling caravan of politics, is a decision made by Mrs Sonia Gandhi after re-election in 2009.

Mrs Sonia Gandhi has always been the person in command in the two terms of UPA; she was the power in front of the Manmohan Singh throne rather than behind any veil. She chose the PM; she gave the orders on who got which portfolio; she had the last word on critical decisions; and she was the arbiter when senior ministers did their pirouette with one another, a familiar competitive dance in every hall of power.

When BJP's seats actually declined after five years in opposition, Mrs Sonia Gandhi concluded that BJP had become an irreparably damaged brand. The stage, she and her advisers thought, was set for Congress to remain in office for the foreseeable future. An UPA 3 was a common refrain within the wider Congress punditry of Delhi till even a few months ago.

There was, consequently, no particular reason to hurry Rahul Gandhi towards Dr Manmohan Singh's chair. He could remain on a well-financed holiday for another few years, emerging only in time to campaign for 2014. The young heir was missing from action even when the youth of the country were on the streets, venting their rage, as over the horrific instance of rape in Delhi.

But Mrs Gandhi, wisely, also recognised that there was a serious danger in leaving opposition space untenanted. This however induced a fatal mistake. She decided that she, and the Congress party, would act as the pretend-opposition while Dr Singh continued to behave as the pretend-government. Two instances will serve as illustration.

When Dr Singh, aided and abetted by officials like Shivshankar Menon and M.K. Narayanan, made a totally unwarranted concession to Pakistan over an alleged Indian role in the Balochistan insurrection during the 2009 nonaligned summit at Sharm el Sheikh, Mrs Gandhi publicly censured the PM she had selected. But she did nothing to actually change the PM's soft policy towards Pakistan. Second: During a budget debate in the Lok Sabha, she ostentatiously applauded the populist points made by the Marxist MP Gurudas Dasgupta. Once again, in actual practice she did nothing.

The anecdotal evidence from the ground after more than a hundred constituencies have polled, is that Congress is sinking without much trace. The voter is taking a call on what Modi will do in the future, for jobs and the economy.

You can always see a boomerang hurtle away; you rarely see it on a return journey. This thin duality did not work. But the Congress establishment was so pleased with itself over the management of Delhi politics, that it either missed or underestimated the real challenge—a subaltern earthquake with Gujarat at its epicentre.

Narendra Modi did induce a degree of unease among Congress leaders, but they thought it was a problem that could be defused by character assassination. And so we witnessed in the past decade the most intense scrutiny ever done on any Indian politician since 1947 through police, courts, academia, media and NGOs. The aim was never really to discover the full truth about the Gujarat riots, but only to establish somehow, anyhow, that Modi was personally culpable.

Such was the frenzy that every irony was lost. Even today, we do not seem sufficiently aware that Congress continues to protect and reward the principal accused in the 1984 riots, Sajjan Kumar, and others like Jagdish Tytler.

This effort floundered when nothing was found that could establish personal culpability. But in the process, demonisation became the template weapon. This is now a staple of Rahul Gandhi's campaign, and little changes despite the fact that the electorate is cold to this stream of hot air. The anecdotal evidence from the ground after more than a hundred constituencies have polled, is that Congress is sinking without much trace. The voter is taking a call on what Modi will do in the future, for jobs and the economy.

The prospect of electoral disaster has unhinged Congress rhetoric even further. When all you have in your arsenal is questions of a marriage that was arranged by impoverished parents in another age, and which led to virtual separation by mutual consent, then you are truly descending to personal depths which Indian electoral politics has avoided for more than six decades. At least one senior Congress leader from Gujarat has asked his party to desist from such tactics.

This election is about jobs, jobs, jobs—and jobs for everyone. It is about development up and down the line. It is about rescuing a national economy turned moribund by governance that lost its way between the confusion of duopoly and the inertia of complacence. It is about turning the young into a powerful engine of growth, rather than abandoning them outside the station. The person who drove the car on a recent trip to Mumbai put it succinctly: if this kind of governance continues for another five years, the middle class of Mumbai will disappear. He considered himself middle class, and was staring at the possibility of poverty.

This election is about India's revival. That is why the young are voting for change.

NEVER ON A SUNDAY

Among the campaigners, one absent candidate

19 April 2014

Every so often small facts light up a large truth. One such nugget appeared in last Monday's *Indian Express*. This newspaper tracks, within many layers of election coverage, where any principal campaigner has been the previous day. And so there was a record of Narendra Modi chopper-hopping through Karnataka, reviving BJP in a state where the party has seen highs and lows through a few turbulent years; L.K. Advani was in Gujarat; Arvind Kejriwal was raising a bit of dust on road-shows in Punjab; and so on and so forth.

Where was Rahul Gandhi? The paper had a simple, even bland, statement: 'No public engagements'. It was an answer, but not an explanation. The likeliest reason, judging by personal history, was that Rahul Gandhi was taking a day off because it was a Sunday.

There is more than one reason why Rahul Gandhi seems to have faded from public discourse during a dramatic campaign season; but one cannot avoid the nagging suspicion that the Congress star is averse to any excessive workload. Nor does he have much to say beyond inanities sprinkled through his script by pen-pushers.

TOWARDS A NEW CULTURE

The culture of the Indian subcontinent has inevitably been influenced by the spirit of the oldest of the world's dominant faiths, Hinduism, and its youngest, Islam.

THE ANSWER IS GANDHI

One should value a neighbour's sentiment as much as one's own

12 February 2006

The publication of the gratuitously offensive cartoons by a Danish newspaper against the Prophet of Islam has already resonated through contemporary events. It will also echo into the future.

The first question must surely be the simplest one: why?

More than one answer has been offered. An editor of the paper appeared on European television and said, primly, that the cartoons were not meant to hurt Muslims but only to represent, through an image, that a number of Muslims had become terrorists. This is the sort of argument that sounds reasonable until you pare open the first layer of deception. If that was the intention, why not use an image of Osama bin Laden? If you want to condemn a racist Christian, you don't use an image of Jesus Christ, do you?

Then there is the 'freedom of the press' argument, a view endorsed so strongly by the media of continental Europe that sensible publications like *Le Monde* have reprinted the cartoons twice. Far be it for me to decry press freedom. It is my bread and butter. But freedom of expression never comes without responsibility. Denmark has laws that restrict excess. Section 266B of the Danish penal code says: 'Any person who publicly or with the intention of dissemination to a wide circle of people makes a statement or imparts other information threatening, insulting or degrading a group of persons on account of their race, colour, national or ethnic origin, belief or sexual orientation, shall be liable to a fine, simple detention or imprisonment for a term not exceeding two years.' Section 140 adds, 'Those who publicly mock or insult the doctrines or worship of any religious community that is legal in this country, will be punished by a fine or incarceration for up to four months.'

The reason for such legislation is not a record of abuse against Islam, but a history of virulent anti-Semitism. There are laws in Europe by which anyone denying the Holocaust can end up in jail. Excellent. Then why is the Danish Prime Minister, Anders Fogh Rasmussen, pleading helplessness? He could have easily referred the matter to his own country's judiciary and awaited their decision. During the long months when nothing happened over the cartoons this would have been sufficient to calm Muslim unease over the insults. The cartoons appeared on 30 September. There was no public reaction in October, November, December and most of January. There was some official reaction. The Saudi and Libyan governments withdrew their ambassadors. Eleven ambassadors of Muslim countries wanted to talk to the Danish PM. They got a polite letter which they construed as a snub.

It has now emerged, thanks to a story in the *Guardian*, that the same Danish newspaper rejected a series of cartoons against Jesus some three years ago because they were deemed to be offensive. It was the correct decision. Journalists like the editor of the German publication *Die Welt*, who has gone on record to say that the publication of the cartoons is 'at the core of our culture' would not find enough freedom in his press to publish a cartoon (produced in a British newspaper, the *Independent*, in January 2003) showing Israeli Prime Minister Ariel Sharon dining off Palestinian babies. I would not publish it either. But editors of continental Europe have suddenly broken into paroxysms of moral indignation at any attempt to question their right to publish offensive cartoons against Islam.

The *International Herald Tribune* of 9 February reported that Fleming Rose, cultural editor of *Jyllands-Posten* (the Danish newspaper that started the controversy), told CNN that his paper was ready to publish cartoons of the Holocaust that were being encouraged by an irresponsible Iranian newspaper, as if two wrongs added up to a right. His newspaper, however, quickly denied any such intentions.

I was in Britain last weekend when this storm was raging. British papers did not publish the cartoons, although there was doubtless pressure to do so. The BBC did a typical weaselly sort of fudge, showing a bit and then removing the image so that it could claim to have it both ways, but no one was very impressed. Instead, newspapers across the ideological spectrum, from the *Observer* on the left to the *Sunday Telegraph* on the right, published argued that we should respect each other's faith. Because of its restraint, British Muslims today feel closer to their country.

The Danish Prime Minister began to perspire only when Muslims started to boycott Danish products. His God is commerce, so the only retribution he understands is disrespect to sales. Muslims who think that violence is the answer, have got it wrong. Violence is wrong in itself, and counterproductive. A boycott of Danish products is far more productive.

Who did we Indians learn this from? Mahatma Gandhi, of course. His challenge to the British empire began with a boycott of British goods. It is only when he made a bonfire of the coloniser's cloth did the world's mightiest empire begin to shiver. It is not too difficult to live without Danish cheese, or even Bang and Olufsen. One would, in fact, like to extend the logic. If you have to buy a European product, buy British. That would be a nice way of saying thank you.

Mr Danish Prime Minister: Do not worry about the enemies Denmark has made. Worry instead about the friends Denmark has lost.

A HOUSE OF GOD IN TELINIPARA

A small town shows the way to living together

5 October 2008

On 2 October, Gandhi's birthday and Eid launched the annual Bengali festive season that will last into the third week of the month. Eid in India is determined by the visibility of the moon; the Saudis, who check the sky with technology, celebrated the end of Ramadan a day earlier. Since one of the many definitions of Indian secularism is proprietary rights over holidays, some Calcutta companies shut down on 1 October. The origin of holiday is 'holy day'. Bengal has always been holier than thou.

Sour brains who rearrange life by the calculus of productivity miss the point. Bengal understands GDP (Gross Domestic Product) but values GDH (Gross Domestic Happiness). Economists will never understand the power of the embrace, common to both Durga Puja and Eid. Every human being is an equal in an embrace.

That is the first gesture after the Eid prayer. I spend Eid at Telinipara, some 30 miles north of Calcutta along the jute-mill-dotted banks of the Hooghly, where I was born.

The men of our family walk together to the Chhoti Masjid (Small Mosque) with heads bowed. This is not due to any excessive humility.

We have to avoid stepping on pats of still-wet cow dung. Early risers have first use of public facilities. The municipality has sprinkled white disinfectant powder along the drains on either side, a practice started during the British Raj and followed twice a year, during Eid and Bakr-Eid. The cows were oblivious of municipal concerns even during British rule.

The official name of the mosque is the rather grandiloquent Masjid-e-Ibrahim (Mosque of Abraham); its popular name is more appropriate, although it has become a bit larger since last Eid. This need has been felt for more than a decade, with the increasing population of Telinipara, but it became possible only when the owner of the huts adjoining the mosque sold his property to the mosque.

Like any public institution, the mosque was strapped for cash. The owner gave it for less than the market value, despite higher offers. He was a Hindu. He was happy to take less because, in his words, the mosque too was '*Bhagwan ka ghar* (God's house)'. Five hundred bags of cement came as a gift from a renowned Calcutta Marwari business family. Neither made the contribution because they expected their names to appear in India's largest English newspaper.

The maulvi leading the prayer was an angry young man. He offered an answer to a major dilemma of dialectical spiritualism. If Islam was the chosen faith, and Muslims Allah's select people, why were they mired in poverty when non-believers in the West were flooded with riches and comfort? True wealth is not what you see in this life, but what you will be rewarded with in heaven. He went on a bit about the pleasures of heaven, not forgetting the heavenly wine that will not leave you with a headache. And his route to heaven was a trifle severe, demanding abstinence even from music. But his argument was a placebo, a calmative for a community bewildered by questions.

Later, around ten, enthusiastic young men of my mohalla took me to their single-room club, fed me sandesh bought from Bijoy Modak's excellent shop, and asked me for '*nasihat*'. I had no advice to offer, just the essence of some experience along the road from Telinipara to Delhi. The pedlars of violence have nothing to offer but self-destruction, I said, and there were nods of agreement. The rungs of an upward ladder are a modern education; and education is the equal right of both boys and girls. The horizon will be outside reach, and the community remain fractured as long as there is gender bias. The young must leave the mistakes of their parents behind. We Indians laugh and cry in Urdu and Hindi and Bengali, but we rule in English. The language of economic and administrative power is English, so learn English.

The young men were ahead of such advice. They were determined to add a room to the club, which would serve as a library and a tuition centre for those who showed promise but did not have the means to fulfil their promise.

Later, a father brought two teenage daughters and reminded them that they wanted to tell me something. Their eyes just a trifle hesitant, but growing with confidence, they said they would be giving their Madhyamik examinations next year, and were determined to go to college. The father beamed with pride. Elsewhere a mother was spending what for her was serious money to get her child into kindergarten in St Joseph's Convent in Chandannagar, which was my first school. I chatted with a student of Aligarh University; she is in her second year, studying statistics. Her English diction was perfect. In another conversation men marvelled at the fact that there was now a fortnightly market in our mohalla where goods worth lakhs were bought. Women were the big spenders. Only 10 per cent of the milling shoppers were men, and they had come as bodyguards, someone said with a very hearty laugh.

This is not yet a gender revolution, far from it. But this is the first hint of a gender insurrection.

When I was in my second year, a student of Presidency College, this small street of Telinipara had descended into desolation through communal violence. On one black night, nearly every mud hut was set ablaze as Hindus and Muslims chased each other with spears, swords, country revolvers, kerosene and matchsticks. They are back together now, the past lost in conscious amnesia.

More than three decades ago, the Chhoti Masjid had become a refuge for Muslims seeking shelter from Hindus. It has become a Bari

Masjid today, with help from Hindus who believe that this too is a house of God.

India may lose itself in Delhi and Mumbai and Bangalore and Ahmedabad, but finds itself again and again in millions of Teliniparas.

THE MANY BATTLES FOR DEOBAND

If Deoband remains honest to the ideals of its founding fathers, it will lead the way to reform

30 January 2011

One of the great follies of the contemporary world is the conversion of the priest, of any faith, into a cartoon character. And so the imam is caricatured with an elongated beard and twisted eye; the pandit has an exaggerated tuft, obese stomach and gloats; the Christian father wears a sanctimonious air barely disguising a leer. This nonsense is largely due to the decline of religion in the ebbing moral universe of modern man, and partly due to the existence of a radical extreme at the edge of every clerical class, which justifies violence in the name of a higher power.

Faith—mosque, temple or church—has been a traditional sanctuary of the people in their constant struggle against innumerable forms of autocracy and dictatorship through history. The institutions of God provide a comfort zone to the individual persecuted by institutions of man, particularly during moments of distress. Faith is often a symbol of resistance, as autocratic regimes are discovering today when the streets are alive with long-overdue protest against smug dictatorships that confused their intelligence services with intelligence.

Competent governments, whether of dictators or democrats, have understood the power of the clergy and chosen a dual response: repression of the radical extreme and a continuous attempt to co-opt others into the establishment through a less than discreet combination of flattery and bribery. The real test for the clergy comes not during periods of relative calm, but during phases of social and political oppression.

If we want to understand the influence of the ulema among Indian Muslims, particularly in north India, then we must remember the sterling part they played in the age of decline, the 19th century, when every other of pillar of sustenance crumbled, either eaten by the worms of decay and decadence, or defeated by the rising force of British arms. It was the clergy that held the community together, even as its radical wing, led by students, or *taliban*, of the seminary of Shah Waliullah launched a jihad for the restoration of political power. That war failed. Those who did not go to war provided a greater service through leadership at the micro level to a community that was under such economic and social pressure that it feared the loss not only of sustenance but also its most cherished elements of language and culture. Out of such trauma emerged an institution like the Dar-ul-Uloom at Deoband, nearly a century and a half ago.

Deoband's founders refused to accept a single rupee as donation from the British; its small band of teachers and students ate what the local community offered. Mahatma Gandhi recognised not just the theological importance of this seminary but also the empirical influence of its grassroots connections. Deoband was the antithesis of the elitist nawab-and-landlord-dominated Muslim politics of the early 20th century.

Deoband is often demonised by a Western-influenced discourse. Yes, there is a fringe that has converted Deoband into a fatwa factory for regressive pronouncements; and some of its influences have been distorted to justify violence. But every great centre of education produces a few children who dishonour their intellectual parent. Deoband is a tremendous resource for those Muslims who do not have the advantage of birth or lineage. It is the hope and dream not only of those who want to serve Allah through the mosque, but also of young men who see in its educational repository a chance for a better life. The place it commands in the affections of Muslims makes Deoband a power centre; and where there is power, there will be politics. What we are seeing at the moment is a political battle between factions, and the vested interests that feed off them, for the control of Deoband.

There are many reasons for the unrest generated by the appointment of Maulana Ghulam Mohammed Vastanvi as *mohtamim*, or virtual vice chancellor. Vastanvi is a remarkable maulana who started a school with just six students in a tribal region on the Gujarat–Maharashtra border in 1979, and built it into an institution with 200,000 students across the country. This is why he is the first person from outside the immediate UP region to be given this honour and responsibility. His presence promised the reform that students thirst for; but it also threatened to upset the cartel that has used Deoband to squeeze out personal benefits from Delhi and abroad. These deep-seated interests would have challenged Vastanvi on any pretext; they found an emotive one.

Deoband is, as has happened before, at a crossroads. If Deoband has become the property of a clerical group that wants to exploit this great name for its own greed, then Vastanvi will be driven out. If Deoband remains honest to the ideals of its founding fathers, then it will lead the way to educational reform and open thought that can turn an underprivileged Indian Muslim child into a privileged adult.

THE ASSAULT ON COEXISTENCE

In the fight against fanaticism, we need leaders who maintain the sanity of good doctors in the face of havoc

23 September 2012

What is common between the criminal complaint against Rabbi David Goldberg for circumcising Jewish boys in Hof, Germany; the ban on minarets in Switzerland; the continual attempts by some European publications to offend Muslims with cartoons; the effort to convict a young Christian in Pakistan for a blasphemy she did not commit; an attack on a mosque in Missouri, USA; or, most vicious of all, the recent anti-Islam film that injects lies and malice into public discourse?

None of them is designed to destroy the existence of the 'other'. Their purpose is to poison coexistence, the fundamental basis of civilised living.

There is no rationale that can justify any of these instances. Rabbi Goldberg was not trying to circumcise non-Jews; he was practising his own faith. To target minarets in Switzerland as a cultural crime in an age of skyscrapers is manifest prejudice, of the sillier sort. Provocative European publishers are not defending freedom of speech, which is their much advertised explanation, since nowhere in the democratic world does the right to publish include the leeway to defame, particularly when a lie can lead to public disorder. The Pakistani child was a victim, not a perpetrator—of fanatics who wanted to punish her and her kin for protecting Christianity in their theocratic environment. The bilious film about the Prophet of Islam was not made by a filmmaker, but by a bigot determined to provoke a violent reaction that would confirm in many innocent or naïve minds the image of Islam as a fountainhead of violence rather than what the word actually means, which is peace. The barbarians who killed four American diplomats in Libya duly obliged: hatred breeds hatred in an escalating cycle.

Even the most dramatic example of pure, unadulterated terrorism, the destruction of New York's twin towers on 9/11, was initiated not to destroy America's existence, which is impossible even within the mindset of a maniac, but to breach an emerging international order of stability founded on mutual respect, and the equality of nations. The planes that headed towards the White House and the Pentagon were not ferrying troops who had been ordered to conquer Washington. Their purpose was to generate fear, hostility and war between the two largest religious communities in the world. They succeeded, but to an extent far lower than the expectations of terrorist masterminds, and yet far more than the young 21st century could stomach. The price has been high.

The Mumbai terrorist attacks in November 2008 had a dual objective: to warp the India–Pakistan engagement, as fragile as it might have been; and to incite violence in India between Hindus and Muslims. It is satisfying to report that the second wish failed spectacularly because Indians understood that such discord would mean a victory for fanatics.

We are also witnessing a rare phenomenon: people outside the state apparatus, working largely (but not always) on their own, can do more damage to social harmony than powerful regiments led by dictators, presidents or prime ministers. There are governments, of course, which are tempted to dip their hands in the sewer for political gain; and you can never rule out the unintelligent intelligence agency which believes in a strategy of destabilising civilian populations. But governments have not, exceptions apart, been in the forefront of these battle lines.

Whatever their nature, despotic, democratic or in between,

governments know that fomenting terrorism inflicts blowback damage. Even when legitimate armies are put on the field, governments calibrate the conflict. When governments fall into the grip of radical ideologues who have left common sense at the club bathhouse, the damage is startling, as was evident during President George Bush's Iraq war.

The most dangerous of today's conspiracies are being manufactured in small rooms lost in the labyrinths of a big city by men who will not become internationally infamous unless they succeed. We do not know how many 9/11s or Mumbai attacks have failed, but just the thought is sufficient for a shudder. Failure is not any hindrance to fanatics. They are now being lured by the siren outreach of a miraculous technology that continues to breed new tools by the day. Prevention is the full-time job of innumerable police forces, while no one has any real clue about what might constitute a cure.

This war has to be fought where it is being incubated, on the street, and in the mind. We cannot afford politicians who seek votes from a sewer. This is a malaise, an infection, a plague, a crisis that demand leaders who maintain the sanity of good doctors in the face of havoc Violence can begin with the word, and every word must be chosen wit care.

GUARDIANS OF THE PULPIT

There is nothing exclusively Islamic about male prejudice

13 January 2013

It is silent. It is complex. There is unease but no outcry. There is diffidence, and uncertainty because it seems to carry sanction—not of faith, but of some of the faithful.

The culture of the Indian subcontinent has been inevitably influenced by the spirit of the oldest of the world's dominant faiths, Hinduism, and its last, Islam. Religion begins as a social revolution, a liberation movement against existing inequity. Religion is inspirational in the voice of prophets and the sermons of saints. What it becomes, centuries later, in the control of its self-appointed guardians is another story.

On 2 January, the Delhi edition of the *Times of India* tried to rescue one such narrative from the many layers of fog we use as a blindfold. Kamini Lau, an additional sessions judge, denied anticipatory bail to a certain Maulvi Mustafa Raja, who abetted in the abduction of a young girl by the accused, Nadeem Khan, by performing a nikah between the two although Khan was already married. The ceremony did not have the girl's consent, and was conducted in the absence of her parents. The Maulvi argued that Muslims were permitted four wives. Judge Kamini Lau noted, forcefully, that Islam permits polygamy under

certain conditions but does not encourage it; and no nikah can be legitimate without the woman's consent. She added that Muslim countries such as Turkey and Tunisia had made polygamy illegal. She could have also said that the present Turkish government of Recep Tayyip Erdogan, widely described as 'Islamist', had also made rape within marriage a criminal offence, and awarded life sentence for 'honour killings'.

Kamini Lau did not mince her words. Nadeem Khan had raped the girl, and Maulvi Raja was accessory to the crime.

Perhaps the court order was as clear as it was because the judge was a woman.

It is axiomatic that religions have differences, or they would not be different. But every faith has one thing in common. All priests are men. Religious law and practice is determined by men, whether a faith believes in monotheism or polytheism, whether it worships the divine as an image or as a spirit. Only a man becomes a Pope, Shankaracharya, Dalai Lama or Shaikh ul Islam; and only men are in their robe-clad armies. There has been some reform in patches; but the Church of England was unable last year to permit women priests to rise to Bishop. A faith may split into sects. Sunni and Shia may quarrel till eternity over the successor to the Prophet, but it is the men who do the quarrelling.

Behind this bias is a conscious or subconscious conviction that women are inferior; and, in its more basic form, that semen is profound and powerful, while menstruation is unclean. Sex is a gender right, a form of domination. This bias has slipped into more than one religious text.

All doctrines understand that law should be adjusted to circumstance. Islamic law specifically accepts this evolutionary process. Would religious law have evolved differently if women had been high priests? Hinduism permitted unlimited polygamy in India and denied inheritance until the reforms pushed through in 1955 by Dr Babasaheb Ambedkar and Jawaharlal Nehru against strong opposition from within the ruling party, in legislation known as the Hindu Code Bill. When Nehru was asked in 1962 why he did not attempt reform on polygamy in Muslim law, he replied that the time was not right in the mid-1950s. The time was not right in the 1980s either when a widow from Bhopal, Shah Bano, demanded a pittance from her ex-husband as maintenance after divorce. The court granted her this pittance; Parliament overruled the court.

The high priests of Islam have never had a problem tweaking a religious injunction when they want to. The specific punishment for theft is cutting off the hand. No mullah or politician in India leads a mass agitation to insist that every convicted Muslim thief should have his hand chopped off. But ask for reform in laws to ensure equality for women, and Muslim politicians will suddenly declare that Islam is in danger. It is not Islam which ever has been, or ever will be, in danger; but male hegemony is hopefully under threat.

There is nothing exclusively Islamic about male prejudice. Listen to some Hindu savants rise from their pseudo-yogic perch to preach that women must share the blame for rape. They are joined by a politician like the Samajwadi Party's Abu Azmi; what unites them is not shared faith but shared prejudice. When they blame the West, they are not fearful of geography; they are terrified of modernity. Modernity is not singing English songs and wearing jeans. That is a cartoon view. Modernity is equality, political and social.

India has taken only the first steps towards that horizon. The churn, conflict and vicious rhetoric prove that conservatives will not surrender their stranglehold easily, and they still control the pulpit and the propaganda. Change is visible, but the long war has merely begun.

JULY IS A VOLATILE MONTH

Equal honour to every faith is a pillar of Indian civilisation

27 July 2014

Sir Jadunath Sarkar, the eminent historian, records that in 1679 Shivaji sent a letter to the emperor Aurangzeb protesting against the imposition of jizya during a time of great hardship. The Maratha icon pointed out that Aurangzeb's predecessors, Akbar, Jahangir and Shahjehan, also had the power to levy this discriminatory tax on non-Muslims, 'but did not give place to bigotry in their hearts, as they considered all men, high and low, created by God to be examples of the nature of diverse creeds and temperaments'. In a memorable admonishment, Shivaji reminded Aurangzeb that the Quran called Allah 'Rabb ul alamin, the Lord of all men, and not Rabb ul muslameen [only the Lord of Muslims] . . . To show bigotry for any man's own creed and practices is equivalent to altering the words of the Holy Book . . .' Sir Jadunath dwells on this remarkable letter in both *Shivaji and His Times*, as well as in his *History of Aurangzeb* (Volume 3). Equal honour to every faith is a pillar of Indian civilisation; and it is this common moral and cultural inheritance that provides the enduring inspiration for our Republic. Shivaji's 17th century letter could serve as a preface to India's 20th century Constitution.

It is not the job of a column to lecture, let alone pontificate, but there are occasions when a reminder is apposite, even if the scale of an MP's provocation is minor compared to the far-reaching impact of an emperor's prejudice. The irrational, almost schoolboy-bully, anger of a few Maharashtra MPs who were served disagreeable food in a government hostelry is an immature misdemeanour rather than government policy, but we must take it seriously, for the edifice of India's democracy is built by the innumerable bricks of individual and collective rights.

It is perfectly true that a man's religion is not written on his face, as an MP who sought to thrust a *chapati* down a Muslim server's mouth at the Maharashtra Sadan in Delhi pointed out. But in which script does one write the language of human dignity, the language that Shivaji made his creed? The question is particularly appropriate when the relevant MP claims to wear the mantle of Shivaji. We are talking of more than an affront to a particular religion; it was brash display of the arrogance towards a much larger community of the poor. This was negation of the central message of Prime Minister Narendra Modi's election campaign, where he repeatedly stressed three core themes and reiterated them during his first major speech in the Lok Sabha: the foremost responsibility of a government is to work for the poor; development and jobs must go to every Indian, including minorities ('If one organ of the body remains weak, the body cannot be termed as healthy. We are committed to this ... We don't see this as appeasement'); and that India can become a modern nation, with double-digit growth, only when we make development into a mass movement, in the manner that Gandhi made the freedom struggle into a mass movement. The volatile variations that are now rising across public debate could throw the government off-message.

Some of the volatility is predictable if not explicable. The election results were an earthquake, and the after-shock tremors will trouble the earth for a while. There will be a fringe which claims justification for its views in the results. A few carpetbaggers will imagine that they can improve their chances of preferential treatment during the distribution of rewards by pandering to the fringe. But marginal facts should not be confused with a central reality. A government can only be run from an inclusive perspective. Home Minister Rajnath Singh did well to reassure Parliament, and the nation, that such behaviour was unfortunate, and by implication unacceptable.

There are practical dangers in veering off-message. Politicians might be surprised to discover that voters have become volatile as well. Voters want delivery on what they were promised at campaign time; they are not interested in the sudden spout of a new rhetoric. Voters are not doctrinaire; they want jobs and homes and electricity and water and lower vegetable prices, and they want it sooner rather than later. They enjoy the luxury of electoral options, and have the ability to recognise a leader who they believe will deliver better than the competition. In state elections, candidates for Chief Minister will influence the outcome significantly. With power comes responsibility, of course; with responsibility comes a face and a name.

Narendra Modi has inspired a pervasive hope that the politics, language and governance of an arid past is behind us. No one expects results to be immediate, or transition to be easy; but the country senses an absence if he shifts to the background for even a week or a fortnight. The travails of July will soon be over. August needs a return of that fresh breeze.

A PETTY FEUDAL AT JAMA MASJID

A mosque is not private property

9 November 2014

When ignorance marries bluster you get a functioning blunderbuss. Every scattershot gun should come with a safety catch, but human behaviour so often becomes vulnerable to the ego of a weak mind.

Muslims claim, with justified pride, that the age of *jahilya*, or ignorance, ended when the message of Islam came to the Prophet Muhammad in the desert city of Mecca. Regrettably, *jihalat* still lingers in parts of the Muslim world. It has found a temporary sanctuary in Delhi's Jama Masjid, the iconic symbol of Indian Islam.

If the bluster of its Imam, Syed Ahmad Bukhari, were nothing more than self-inflicted wounds, it would not matter so much. But Bukhari gets media space, thanks to his position, and thereby affects the wider perception of Indian Muslims. When he claims that he will not invite India's prime minister to his 19-year-old son Shaban Bukhari's so-called investiture ceremony, but would like Pakistan's leader to be present, Ahmad Bukhari is guilty of many varieties of stupidity. Indian Muslims relate to their country's leaders, not to those of a foreign nation. But this is an appropriate moment to ask another question.

Since when has a mosque become, in Islamic doctrine, private property? Who has given the Bukhari family genetic rights over India's most glorious mosque? Who has allowed him to pocket all the revenue from that institution, and use it for a lifestyle that is anything but pious? The mosque is wakf property, and therefore owned by the Delhi Wakf Board. Bukhari claims a hereditary right to the Imam's position because an ancestor, sixteen times removed, was made Imam by the emperor who built the mosque, Shah Jehan. That is an illegitimate argument because of both religious practice and a democratic environment. If that principle were applicable, Shah Jehan's woebegone heirs should send an application for the ruler's job in Delhi.

A mosque is always owned by the Muslim community, for which it was constructed. The first mosque was built by no less a person than the Prophet Muhammad in his adopted city, Medina. This glorious mosque is still a magnet for the faithful, wherever they may reside across the world. Did the Prophet bequeath that mosque to his son-in-law Hazrat Ali and his daughter Bibi Fatima? No. Why have Indian Muslims abandoned the precept established by the Prophet himself?

The two holy mosques are at Mecca, where Muslims go on Haj, and at Medina. For fourteen centuries, a succession of Caliphs and Sultans has protected these mosques from external threat and internal turmoil.

Every ruler has described himself as only a servant or custodian of the mosques. When the great Ottoman Sultan Selim the First became caliph, after defeating the Mamelukes, he went to the grand mosque of Alleppo for Friday prayers. The nervous Imam described Selim as an overlord during the sermon. Selim corrected the cleric immediately. He was only a servant, said the Caliph.

The Imams of Mecca and Medina do not possess hereditary rights. They are appointed by an order of the Saudi court, and can be changed in their lifetimes. The selection criterion is familiar: knowledge of the Quran and Sunnah, combined with piety in character. But in Delhi's Jama Masjid, we have permitted a dynasty to prevail. This is anathema to Islamic practice.

Why? No one really knows. The true answer is the community's inertia.

There are countless mosques in India's cities, towns and villages. In each one of them an Imam is chosen by the will of the community, through the mosque community. This principle should be applied to Delhi's Jama Masjid as well, for, to reiterate, the place of worship belongs to the congregation, not to the person who leads the prayers. It is up to the Muslims of Old Delhi to establish the democratic process through which they elect the mosque committee, and then empower the elected body to choose the Imam for regular terms.

Perhaps it is also time media and politicians stopped catering to the arbitrary whims and fancies of an interloper like Ahmad Bukhari by according him importance. Who, after all, does he represent except himself? Would he ever dare contest an election in his local constituency? We might then find out precisely how much support he has in his own area. We could even test the trust he commands in an even smaller constituency, his congregation. I have little doubt that he would lose.

Institutions must be protected through institutional mechanisms. Bukhari has set himself up as some sort of petty Nawab of Jama Masjid, rather than as an Imam who serves the people. People have been afraid to intervene largely because they do not know how to go about it. The Bukharis have, in effect, acquired squatters' rights.

It is time that honest Indian Muslims decided who is a good Imam, instead of a devious Imam deciding who is a good Muslim.

THE FOURTH GREAT WAR, FOR MODERNITY

Any failure of modernity is an invitation to an imagined past

30 November 2014

Wars begin with a preamble, mostly confused, and end with a postscript, often bitter. The link between Versailles in 1919 and 1939 is standard knowledge. The Cold War began at Yalta, where Europe was divided between victors who then mobilised to protect what they had won. If the Cold War ended with Soviet defeat in Afghanistan, then that is precisely where the war against terrorism began.

It should not come as a surprise that allies in Afghanistan turned on each other almost immediately after victory. The conquerors of 1945 did much the same. But if America and Europe are shocked by the sudden swell of Islamism, it is only because they ignored the second narrative of 1919, the dismemberment and colonisation of the last great Muslim empire, the Ottoman Caliphate. After a troubled century, the First World War has looped back to link with the fourth.

Less than seven decades before 1919, Britain had buried what was left of the Mughal empire on the Indian subcontinent, home to the largest ethnic Muslim population in the world. (The more ribald Victorian politicians teased their Ottomans with the thought that

Queen Victoria was the real Caliph, since she had far more Muslim subjects.) In 1919, a startling thing happened: every single Muslim land was colonised or occupied by Europe. The humiliation was almost too much to bear.

As Muslims from the Ganges to the Nile searched for revival, they also took comfort in lament. A powerful motif was the romance of the Caliphate, which became more glorious in memory than it had ever been in reality. The Caliphate represented security for Islam and its holy cities in an age when Muslims were under siege; it was an emotional symbol of glory; and its law, Sharia, was reassuring to Muslims who perceived it as a safety net against the potential tyranny of their own despots. In India, Mahatma Gandhi used the high-voltage appeal of the Caliphate to draw Muslims into his mass campaign, between 1919 and 1922, against British rule. The ultimate irony, of course, was that Turkey abolished the Caliphate in 1924.

Turkey, under Mustafa Kemal, took a rational route into the 20th century. It recognised that Caliphs, like the Hapsburgs and Tsars, belonged to an age that had outlived its utility. The Indian Muslim elites eased their anxieties by carving out, with a British knife, a separate state in 1947, Pakistan, a unique country that straddled either side of a subcontinent and fondly believed that faith could unite what God's geography had divided. Pakistan could have become a Turkey in South Asia; instead it attempted to mix theocratic impulses with democratic intentions, and succeeded in achieving the worst of both worlds. Pakistan became the first Islamic state in the post-colonial era, and, inevitably, a sanctuary for myriad terrorists flying the flag of jihad in order to gain popular legitimacy.

The Arab world was cut and stripped with abandon by its British and French masters after 1919, and turned into a haven for neo-colonisation. Neo-colonisation, of course, is the grant of independence on condition you do not exercise it. This might have worked if it had been accompanied by economic empowerment and democratic freedoms, but perhaps the suggestion itself is a contradiction. Family systems soon blurred the difference between personal wealth and national resources. Every experiment, whether born on the left or right, gravitated towards soft or hard dictatorships. The West did not help by using war, or regime change through more insidious means, to protect its domination.

Any failure of modernity is an invitation to an imagined past. As other models, from royal paternalism to Nasserite populism, to Baathist liberalism, to Army despotism, and finally a brief upsurge of democratic spirit, collapsed, or were suppressed, the last idea standing was a return to faith. Except that no one quite knew what this meant in a contemporary context. What transpired was less the faith of Medina and more the reinvention of thinkers like Abdul Wahhab in Arabia and Shah Waliullah in India, who fed insecurity and extremism into despair to arouse a jihad that has become demented in its search for chaos wrapped in the illusion of liberation. The degeneration has been swift. Today the region between Pakistan and north Africa is an arc of turbulence, in which most governments survive in isolation while nations spin out of control.

A fundamental requirement of jihad in Islamic theory is that it can only be declared by the state. The dangerous proliferation of maverick jihad is evidence of the dangers when practice abandons theory. This, however, is little solace to this jihad's targets: the 'far enemy', principally America; the 'near enemy', or those hostile to them in their immediate environment; and the 'third enemy', countries which 'occupy' Islamic space. India and China (because of Muslim-majority Xinjiang) are in the last group.

When, or how, this war will end is difficult to assess. But we can be certain of this: it will devastate Muslim communities long before it damages others.

FOUR POETS: CHAPTER AND VERSE

Four Urdu greats mark the swivel points of pre-Independence Muslim history in India

Islam came to India long before Muslim rulers arrived; in the 7th century, through seafarers and traders in both south and north, and merged into the cultural landscape, adopting, without controversy, local languages, and adapting, without fuss, many of the indigenous lifestyle habits. There was nothing particularly unique in this. When Persians accepted Islam in the early years, they did not change their language to Arabic; and when Indonesians became Muslims many hundreds of years later, they did not jettison their traditions or culture. Nor were they expected to. Ibn Batuta, who left Tangier in 1325 and returned home 29 years and 75,000 miles later, maintains a poker face when he describes Muslims he met in the Maldive Islands: 'The[y] . . . are upright and pious, sound in belief and sincere in thought; their bodies are weak, they are unused to fighting, and their armour is prayer. Once when I ordered a thief's hand to be cut off, a number of those in the room fainted.'

And then he adds, with a hint of the censorious Qadi: 'Their womenfolk do not cover their hands, not even their queen does so, and they comb their hair and gather it at one side. Most of them wear only an apron from their waists to the ground, the rest of their bodies being uncovered. When I held the Qadiship there, I tried to put an end to this practice and ordered them to wear clothes, but I met with no success'. He notes with wonder that their ruler was a woman, called Khadija.

Local cultures easily absorbed Islam. Sufi missionaries who lived the message, and through their example and teaching spread the faith, preached that all human beings, cultures and colours were equal before Allah. And so in 14th century Bihar, Sharafuddin Ahmad ibn Yahya Maneri saw nothing wrong with vermilion; and in 18th century Sindh, the mystic poet-diving Shah Abdul Latif could celebrate his love for yogis in his poem, Ramkali. These are not random examples. They illustrate a substantive truth.

Muslim dynasts seized power in Delhi some 500 years after Muslims came to India. The history of those first five centuries has been buried under ignorance (understandable, for there are few records of that period), indifference, and the depressing fact that history is generally the record of kings and conquests.

The first Arab army landed near today's Karachi in 711, in the same year that Arabs won their famous victory in Spain. But while there was an earthquake in Europe whose tremors have not ceased, the Arab invasion of India did not travel much beyond the sands of Sindh. It was another three centuries before the plundering meteor, Mahmud of Ghazni, expanded his domain to Lahore, and marched deep into central India, looting cities and temples, including Somnath, in search of wealth. It was not until Turkish clans began to dominate the world of Muslims that what is known as Muslim rule was established in India. It was an era of a major surge of Muslim arms across Asia. In the west, Turkish regiments played a critical part in the re-conquest of Jerusalem in 1187 and the historic defeat of the third crusade, led by Richard II and Francis I, in 1192.

In India, 1192 would prove a decisive moment as well, for Prithviraj was defeated by the Afghan ruler Muhammad Ghori. Credit for the Delhi Sultanate, however, must go to a Turki general, Qutbuddin

Aibak, who was called a Slave King because he had once been a slave of the Qazi of Nishapur, before being purchased and freed by Ghori. By 1194, Aibak had conquered a parallel power centre of north India, the kingdom of Jaichand, after another momentous battle, at Chandwar in Etawah, on the banks of the Jamuna. He then marched into Gujarat; by 1199, the Turks had taken Bihar and Bengal. That was the broad expanse of Muslim empires, through significant highs and lows, till the death of Aurangzeb in 1706. By the time the Mughal dynasty was declared formally dead in 1857, the rule of Padishah Shah Alam, according to a popular ditty, had been reduced to a stretch from Delhi's Lal Qila to Palam. More than pride was wounded by that phrase. It marked a seminal turn in the thought process of Indian Muslim elites: they entered an age of depression.

The portrait of this multi-ethnic Muslim community is best drawn not from the features of kings but by the lines of poets. Four great Urdu poets mark the swivel points of this history: Amir Khusrau, Mirza Ghalib, Akbar Allahabadi and Sir Muhammad Iqbal.

Khusrau was born at Patiyali in 1253. He died of a broken heart in 1325, unable to bear the pain of the death of his *pir*, Delhi's iconic Hazrat Nizamuddin Auliya. Khusrau's deep devotion to Hazrat Nizamuddin merged seamlessly into the larger Indian consciousness. His glorious verse is the work of a smiling sufi, the poet who defined the identity of the Indian Muslim as both Indian and Muslim. His geet and qawwali belong to the genius of the land; although a Turk by descent, he proudly claimed that the music of India had made him an Indian. It was not the sword that kept him in India, but soil and song. He rejoiced in the images and diction of India. 'I am an Indian Turk,' he said, 'and my answers are in Hindwi.' Professor Mohammad Mujeeb, former vice-chancellor of Jamia Millia and author of the definitive *The Indian Muslims* (George Allen and Unwin, London, 1967), notes in the seminal work: 'In one of his historical mathnawis, the Nuh Sipahr, or the Nine Skies, Khusrau has devoted a whole section, The Third Sky, to the description and praise of India and Indians. He likens India to Paradise, and shows that because of its fruits, flowers and climate, it is better than any other country. The Indians excel in science and wisdom; they are inventors of numerals, the creators of the *Panchatantra*, the great book of worldly wisdom that has translated into Persian, Turkish, Arabic and Dari; their music surpasses the music of any other country.'

As a court poet he had to often write like a courtier, but he is not remembered for his panegyrics, but for his lyrics of the people. His *geet* is still a staple of wedding music. His songs like '*Chaap tilak sab cheeni*', '*Achche banne mehendi laawan de*', '*Hare hare baans*', '*Amma mera bawa ko bhejo*', '*Kahe ko biyahi bides*' and '*Mohe rakh le tu aaj ke din*' touch the soul of the Indian experience; not least was the music of lament at the departure of a bride. Khusrau's songs helped create the dialect and dialectic of harmony between Muslims who had begun to settle in India and its older inhabitants. Aitzaz Ahsan, the eminent lawyer-politician of Pakistan, narrates a story about Khusrau's virtuosity with verse in the language of the people that has become part of north India's folklore. Once, on the road, a thirsty Khusrau asked some girls at a well for water. They teased him, saying they would only do so to hear '*charkha*', '*kutta*', '*dhol*' and '*kheer*' (wheel, dog, drum and a sweet) in the same couplet. Khusrau's response was instant:

> '*Kheer pakai jatanon se, charkha diya jala,*
> *Aya kutta kha gaya, tu baithi dhol baja.*'
>
> (You cooked kheer with so much effort and burnt your wheel as fuel;
> a dog came and ate it up, now sit and beat your drum!)

The poet got his drink. Of water.

If Khusrau sparkled with the energy of a new fire, then Asadullah Khan Ghalib was a philosopher searching for the mysteries of a dying flame. His life spans the dusk of Mughal departure to the dawn of British domination. He was born in Agra in 1797, and died in 1869, the year of Mahatma Gandhi's birth. Ghalib's is the poetry of loss; of questions and uncertainty that overtake Muslims as their complacency is exposed by the rise of the British flag. Proximity makes the pain more intense for a Dilliwallah. Ghalib is the helpless courtier of a court that has become impotent, in a city that was destroyed in his father's time, when the Persian invader Nadir Shah massacred Hindus and Muslims in 1739, and would suffer a second traumatic massacre in his own life, when the British emptied Delhi after 1857. In 1739, all that the lethargic debauch Mughal Muhammad Shah Rangeela could do was tell the messenger who brought news of Nadir Shah's advance, '*Hinuz birau! Dilli dur ast!* (Go away, Delhi is too far!)'. In 1857, there was nothing left to say. Ghalib's great predecessor, Mir Taqi Mir, had already written Delhi's obituary:

> '*Dilli jo ek shahar tha aalam mein intikhab*
> *Rahte thhe muntakhib hi jahan rozgar ke*
> *Us ko falak ne loot ke weeran kar diya*
> *Ham rahne wale hain usi ujre dayar ke.*'

> (Delhi once was a city without parallel, in which the best and brightest lived. Fate has looted and desolated that city; I am a citizen of that ruin.)

Regional satraps had weakened Mughal rule much before the British delivered the coup de grace. Eight years before Ghalib was born, the sadistic ruler of a principality called Najibabad, Ghulam Qadir Rohilla, enjoyed Raqs-e-Bismil, or the dance of death, in the Red Fort: the sight of a beheaded twitching in its last throes as a red hot iron tray was placed on the severed neck and the heat prolonged the torso's agony. When the hapless Emperor Shah Alam told the rapacious Rohilla that he could not open up any hidden treasure because there was no treasure left, Rohilla threatened to blind him. These eyes, cried Shah Alam, had done nothing for 60 years except read the Quran. Rohilla planted his foot on the nominal sovereign's breast and gouged out the royal eyes. Princesses of the palace were ordered to dance before the usurper; they did. He pretended to sleep to see if any dancing princess from the House of Timur would avenge the insult by trying to kill him, but no one dared.

Wit is the balm for defeat and despair. I would have been a prophet, writes Ghalib, were I not a drunkard:

> '*Yeh masaail-e-tasawwuf, yeh tera bayaan Ghalib,*
> *Tujhe ham wali samajhte jo na baada khwar hota.*'

(Your matter is mystic, your style inimitable, Ghalib; I would have called you a prophet, were you not so fond of wine.)

Ghalib had to beg for a pension from the British after 1857.

'*Ghalib wazifa-khwar ho, do shah ko dua*
Woh din gaye ke kahte thhe naukar nahin hoon main.'

(Ghalib, you are a seeker of pensions, pray for the king; Gone are the days when you proudly said that you were not a servant.)

And when the British magistrate who sanctioned pensions asked if he was a Muslim, which would have left his begging hand empty, Ghalib, tongue firmly in cheek, answered that he was half a Muslim: he drank wine, but did not eat pork. In any case, it was an age in which the priest had become a drunkard.

There is no fulfilment, even in love.

'*Yaar se ched chali jaaye, Asad,*
Gar nahin wasl to hasrat hi sahi.'

(Keep on teasing your love, Asad; if there is no union, at least there is longing.)

'*Muhabbat mein nahin hai farq jeene aur marne ka*
Usi ko dekh kar jeete hain jis kafir pe dam nikle.
Kahan maikhana ka darwaza, Ghalib, aur kahan waaiz,
Par itna jaante hain, kal woh jaata tha ke ham nikle.'

(There is no difference between life and death in love; after all, I live only to see the infidel I would die for. Where is the door of the tavern, Ghalib, and where the preacher; but this I know, yesterday he was leaving that door when I entered.)

Ghalib spoke for a once-glorious community that now barely deserved the respect of memory:

'*Hue mar ke ham jo ruswa, hue kyon na gharq-e-darya,*
Na kabhi janaaza uthta, na hoi mazaar hota.'

(When I died, why didn't I drown? There would then have been neither funeral nor grave.)

If Ghalib was a prism, Akbar Allahabadi was a mirror. Appropriately, he would become known as Lisan al-Asr, or the Voice of His Time. Ghalib was still alive when Akbar was born, in 1846; he died in 1921, at the very height of Mahatma Gandhi's impassioned, historic non-cooperation, or Khilafat, movement when Hindus and Muslims abandoned their differences in common cause against British rule.

The last illusions, destroyed in 1857, gave way to nostalgia or bravado as Muslim leaders began to search for a fresh way forward. This was opportune diet for a satirist, and Akbar Allahabadi was satirist par excellence. He castigated rabble-rousers, double-tongued clerics and the peacock strut of modernists dressed in English plumes with equally sharp scalpels. He was not an ideologue or theoretician, but his sharp pen exposed the duplicity and injustice of imperialism as well as the subservience of its fellow travellers. Sir Sayyid Ahmad Khan, the founder of Aligarh Muslim University and leader of the pro-British movement, was never too lofty to escape his laughter. He readily acknowledged his own contradictions. He owed his livelihood to the British. His first job was as a clerk in the construction company that built the bridge over the Jamuna in Allahabad. He soon applied for a job as copyist in a court, got it, learnt English, and quickly rose to become revenue officer. Seeking better society, he studied law and became a successful lawyer. The powers that were named him to the bench, and by the time he retired in 1903, he was a judge in the small causes court.

But his personality was not quite as boring as such a biodata suggests. He spent a good deal of his income on courtesans, and his poem on the joys of drinking is part of popular music to this day: '*Hangama hai kyon harpa, thodi si jo pee li hai, Daaka to nahin daala, chori to nahin ki hai.*' (Why is there such a fuss when I have drunk just a little? I have not committed a dacoity, or stolen from anyone). The last line is memorable: '*But ham ko kahe qaafir, Allah ki marzi hai*' (The idol has called me an infidel—such is the will of Allah!).

His point was to survive British rule without losing identity or hope. Professor Mohammad Mujeeb, an admitted fan of Allahabadi, notes the dilemma of a person 'who's neither Englishman nor coolie': 'The two all-important issues during Akbar's lifetime were: what policy should the Indian Muslim follow in the existing political situation, and how should they maintain their cultural and religious identity amidst the tumultuous forces let loose by the civilization of the West. 'The master is turned slave, such is the will of fate; The owner of the palace is now keeper of the gate.' He was too realistic to take refuge in apologetics, and recite to the 'keeper of the fate' the glories of the those ancestors of his who lorded it in the palace.

If Akbar Allahabadi served the English without too much remorse, he also satirized Englishness remorselessly. The threat to Indians, both Hindu and Muslim, was not only from English rule but also from Western culture.

> '*Kahan ke Muslim, kahan ke Hindu, bhulai hai sabne apni rasmein*
> *Aqeede sab ke hain teen-tehrah, na Gyarwi hai na Ashtmi hai.*'
>
> (Where is the Muslim, where is the Hindu? Both have forgotten their rituals; belief has scattered, there is neither the 11th nor the 8th [religious days observed by Muslims and Hindus].)

Even Allah had been forgotten. His most famous couplet is still a staple of conversation among those who know Urdu:

> '*Raqeebon ne likhwai hai ja ja ke thane mein,*
> *Ke Akbar naam leta hai Khuda ka is zamane mein.*'
>
> (Rivals have gone repeatedly to file police complaints, That Akbar takes the name of God in this age.)

He could laugh at himself:

> '*Tayyar thhe nimaaz pe hum sun ke zikr-e-hoor,*
> *Jalwa buton ka dekh ke neeyat badal gayi.*'
>
> (I was ready for prayer when I heard of the houri; alas, the sight of idols changed my mind.)

Like so many Muslim poets before and after him, he sliced the pomposity of dubious priests. He might not have the lyricism of Daagh Dehlvi, who wrote, '*Waaiz sharab peene de masjid mein baith kar, Ya woh jagah bata de jahan Khuda na ho*' (Priest, let me drink inside the mosque, Or tell me a place where God does not exist). But Akbar could send a message forcefully enough:

'Mujh ko khush aati hai masti, Shaikhji ko farbahi
Main hoon peene ke liye aur woh hain khane ke liye.'

(I am happy when delirious, the Shaikh when he is fat; I was meant to drink, and he was born for gluttony.)

When gloom descends there is always the comfort of fatalism:

'Tumhen is inquilab-e-dahar ka kya gham hai ai Akbar
Bahut nazdik hain woh din na tum honge na ham honge.'

(Why are you worried about this revolution, Akbar? Soon enough neither you nor I will exist.)

'If Akbar attempted any systematic thinking, it was in relation to imperialism and imperialist policy in India,' writes Mujeeb. 'There could be no question of equality between the dispossessed Muslims and the English rulers of the land, even if Sir Sayyid and his group achieved some apparent success socially and a few score Muslims found employment under the government. In fact, this made the position of Indian Muslims worse. In a bitter vein, Akbar says he can see nothing on which to congratulate the performing monkey; if at all, the trainer ought to be complimented. The poet could create the impression that he was indifferent to the fate of the Indian people as a whole. But that would be far from the truth. He deplored Pan-Islamism; he was sure that the Muslims could not make a separate deal with the British; he ridiculed the illusions and the essentially servile attitude on which Muslim politics was based. He thought it absurd and painful that Muslims should make merry over the reverses suffered by the national movement because it was preponderantly Hindu.'

Sir Muhammad Iqbal (1876-1938) is the only one of the four Urdu poets to have received a formal Western education. The nation and his community were his abiding concerns, and it is not surprising that, over time, the two streams began to mingle and then merge. If Akbar Allahabadi wrote about Muslims, then Iqbal wrote as a Muslim. He was intensely political, and thereby represents the excitement as the

British, in collaboration with elitist leaders, offered political options. He was sentinel, guardian, preacher, visionary, judge, revolutionary and Cassandra as and when he felt that the moment suited a particular role.

> '*Watan ki fiqr kar, nadan, museebat aane wali hai,*
> *Teri barbadiyon ke mashware hain assmanon mein.*'

And:

> '*Na samjhoge to mit jaoge ai Hindustanwalo*
> *Tumhari dastan tak bhi na hogi dastanon mein.*'

(Worry about the nation, innocent; trouble lies ahead; your destruction is written in the skies. And: If you do not understand, Indians, you will perish; even your history will not find a mention in history books.)

His evolution from intense nationalism to separate solutions for Hindus and Muslims—although he never advocated the kind of partition that came about in 1947—was stern and, typically, sincere. '*Patthar ki mooraton mein samjha hai tu Khuda hai, Khaq-e watan ka mujhko har zarra devata hai.*' (You see God in idols of stone; I see divinity in every particle of my country's dust.) For the aesthete, Iqbal has much to offer; for the thinker perhaps more. But the Muslim *qaum* turned him into a leader because of his seminal, and most famous, verse-sermons, '*Shikwa*' (The Complaint) and '*Jawab-e-Shikwa*' (Answer to the Complaint).

The Muslim complains to Allah: why have You forsaken the faithful? The question reflects low self-esteem in an age of defeat; loss of political and economic power; bewilderment at descent from invincibility to impotence; and an inability to fashion an intellectual and social agenda for revival. It was a generation that had witnessed the collapse of the last two great Muslim empires, Mughal and Ottoman, before European imperialism. Many Muslims, including Iqbal, also saw as a continuation of the conflict between Islam and Christianity. Ironically, elsewhere, Iqbal has answered this precise question more robustly: '*Khudi ko kar buland itna, ke har taqdeer sey pehley, Khuda bande se yeh pooche bata teri raza kya hai*' (Make your will so strong that before writing your destiny, God asks you what you want written). But the Bulgarian/Slav armies were at the doorstep of Ottoman Istanbul when Iqbal read out '*Shikwa*'. He told depressed Muslims what they wanted to hear, and injected a magical quality into historical narrative. A few verses will illustrate:

> '*Ai Khuda! Shikwa-e-arbab-e wafa bhi sun le*
> *Khu gare-hamd se thora sa gila bhi sun le.*'
>
> (O Lord! Listen to a few complaints from your faithful, among the choir of hymns around you.)
>
> '*Thhe hameen ek tere maarika aaraon mein!*
> *Khuskiyon mein kabhi larhtey, kabhi daryaon mein*
> *Dee aazanein kabhi Europe ke kalisaaon mein*
> *Shaan aankhon mein na jachti thi jahadaaron ki*
> *Kalma parhte thhe ham chaon mein talwaron ki.*'
>
> (We fought every battle for You, on desert, on sea; the azaan was heard in Europe's churches and on the burning sands of Africa. The world envied Your glory when we recited the kalima under the shade of swords.)

And:

> '*Aa gaya ain larhai mein agar waqt-e-namaaz*
> *Qibla ru ho ke zameein-bos hui qaum-e-Hijaaz*
> *Ek hi saf mein ho gaye Mahmud-ayaz*
> *Na koi banda raha na koi banda-nawaz,*
> *Banda-wa-sahab-wa-muhtaj-wa-ghani ek huey*
> *Teri sarkar mein pahunche to sabhi ek huey.*'
>
> (In the midst of battle when the call came for prayer, we turned towards Mecca and bowed before You. In one line stood all, there was no ruler and no slave. Great, meek, mighty or rich, we were all equal before You.)

Allah's answer is simple: I have not forsaken Muslims, Muslims have forsaken me. Muslims were now embarrassed by namaaz and the Quran: '*Jalwa-e-Tur to maujood hai, Moosa hi nahin*' (The miracle of

Mount Sinai is still there, but Moses is missing). All that Muslims now did was wring their hands and wallow in self-pity (*'Haath pe haath dhare muntazar-e farad ho'*). The description of moral decay is scathing, the admonition scalding. But then the mood turns, and Allah becomes both forgiving as well as well as inspirational: He returns to the Muslim, as it were, on condition that the Muslim return to Him. The last verse is promise of renewal, if but Muslims could return to the fundamental principles of their faith:

> *'Aql hai teri sapar, ishq hai shamsheer teri*
> *Mere darwesh! Khilafat hai jahangir teri.*
> *Masiwallah ke liye aag hai taqbeer teri*
> *Tu Mussalman hai to taqdeer hai tadbeer teri*
> *Ki Muhammad se wafa tu ne to hum tere hain*
> *Yeh jahan cheez hai kya! Loh-wa-qalam tere hain!'*

> (Intellect, reason and compassion are your sword; My servant! The world is your Caliphate. 'God is Great!' is your inspiration; you are a Muslim, your fate is your fortune. Be true to Muhammad, and I will be true to you. This world is a mere nothing—unseen worlds are yours!)

It was a call for Muslims to turn to religion; instead they turned to religiosity. But that is another story, a tragedy that continues to unfold more than a hundred years after Iqbal thought that between a complaint and an answer he had found a denouement.

A CONDITIONAL CALIPHATE

Mahatma Gandhi's short-lived support for an Islamic state

16 December 2014

Lost in the outcry over the Islamic State of Iraq and al-Sham's (ISIS) recent declaration of a caliphate in Iraq and Syria is the fact that Mahatma Gandhi was the first modern leader to demand a caliphate for Muslims. In 1919, determined to unite Hindus and Muslims to challenge British rule, Gandhi formed an alliance with a range of Muslim leaders—from clerics to Oxbridge graduates to poets and businessmen—in an aptly named Khilafat, or Caliphate, movement.

Gandhi did not actually believe in a caliphate. His support was tactical. He reached out to Indian Muslims at a moment when they were vulnerable. They were struggling with uncertainty over their fate after the collapse of the Mughal dynasty in 1857, as well as with the despair they felt after the fall of the Ottoman Empire at the end of World War I. The Ottoman caliphate had been the last symbol of Islamic power, and after its defeat, all Muslim lands were either a European colony or under occupation. Even the holy cities of Mecca and Medina had been lost. Therefore, for Indian Muslims, the caliphate became an ideal more powerful in memory than it had ever been in reality. A mournful lament—'Islam in danger!'—morphed into a powerful war cry.

Gandhi, a devout Hindu, had consistently maintained that politics without religion was immoral. He saw nothing wrong with the Muslims' emotionally charged expressions of faith as a vehicle for protest. He did, however, force Muslim leaders to accept two conditions in exchange for his allegiance: nonviolence and his undisputed authority as the 'dictator' of the whole independence movement. (At the time, the term 'dictator' was still associated with its original meaning of dictation.) Gandhi famously took orders from only one source: his own conscience. India's Khilafat movement, which was folded into Gandhi's campaign for non-cooperation, thus became the only jihad in history that was both nonviolent and led by an 'infidel'.

But as the tempo of mass mobilization picked up, passions rose. Violence entered the Muslim rhetoric and, eventually, practice. In 1921, at the height of Gandhi's movement, which involved nonviolent forms of civil disobedience against the British Raj, a rogue group of Muslims attempted to establish a small caliphate in southern India. They killed or forcibly converted hundreds of Hindus. The British put down the uprising, but the cost was high: 2,337 Islamic rebels were killed and 45,404 were sent to prison.

In a separate and unrelated event on 5 February 1922, in the village of Chauri Chaura in Uttar Pradesh, a mob of protestors clashed with police and torched a police station, burning to death 21 constables who were trapped inside. Gandhi, shocked by the violence, abruptly ended his campaign for nonviolence without consulting the Muslim leadership. Satan, he explained, had taken over.

The Muslim leaders felt betrayed. They condemned Gandhi as a coward and never forgave him, no matter how much evidence Gandhi offered over the years that his heart, mind, and, indeed, life were still committed to Hindu and Muslim unity. A strong view emerged among Muslim leaders that they should never again surrender power to an idol-worshipper, as they called Gandhi. Ironically, in 1920, when optimism for Hindu and Muslim unity was at its peak, Gandhi had predicted that such an opportunity for partnership would not come again for 'one hundred years'. History proved him right.

Gandhi did not foresee the long-term implications of theocratic revivalism among India's Muslims. Nor did he fully understand a dangerous deviation that emerged from within his own movement. Just before the Khilafat movement began, Muslim clerics nominated an Imam-e-Hind, or an Imam of India, who would command the spiritual and political allegiance of Indian Muslims within a larger Indian state once India achieved independence from the British. This nation within a nation concept withered when Gandhi disbanded his non-cooperation campaign, but the passions that propelled it remained. In the late 1930s, Muslim leaders revived the slogan that Islam was in danger—not, this time, from British imperialists but from Gandhi and the Hindus. They dismissed Gandhi's vision of a modern, secular state as incompatible with Islam. In 1947, the sword of Islam, with some cooperation from the British, carved out the first contemporary Islamic state: Pakistan.

Democracy got off to a false start in Pakistan; liberal ideas may have made it into the new country's first constitution but not its legislature. In its first decade as a new state, Pakistan was characterized by violence and disorder. Within ten weeks after its birth, it launched a war with India over Kashmir. After three years, its prime minister, Liaquat Ali Khan, was assassinated, destabilizing the government and opening the door for turmoil and subversion; within a decade, the eastern wing of the country was seething with secessionist sentiment. And after 11 years, there was a military coup—evidence that Pakistan was a fragile idea with dysfunctional borders. The instability also revealed that Islam was insufficient as a basis for nationalism. In 1971, after a bloody war of liberation, eastern Pakistan broke off into Bangladesh. Ethnic and sectarian battles continue to ravage the country, particularly in its largest city, Karachi, and across the wide swath of territory west of the Indus.

Paradoxically, Pakistan's disintegration reinforced the view among many Muslims that Islam was the only basis for the integration of an ethnically diverse nation. But the centres of power and public institutions that supported the idea of Pakistan as a theocratic nation merely turned it into a haven for terrorist militias that used jihad as a means to extend

'Islamic space'. Pakistan has now turned into a jelly state, constantly quivering from political instability.

Indeed, out of that chaos emerged a second Islamic state: Taliban-controlled Afghanistan. As the United States learned, after paying a heavy price in blood and treasure, Pakistan provided sanctuary to Osama bin Laden. And today it is guardian of Mullah Omar, leader of the Afghan Taliban, who runs his war against NATO and Kabul from safe houses in Quetta and other clandestine locations.

ISIS is the third manifestation of Sunni theocratic revivalism. The ideological impetus for today's expanding jihad comes from the eighteenth-century theologies of Shah Waliullah of Delhi and Muhammad ibn Abd al-Wahhab of Najd in Saudi Arabia. Both scholars offered a vision of a caliphate reborn with a leader who would be true to the original principles of Islam and cleanse it of 'impure' practices and 'heresies' such as Shiism. Their modern-day followers took the next step backward, and under takfir, condemned any non-Sunni Muslim as an apostate or an infidel. As a result, Shia are constantly being gunned down in Pakistan by Sunni terrorists.

The thirst for purity is also a thirst for blood. These advocates of Dar al-Harb, or the House of War, are happy to burn their own house down since, for them, it would only clear the 'rot'. Jihadists categorize their enemies in three groups: the far enemy (principally America); the near enemy (foes at home or in the region); and countries that have occupied 'Islamic territory' (Israel, India, and now China, thanks to its Muslim-majority province, Xinjiang). Although al Qaeda is concerned primarily with the far enemy, ISIS' priority is to defeat the near enemy, the Shia, and to eliminate all non-Muslims from the region, even though support for ISIS has grown international. Recent intelligence reveals that there could be as many as 20,000 foreign fighters working for the terrorist group.

These parallel and overlapping conflicts, connected by the thread of Islamic theocracy, have destabilized the vast region that stretches from Pakistan to north Africa. We are, whether we admit it or not, in the midst of a fourth world war. World War I ended where World War II began: in Versailles. They were, respectively, battles against imperialism and fascism. The third, the Cold War, emerged out of disagreement over the future of Europe at Yalta. It was fought between the victors of War World II over the spread of communism. It ended with the Soviet defeat in Afghanistan, which is exactly where the fourth began—the war against terrorism, which is a conflict between democracy and theocracy.

Today, the Muslim countries that emerged out of the Mughal and Ottoman empires have been unable to come to terms with many requirements of a modern state, principally democracy, but also with freedom of faith, gender equality, and economic equity. Such failures are an invitation to an imagined past in the form of a caliphate or, in the case of suicide bombers, an imagined future in paradise.

The tragic irony is that Islam historically flourished precisely because it left space for pluralism in faith and politics. Verse 2:256 of the Quran unambiguously states, 'There shall be no coercion in matters of religion.' The Prophet Muhammad banned female infanticide, a common practice at that time, and Quranic law gave women inheritance rights. As for the concept of jihad, only a state can declare a holy war; the maverick jihadism that we see today is evidence of chaos rather than the realization of Islamic doctrine. If Islam is in any danger today, it is from rogue Islamists who fail to recognize that the former glory of the Ottoman caliphate grew out of its policy of tolerance, such as providing refuge for Jews fleeing the inquisition in Spain and Portugal. Long before the closed-minded caliphate of ISIS and its allies can hurt their declared enemies, they will devastate the faith of the faithful.

INDIA AND PAKISTAN: THE POISON OF CONFRONTATION

India and Pakistan are walking on different pavements on either side of a street that has caved in to become an abyss.

A CHANCE THAT CAME, AND WENT

On both sides there was great faith in the idea that if only India and Pakistan cooperated, they could leap towards prosperity

1 July 2001

During that brief period when they were Prime Ministers at the same time, Rajiv Gandhi wanted to give Benazir Bhutto a welcome in India such as no visiting dignitary had ever received. Was this innocence or overconfidence? Some of the starry-eyed even had visions of a handsome Gandhi and a beautiful Bhutto making a perfect pair on the ramparts of Red Fort while they declared peace before captive television cameras and liberated masses while their aides filed applications for the next Nobel Peace Prize. The opening moves between the two leaders had been promising. Rajiv Gandhi had taken the initiative, sent Ronen Sen to prepare the ground, and the two signed an agreement promising no first attack on each other's nuclear installations.

We are talking of the 1980s. That was another era, much more distant from today than the lapse of a mere decade would suggest. For one, so many of the principals are dead. Rajiv Gandhi. Zia-ul-Haq. Najibullah. Even the Soviet Union is dead.

In 1985, when Rajiv Gandhi was elected, there was much debate in Delhi about whether peace with Pakistan could be better negotiated with the leader of a military coup, General Zia-ul Haq, or an elected leader of a democratic order. No one could estimate how long this wait could be. General Zia made more than one effort to open a peace front with India. Like any sensible military man, he had both a deeper knowledge and a consequent respect for the abilities of the enemy. Even when Pakistan lost a few posts on the Siachen glacier under his watch, he did not order expensive (particularly in human terms) retaliation; instead, he dismissed what had been lost as ice and stones.

General Zia's focus was intensely engaged in his dream war against the might of Soviet troops in Afghanistan. He was funded by the CIA and Saudi Arabia, which meant hard cash without any questions asked. It was a war that the Soviet Union could never win and Pakistan could never lose. General Zia had a post-victory vision of a grand alliance of Muslim countries between Pakistan, Afghanistan, and all the Muslim Central Asian republics that would soon, he had no doubt, prise themselves away from the Soviet empire. He was not wrong about the consequences of a Soviet defeat in Afghanistan but this Islamic alliance was opium smoke. It had no basis in the realities and interests that govern relations between nations.

Zia's India policy was nuanced by this imperative: he wanted to finesse Kashmir through Punjab. All through his term the Valley was at peace, and kept its undercurrents under control. Punjab was on fire, and General Zia always kept a supply of fresh matchsticks nearby. Officially, he claimed the virtues of a peacenik, arguing that he could not fight on two fronts, and throwing more than one ball (occasionally a cricket ball) towards India for Delhi to pick up.

Rajiv Gandhi was cool to the General, treating Zia's overtures with a disdain that bordered on condescension. But there was an unmentioned element as well. Zia was not quite 'one of us'; Benazir Bhutto was. There was social bonding between the Nehru–Gandhis and Bhuttos, helped by a shared Oxbridge culture.

Rajiv Gandhi was eager to see if this could be turned into a political asset. He extended a Saarc summit in Islamabad into a bilateral. On their first evening in Islamabad, the Gandhis (including Sonia, Priyanka and Rahul) dined alone with the three reigning Bhuttos: Benazir, her mother Nusrat and her husband Asif Zardari. Both told their delegations later that politics was off the menu, and that they had fun. It was entirely believable.

There was agreement in that first summit on nuclear installations, and some progress towards a common position on NPT. Rajiv Gandhi suggested that secret negotiations should continue between officials: the 'invisible' dialogue. More visible would be talks on reduction of conventional arms and Siachen. Rajiv urged free flow of information, travel and popular-culture exchanges. Benazir on her part stressed that only a control of the arms race between the neighbours could alter the 'poverty heritage'. As is evident, there was no shortage of good English metaphor. Benazir mentioned Kashmir; Rajiv responded with silence. He realised that this silence was not playing well back home. Later, he stopped over in Pakistan on the way back from a non-aligned summit in Belgrade. When asked about Kashmir at a joint press conference, he was vehement that it was an integral part of India.

When V.P. Singh became Prime Minister in November 1989 he inherited a Kashmir that made Punjab look manageable. In a few unbelievable weeks the peace of the Valley was gone, not to return till the moment of writing. The first major incident was the kidnapping of his home minister Mufti Mohammed Sayeed's daughter; that was how Kashmir welcomed the first Kashmiri home minister of India. The government traded militants for the hostage. Farooq Abdullah resigned. Bullets began to ricochet through the city and the Valley. The Mirwaiz was killed. His funeral became a protest demonstration against India. Police opened fire, killing more than they would admit. V.P. Singh sent Jagmohan as governor, who in turn instituted a harsh regime.

Rajiv Gandhi tried to keep some semblance of the momentum he had created with Benazir Bhutto alive. During a visit to Namibia, where both he and V.P. Singh were present, he introduced the new Prime Minister to Benazir's national security adviser Iqbal Akhund. The message that V.P. Singh repeatedly received from Benazir was that she—and implicitly Pakistan—had nothing to do with the uprising in Kashmir. She even sent a special emissary, a man who is back in the news, a former high commissioner for Pakistan in Delhi, Abdus Sattar.

Both V.P. Singh and his foreign minister Inder Gujral could hardly disguise their cynicism about such assurances. The irony is that Benazir Bhutto's ignorance may have been genuine.

Rajiv Gandhi and Benazir Bhutto shared at least one problem. Because they were elected to power they assumed they understood the complexities of power. In fact, both inherited an election victory with the martyrdom of a parent. Both needed to learn on the job, and took too long to do so. Destiny made them Prime Minister when they were young, and then snatched time away from their grasp.

Rajiv Gandhi's government had frayed at both the edges and the centre when he launched his Pakistan initiative; his own credibility had soured. However, there was no objective reason for any dramatic or radical rethink on Kashmir in the late 1980s: the problem of Kashmir waxed only after Rajiv began to wane.

Benazir Bhutto's naïveté may be understandable in retrospect but that hardly makes it more forgivable. Worse, she learnt nothing from the dismissal of her first government, within a year or so of Rajiv's defeat. She thought that she had been removed because of her rapport with Rajiv Gandhi and her Indian manoeuvres. That was a symptom, not a cause. No one in Pakistan's Establishment could have seriously considered her unpatriotic; she had no reason to be. Her problem was her visceral hatred of the army that had supported the hanging of her father and kept General Zia in power, and her suspicion of the army as an institution and its senior officers as a permanent enemy. She could not coexist with an army that had become a major power centre in Pakistan. General Zia had used his ten years to create political space for the army; this fitted well with a demographic fact, that a quarter of Pakistan now has some economic interest in the armed forces either through immediate or past employment of some member of the family. She jostled with this powerful force instead of accommodating it. She had neither the party cadre nor sufficient reserves of sustained popular support to take on the army. She overestimated herself. But when she came to power a second time, again fortuitously, she thought she could appease her tormentors by being holier than thou on India. She became hysterical on Kashmir, using language that would embarrass a jihadi in an effort to mobilise support in an election she would lose to Nawaz Sharif (who kept his cool and advocated better relations with India). Sitting in Delhi at that time was the sphinx P.V. Narasimha Rao. The visual comparison between a ranting Benazir and a pouting Rao as the two dominated their respective obedient television channels was almost funny.

Interestingly, the only time that Benazir Bhutto and Nawaz Sharif cooperated was when they tried to unite against the generals. Benazir was having a baby at the time, and enjoying two honeymoons: one with her husband, and a political one with Nawaz Sharif, who even sent flowers to her hospital bed. The generals were not necessarily better equipped intellectually than their civilian competitors, but they had the enormous base of the one stable institution in a country that has not been able to create a reliable polity.

Hindsight provides a better line of vision. When Benazir Bhutto claimed that she had no knowledge of any Pak help to Kashmiri insurgents in 1989 and 1990 she was only providing evidence of her own impotence. What is clear now is that certain elements, across the arc from Kashmir to Afghanistan, decided to follow up the Decade of Punjab with the Decade of Kashmir. The objective situation was right for this. The war in Afghanistan was over, leaving thousands of trained, motivated and well-armed fighters with no place to go for a holy war. (Many of them continued their holy war in Muslim countries like Egypt and Algeria.) These men could not have been used in Punjab; a jihadi can hardly go to Paradise via Khalistan. But Kashmir could become a battleground for such martyrs, as the killing fields of Afghanistan had once been. One of the perceived problems of militancy in Kashmir had been the Kashmiri's reluctance to indulge in violence. A gun culture had to be induced into the Valley, leaving the rest to the inevitable fallout of a few years of point and counterpoint between insurgents and India's security forces.

Battles take time. They may also be independent of other impulses. Clearly Nawaz Sharif felt some urge to practise what he had preached during the election campaign that gave him an unprecedented majority. While he moved towards Lahore, the parallel policy begun some years ago found its culmination in Kargil. In a remarkable repetition of what had happened in 1990 Nawaz Sharif sent word to Delhi that he was not behind Kargil, although he did not deny complete knowledge of what was happening. Was Nawaz Sharif being disingenuous? Frankly, it does not matter much now.

For those who ran the Kargil sideshow are officially in charge of Pakistan, and they want their own dialogue with India. Is this an invitation to an Abbasid dinner? (The Abbasids seized power in Baghdad after they invited their rivals to a dinner at which they massacred them.)

Prime Minister Atal Behari Vajpayee is, understandably, a little anxious: a man who has felt cold steel in his back is loath to leave it exposed a second time. Is there a rational reason for a change of attitude in the Pakistan Army? Sentiment is best left out of calculations; even if it exists, it is too sloppy to hold anything together. Is there a hard and rational reason to expect sincerity? Yes.

Why? Does the Pakistan Army accept that its policy has failed in Kashmir? No. That is not the reason. Irrespective of what we may feel, Islamabad does not believe that its Kashmir Decade has been a failure. They believe that these ten years have weakened India economically and psychologically. Nor do the generals believe that they were defeated in Kargil, where we had to conquer to win and they had to survive to declare victory.

It was the denouement that was critical. Bill Clinton has now revealed what was known already, that he forced Islamabad to withdraw its own and auxiliary forces from the hilltops where the battle raged. One thing became clear after Kargil; conflict would not lead to a solution. India had the power to reverse any tide. Second, the world was not ready to stand by and watch two nuclear powers battle. Suddenly, the meaning of international intervention, which Pakistan has always wanted, changed. America twisted Pakistan's arm because it had clearly initiated hostilities. The world wants a settlement, not a victory.

This is the world of the 21st century, not of the 1950s or even the 1980s and 1990s.

Equally, India and Pakistan, now rescued from any self-induced sense of insecurity by their nuclear status, are at a point where their people dearly want to leave the poison of confrontation behind and challenge that poverty heritage that Benazir Bhutto spoke of. Who could want nuclear destruction when there is so much to live for? There is so much faith in the idea that if only India and Pakistan cooperated they could leap towards prosperity. It is a dream waiting for its chance. And, of course, the army and the BJP are in power in Pakistan and India.

OUTBREAK OF PEACE

The higher the expectations, the greater the post-conjugal depression

8 October 2006

Any outbreak of peace between India and Pakistan should be handled with almost as much care as an outbreak of war. Paradoxically, now that full-fledged war, of the 1965 or 1971 kind, has been made infructuous by nuclear weapons, peace might be a more dangerous game to play than war. Failed wars can be halted by a ceasefire, as has been the story from 1948 to Kargil. How to handle a failed peace?

Peace has erupted before, sometimes more suddenly than war; sometimes in quiet incremental doses. The Simla Agreement of 1972 did not bring peace. It merely induced indifference between uncertain combatants. General Zia-ul-Haq was rather more successful with his mildly escalating injections of normality (cricket, interviews, a better visa regime), but then he had a vested interest in temporary calm. He could not afford a second front on the east while engaged with the Russians in the west. He was deceptive. He used treacle to camouflage support for secession in Punjab. Zia was a master at eating the cake he was offering.

The last great outbreak of peace was at Agra. The Agra summit between Atal Behari Vajpayee and Pervez Musharraf is proof of that ancient law: the higher the expectations, the greater the post-conjugal depression. President Pervez Musharraf reveals the bitterness of this failure in his memoirs, *In the Line of Fire* (quite a bit of it, incidentally, friendly fire). The fact is that Agra failed because India and Pakistan had not checked whether the words they were using meant the same thing to both sides. That problem remains.

I don't know if Prime Minister Manmohan Singh and President Musharraf consulted the same dictionary when they met at Havana. There was the usual triumphalism when they agreed upon a 'joint mechanism' to fight terrorism. The problem is not about 'joint', however leaky the glue might be, or 'mechanism', however mechanical it might become. They need a consensus on what they mean by terrorism. It would be a pity, wouldn't it, if Dr Singh began preparing his bags for a trip to Kashmir only to find that General Musharraf wanted him to visit Baluchistan? One man's terror, after all, is another man's intelligence agency.

THE GREAT WALL OF SILENCE

Why Pakistan has turned into a 'jelly state'

10 August 2012

What is the difference between Indians and Pakistanis? There is no difference. We are the same people, with similar personality strengths, and parallel collective weaknesses. Why then have the two nations moved along such dramatically different arcs in the six decades of their existence?

India and Pakistan are not separated by a mere boundary. They are defined by radically opposed ideas. India believes in a secular state where all faiths are equal; Pakistan in the notion that a state can be founded on the basis of religion.

The two-nation theory, which was the basis of Pakistan, did not separate all Muslims of the subcontinent from Hindus; nearly as many Muslims live in India at this moment, without any hindrance to the exercise of their faith, as live in Pakistan. Pakistan was created on an assumption, which had no basis in either the political or social history of Indian Muslims, that they could not live as equals in a united, Hindu-majority India. It was a concept that flourished in the wasteland of an inferiority complex.

Indian Muslims who rejected this view, like Maulana Azad and most of the learned Deoband ulema, argued that Islam was a brotherhood, not a nationhood; they pointed out that faith belonged to God, and nations to men. They offered empirical evidence: if faith was sufficient glue, why would there be so many Arab countries? Muslims who fought for Indian unity were swamped by the high passion of a separation dream that acquired, in the imagination of its advocates, the attributes of an earthly paradise. It took three decades for that cold judge, time, to deliver its first verdict. The two-nation theory collapsed in 1971, when the majority of Pakistanis broke away to form Bangladesh, an ethnic entity.

Conventional wisdom in the 1950s, particularly of the kind which presumed that 'natives' were insufficiently evolved for the higher reaches of political thought, was certain that India's idealistic one-nation theory was the bubble that would implode, and Pakistan would stabilise and prosper. Although its polity collapsed within ten years of freedom, Pakistan seemed to offer, initially, a more positive social and economic environment. But as its raison d'être began to unravel in the mid-1960s, Pakistan's leaders learnt the wrong lesson from experience. Instead of moving away from theocracy, they clung to it as the abiding rationale for survival.

Ironically, Muhammad Ali Jinnah, the suave and brilliant barrister who had turned a whisper of the 1930s into the storm of the 1940s, and created Pakistan on the slogan that Islam would be in danger from Hindus once the British left, was the first Pakistani to recognise the perils of the idea he had incubated. In his private thoughts and at least in one major public speech, his first before the Pakistan Constituent Assembly in the second week of March 1947, Jinnah envisaged Pakistan as a secular state with a Muslim majority. He never deigned to acknowledge Gandhi, of course, but it would have been a mirror image of India: Gandhi wanted a united, secular state with a Hindu majority. There was a critical difference, however. Jinnah's state was exclusive; Gandhi's India was inclusive. The point of departure came in the mid-1930s: Gandhi and the Congress fought the British for the freedom of India; Jinnah and the Muslim League fought the Congress for the freedom of Pakistan. The British acted as brokers, and they did not leave without taking their brokerage.

The idea of India as a pluralist democracy was enshrined very quickly into the document that is the spine of Indian nationalism: India's Constitution. The debate over whether Pakistan should be an 'Islamic state' began to simmer and cartwheel as it came to the difficult part: what precisely did an Islamic state mean? The Justice Munir Commission, set up in the 1950s after the Lahore riots against the Ahmadiyya sect, offered some advice: an Islamic state was a mirage; in any case, it was no business of the state to define who a Muslim was. But wisdom has rarely deflected ideologues from their relentless march towards the extreme. The father of Pakistan, Jinnah, was soon ambushed and overtaken by the godfather of Pakistan, Maulana Maudoodi, creator of the Jamaat-e-Islami, who did little for the Pakistan movement, but once it had been founded, turned it into fertile ground for his dialectics as well as his foot soldiers. The Jamaat is a tailpiece in electoral battles since the voter does not trust the mullah with governance, but its influence on the ideology of the state is in consistent ascent.

Maudoodi's extremism, and the inability of Islamabad to do anything about his heirs like terrorist Hafiz Muhammad Saeed, has not only undermined Indo-Pak relations but also infected the social rubric of Pakistan. Textbooks, which once merely asserted Muslim superiority over Hindus and other non-Muslims, now demonise them in the most malicious language. Family and minority laws are caught in a corrosive downward spiral that has little prospect of reversal; and many tribal areas have simply slipped into barbarism. Pakistan has turned into what I have called a 'jelly state' in *Tinderbox: The Past and Future of Pakistan*: Jelly quivers constantly, and unlike butter will never melt away. Since it has an underlay of a terrorist substructure and an overlay of nuclear weapons, it has become a toxic jelly state. India is a prime victim.

The idea of India, conversely, has saved India from its own calamities. The healing power of democracy has eased the trauma of both the northwest and the northeast; the secessionist movement built around fear that Sikhism was under threat in secular India lost ground quickly after a brief and violent upsurge. India emerged from the flames of the

1980s reborn and resuscitated, held together by the promise of modernity: political rights, gender equality, freedom of faith and economic equity. The idea of India has proved stronger than the Indian; the idea of Pakistan is weaker than the Pakistani.

The sunder is permanent. Both partitions—Pakistan's from India, and Bangladesh's from Pakistan—are irreversible. Pakistan's answers lie in the man it remembers only in selective photographs, and whose personal values and ideology it chooses to ignore, Jinnah. There is some evidence to suggest that Jinnah did not fully realise the permanence of the separation; after all, he refused to sell his home in Mumbai, although the Nizam of Hyderabad offered Rs 10 lakh for it, a handsome amount in 1947. Perhaps Jinnah thought that Pakistan would be akin to a princely state of the British Raj, independent, but with open borders. In any case, Jinnah would have been repelled by the fundamentalism that is poisoning the life of Pakistan.

The 'ifs' of history are little consolation for the certainty of reality. In 1947 America was seven seas away from India; today an Indian probably feels closer psychologically to America than to Pakistan. India and Pakistan are divided by a great wall of silence, which liberals are anxious to breach, which ideologues are determined to strengthen, and which people are condemned to suffer.

WHEN FOREIGN POLICY IS A GAME OF HOP, SKIP, JUMP

Dr Singh has only time for inimical Pakistan and cynical China

22 September 2013

Every neighbourhood has its share of hoods. They come with the territory. When geopolitics is involved, one nation's hoods are another's soulmates. That's where is gets complicated.

Hostility is quite straightforward. Provocation has well-set parameters, and response is generally predictable. India and Pakistan are a classic example. Their foreign offices and militaries have developed a calibrated formula: so much ammunition for this much excess. The sabre rattles, and sometimes nicks, but never escalates beyond an almost predetermined point, no matter who is guilty. Life, punctuated by death, goes on.

Delhi, the aggrieved party most times, has factored in swings of an imbalanced pendulum. The sway is not even because the momentum generated by peaceniks falls far short of the conflict engineered by those determined to change the map of India. Sensible governments on both sides realise that while they can be confident no situation will end with the dramatic checkmate of victory or defeat, it remains their responsibility to ensure that the stalemate never decays into toxic war.

It is the relationship with friends that requires both more imagination and harder work. India's diplomats work hard enough, as is only to be expected from the big boys of the subcontinent. But over the past five years they seem to have had little purpose. Purpose is a consequence of policy, and foreign policy has been converted into a game of hop, skip and jump by the Indian government. The results are evident. India generates perplexity or scepticism among those who could be, or should be, friends.

Two examples stand out: Sri Lanka and Bangladesh. I mention them because five years ago our relations with both neighbours were just a few steps away from unprecedented cordiality after having sunk to an historic low.

The nadir in India–Lanka relations came with the ill-prepared military intervention ordered by Rajiv Gandhi, a paradoxical culmination of interference that began with an opposite objective when Mrs Indira Gandhi armed and trained the Tamil secessionist movement led by Prabhakaran. Squeezed into a horrendous trap, India became hated by both the Sinhalas and the Tamils. In January 2009, we stepped out of this poison-pill dilemma when India, guided by a foreign minister, Pranab Mukherjee, who could be both firm and clear, gave total if unadvertised support to Colombo in its final offensive against Tamil separatists. Delhi was quiet, despite pressure from its most important ally, DMK, as Colombo defeated the LTTE and killed Prabhakaran.

This was an excellent investment, which should have created a huge opportunity base for the expansion of mutually beneficial relations. Instead, nearly five years later, there is concern that Prime Minister Manmohan Singh may not attend the meeting of Commonwealth heads of government slated for November. Reason? The UPA is, apparently, worried about the political fallout in Tamil Nadu, where passions have been raised by accusations of human rights violations by the Lanka army during its war against the LTTE. This does not make sufficient sense for two reasons. First, India was complicit in whatever happened in the last phase of the war, for it knew what was happening but deliberately chose to do nothing. Second, if policy is going to be held hostage to domestic electoral mathematics, there can never be either consistency or gain to the national interest.

Bangladesh offered equally dramatic scope, with the comprehensive re-election of Sheikh Hasina. India could ask for no better friend in Dhaka than the daughter of Sheikh Mujibur Rahman, architect and undisputed hero of Bangladesh's liberation in 1971. And yet, through contortions that are a textbook lesson in how to snatch disaster from opportunity, Delhi managed to betray Sheikh Hasina on an issue as sensitive as water. The touchstone is not what Sheikh Hasina demanded, but what Dr Singh promised. Delhi could not honour its word because its management skills were woefully inadequate. There is good reason, therefore, why Colombo is perplexed and Dhaka is sceptical.

A scattershot approach extends its aim to wherever the blunderbuss can swivel. If India had one all-weather alliance in the world, it was with Bhutan. A permanent spring has slid into monsoon, with thunderstorms threatening all the time, even if they do not quite break into a downpour. It requires exceptional dexterity to damage relations with Bhutan, but we have managed to achieve this in the past few years.

If Dr Manmohan Singh's government has time for any neighbour, then it is only for inimical Pakistan and cynical China. The signal to others is simple: Delhi responds to trouble, not to a handshake. A bemused China takes what it can from Delhi, and snubs India when it wants. And an amused Pakistan laughs all the way to that bank called Saarc.

ON PAKISTAN, THE PRESIDENT IS THE VOICE OF INDIA

Pranab Mukherjee asks a tough question

6 October 2013

It is some relief that the latest high-level spat between India and Pakistan revolves around whether Nawaz Sharif described his fellow Punjabi Manmohan Singh as an old village woman carrying tales to Aunty or Uncle Sam.

Not being privy to breakfast chatter in New York, I cannot vouch for the authenticity of a participant's story that was denied with far less assurance than it was reported. One does wonder, though, what precisely that old village woman might have to say about the comparison. Would she take offence?

Dr Singh seemed unaffected, either by this or by the hint that he might have become a *bechara* after Rahul Gandhi's intemperate offensive against him. It says something about the political environment we live in that even a Congress heir believes he can best score some brownie points with the electorate only when he attacks a Congress government.

Lost in our immediate concerns we might be missing another perspective. The meeting between Dr Singh and Sharif was not between a departing lamb and an incoming lion, but probably between two helpless men. It took years for Dr Singh's credibility to weaken. Nawaz Sharif seems to have lost his sheen in just a few months. Both represent weak governments: if Delhi has been grounded, then Islamabad has not taken off.

The two met abroad because they cannot meet at home. But if the purpose was merely to repeat clichés, delivered in pseudo-stern language and heard in stoic silence, why meet at all? Dr Manmohan Singh never asked a question which Nawaz Sharif may never have wanted to, or been able to, answer: what is the reason for the sudden spurt in violence and incursions along the ceasefire line?

Conflict is too complex a dilemma. There are no easy prescriptions. But India and Pakistan have reached a point where even a common effort at diagnosis is not possible. Officially, Pakistan withdraws from any responsibility when it attributes the continuation of Pakistan's war for Kashmir to 'non-state actors'. It maintains, by this formulation, that the state has abandoned war as an option in the struggle for Kashmir.

But the Indian Prime Minister never raised the question that India's President, Pranab Mukherjee, asked during his trip to Belgium and Turkey: where do these 'non-state actors' come from? As he put in a pithy phrase, they do not drop down from heaven. They thrive in Pakistani territory, and they cross the ceasefire line with help from the Pak forces stationed along that line. They are never challenged while on the Pakistani side of the line. Is this help provided with permission from the Sharif government, or is it an independent operation run by the Pak armed forces, who follow their own two-track policy on terrorists?

The reasonable assessment is that Sharif is helpless. He cannot confront his own army; and he will not risk antagonising those powerful vested interests who still believe that India can be bled to slow death. Sharif has made it obvious, by his inaction if not through words, that he has chosen the path of least resistance over Hafiz Saeed, head of the Lashkar-e-Taiba, who orchestrated the Mumbai terrorist attack and continues to nurture assaults against India.

It is possible that given the horrendous resurgence of mass killings, whether of Christians in a Peshawar church or Muslims on a Peshawar street with a car bomb, or Shias across the country, cross-border terrorism in Kashmir might be at the bottom of his priorities. If Hafiz Saeed is a threat to India, then the Pakistan Taliban is a danger to the whole existing establishment in Pakistan. But if that is the truth, then the best course would be to keep the India–Pakistan dialogue on hold at least until both Delhi and Islamabad are in a position to discuss something concrete. The fudge that was offered as a meal in New York only looks more ludicrous when served with such solemn faces.

Sharif and Singh are not fooling their citizens. The people are wiser than they think. But they are fooling themselves.

Indian public opinion is nostalgic for Pranab Mukherjee, not least because Mukherjee understood the mood of street and village and gave voice to it. He is the Prime Minister they did not get, because Mrs Sonia Gandhi would not give him the job. The Congress will never acknowledge this, but privately its leaders are beginning to appreciate the perils of heading into a general election without Mukherjee's counsel and articulation. Mukherjee is as far from a hawk as you are going to get in India, and if he has finessed the government's wishy-washy language it is only because the Indian mood has hardened.

Dr Singh will not be Prime Minister after 2014. Pranab Mukherjee will remain President till 2017. Perhaps there is enough time to arrange a chat between Sharif and Mukherjee.

PAKISTAN IS NO COUNTRY FOR OLD DICTATORS

Pakistan must become a land to which Malala Yousafzai, winner of the Nobel Prize for Peace, can return

13 October 2013

Between Prime Minister of Pakistan, which 16-year-old Malala Yousafzai wants to become some day, and a Nobel winner for peace, which she might have become last week, the former is by far the better option. The Nobel generally comes to worthies when they have long passed their sell-by date. The last peace winner whose name I can recall, President Barack Obama, has not fallen far short of a superpower's quota for international violence. A Nobel gong and a cheque would certainly help Malala; a political career for her would help Pakistan.

Yousafzai is a brave girl, as much for dreaming of a better future as for getting a bullet on a bus on her way to school from those who are wrecking her country, the Taliban. Gender oppression, of the very worst kind, is central to the DNA of Pakistani extremists. Pakistan's Taliban, and its numerous terrorist associates, are a throwback to barbaric times, and a disgrace to the religion they profess.

This has not, alas, diminished their growing influence at the grassroots, or weakened the clamour among Pakistan's political elite for a 'negotiated settlement' with the Taliban. The question that is rarely asked, and never answered, is a simple one: what is there to negotiate? What should be on the agenda in a dialogue with sectarians who have made random murder their principal tactic, and perhaps the central principle of their ideology?

The Taliban and its surrogates want power. Is that on offer from Pakistan's politicians? Does anyone want to appease them with a share of authority in regions northwest of the Indus? Their influence has already crept into legislation to a dangerous degree. No one can stop their rhetoric, blasted into public space through some mosques and public rallies. Can they be bought off with money? Unlikely, as they have enough funds from domestic as well as external sources.

You cannot deal with inconvenient facts by pretending that they do not exist.

If Malala is in a British school today, it is because of them. If she hopes to challenge their vicious grip through elected office, it is because she knows how dangerous they are to the very sanity of Pakistan.

Malala is a teenager. She has every right to dream, particularly since she has been given a second life. Her dreams certainly make more sense than the rambling, shambling fantasies of a 70-year-old has-been like General Pervez Musharraf, who is obviously tired but will never retire. Musharraf can, and probably should, escape to Dubai or America or wherever he can find a few dollars more, instead of looking desperately for power, and posturing as a 'saviour'. Pakistan has moved far beyond him. It is no longer a country for old dictators.

If Pakistan is going to be 'saved' then it needs to become a nation with younger women and men in office, a new band of officials blessed by the fact that they do not carry the burden of recent history. It must become a land where Malala can return home. Malala has everything she could conventionally want at this age in Britain: an education, a future, and the laudatory attention of a British media. But she wants to bring peace to Pakistan, not to Britain. She wants to be a young woman in Lahore and Peshawar, not Bradford or Birmingham, to challenge the forces of misogyny and fanaticism which still command her own streets.

What are the odds that this might happen? Not too good, if one were to be honest. Nawaz Sharif has become Prime Minister at the head of a stable government because voters believed that he could restore calm to a nation whose nerves are on edge, and whose peace of mind has been shattered. So far, Sharif seems to be travelling at a leisurely pace to nowhere. To be fair to him, he still has time. But if Sharif fails, Malala and her generation will have to confront another question: is there nothing anyone can do?

A teenager who nearly lost her life, but never abandoned hope, does not need the counsel of despair. Dreams do not necessarily come true, but then how many get a second life?

HAFIZ SAEED IS PROTECTED BY HIS GOVERNMENT

National interest cannot be parlayed into a minstrel show

20 July 2014

Saints are the exception. Anyone else in the writing business, including those of us at the nether end of the business, can rarely resist the temptations of glory. The danger is obvious: vainglory, that purgatory space where imagination outstrips the boundaries of reality and ego functions on the basis of what we imagine we should be, rather than what we are.

One reveals no secrets when recording that an itinerant Delhi columnist Ved Pratap Vaidik, who enjoyed his fifteen minutes of fame last week after a visit to Pakistan, has declared freedom from the desultory limits of nationalism and repositioned himself as an internationalist in the intellectual category of Rousseau and Karl Marx, the former a philosopher of the French Revolution and the latter an author of the *Communist Manifesto*. That is how Vaidik describes himself on his Twitter account, and who are we to argue? In his ranging role of a world citizen, Vaidik has been advocate of a solution to the vexed problem of Kashmir: a united and independent state.

This, understandably, makes Vaidik Pakistan's ideal Indian. The reception he received during his last trip to Islamabad and Lahore included a chat with our next-door Prime Minister Nawaz Sharif and a very hearty meal with one of the world's most despicable terrorist ringleaders, Hafiz Saeed, who organised the assault on Mumbai in 2008 and continues to live like a lord in Lahore. This information is not confidential either. Vaidik has been talking about it to anyone who has the time to listen ever since he returned to Delhi.

When journalists try and make news rather than break it, they generally offer a butterfly story: it flits around a bit and then dies a quick death, killed by a yawn or a shrug. This is precisely what had happened to Vaidik's tale, until Congress, for reasons that continue to defy political sense, decided that it was something they could beat the government with.

It is possible that Congress, still unbalanced after the heaviest defeat in its history, has not been able to find its thinking cap. But to imagine that it could launch a credible attack on Prime Minister Narendra Modi over terrorism only means that the party is still skewed. No contemporary leader has better credentials than Modi in our ongoing national war against terrorists. His record, as well as his oft-declared convictions, speak for themselves.

It is strange that Congress did not even bother to check the names of Vaidik's companions on this Pakistan tour. It would have discovered its own stalwarts, like Salman Khurshid and Mani Shankar Aiyar, along with fellow-travellers who have received grace-and-favour appointments in Congress regimes because of their relentless criticism of Modi. It says something about the plight of the party that a free kick turned into a self-goal.

One of the depressing aspects of Dr Manmohan Singh and Mrs Sonia Gandhi's decade in power is that they handed virtual control of Indo-Pak relations to busybodies operating under high-falutin masquerades such as Track 2 and Track 3. In the competitive shouting match between peaceniks, Track 1 disappeared. This suited Islamabad brilliantly, for it could sustain the fiction of a relationship without having to answer hard questions about terrorism, particularly after the Mumbai attack mentored and managed by Hafiz Saeed and his allies in the Pak army and its intelligence services. Delhi became a willing party to a game where national interest was parlayed into a minstrel show.

Pakistan was able, in such a simulated atmosphere, to put forward a face it wanted to show, confident that none of the goodwill missionaries was interested in the second, more pernicious, face of the Islamabad establishment. Worse, such interlocutors missed—deliberately or unconsciously—the great changes that were taking place among the social forces in Pakistan. Hafiz Saeed cannot be touched in Pakistan not merely because he is protected by the government. His true strength lies in the support he receives from an increasingly radicalised Sunni population that is dragging Pakistan, step by violent step, towards anarchy in the name of religion. India is but one of the targets. Pakistan has turned into a graveyard for Shias as these self-proclaimed jihadists turn their weapons on anyone who does not fit their version of faith. The irony of course is that the father of Pakistan, Muhammad Ali Jinnah, was a Shia, but don't whisper that too loudly these days. They will begin to shoot up Jinnah's portraits next.

A shallow approach to a complex problem has driven India's relations with Pakistan to a cul-de-sac, and no one quite knows where to go next. A low intensity war continues on our borders, even as the likes of Hafiz Saeed continue to plan another conflagration within India.

What is certain is that Delhi and Islamabad must stop this pretend-dance and grapple with harsh facts. Pseudo-diplomacy and fantasy-peddling have done enough damage.

A TOAST TO STRATEGIC HEALTH

Finding common cause with China

21 September 2014

Once is never enough in the carefully crafted, meticulously guarded language of diplomacy. It is repetition which sets the pace. In his formal address at the banquet hosted by President Pranab Mukherjee, Chinese President Xi Jinping said he was convinced that a 'China-India strategic and cooperative partnership will make even bigger progress and contribute to an even brighter future for our two countries and to progress and prosperity of this region and the world at large'. And then, in a second mention, he raised a toast to this strategic partnership.

Message from Beijing: we will be serious about this discussion the next time our officials meet. So far, this particular aspect of the India-China dialogue has fluctuated on the assumption that each conversation be deemed successful if both sides manage to agree on a date for the next meeting. Presumably that will change.

So where precisely are the regions for strategic cooperation that will help the world at large? Which parts of this very difficult and acrimonious world are we talking about?

The Himalayas, for starters. Progress begins at home. The boundary has been a central problem between the distant neighbours since 1948, when Maoist Communists seized power in Beijing and claimed Tibet for China. After the low point of the 1962 war, India and China climbed quietly to a high point in 1988 with a unique solution to an intractable problem. They accepted that what could not be resolved was best left unsaid, and there was much to discuss about more productive subjects, like trade and travel. A piquant phrase established the contours of this new relationship: 'peace and tranquillity' along the border irrespective of national claims. And so, while the narrative of incursion and excursion continues, no shot is fired in anger. Contrast this with the India-Pak border, where every few weeks shots are fired in rage.

But an unstable boundary does not become stable simply because two nations have agreed it is unstable. This is what Prime Minister Narendra Modi stressed, in his forthright trademark manner, during his talks with President Xi Jinping. His rhetorical analogy was almost Chinese in its nuance: a toothache can immobilise the whole body. There is no significant dispute over half of the Indo-China border, and that section of the line can be settled given minimal will. It is the rest, across Arunachal, Ladakh-Aksai Chin and the part of occupied Kashmir that was gratuitously handed over to China by Pakistan, where the big chill descends. India would like Tibet to gain greater autonomy but has whittled away, over the years, the sovereignty issue.

China will have to accept Arunachal as an integral part of India. We cannot predict what the final agreement will be elsewhere, but there is nothing that cannot be settled with a little quid pro quo.

Can there be strategic cooperation elsewhere while such complex debates take their time?

At the moment, eyes and minds are transfixed upon the mountains, coupled with a sustained glance at the Pacific. But an important area of partnership lies in the immediate west of India and China. Both nations are under threat from the shadow armies and theocratic militias that have blossomed dangerously in the war zones of Pakistan, Afghanistan, Iraq and beyond. Al Qaeda, which is only one of numerous malevolent terror machines, has formally declared war against India.

Prime Minister Modi gave one sharp slap across the face of agent provocateurs when he told Al Qaeda to forget its fantasies about turning Indian Muslims into a fifth column of its illegitimate jihad. His assertion, to Fareed Zakaria in an interview to CNN, that Indian Muslims are patriots and will live and die for their nation is powerful affirmation of the PM's faith and convictions, which will reverberate across the world. But there is far more work ahead.

China is also under siege. Beijing, after underplaying this threat for tactical reasons, is beginning to appreciate that self-appointed 'Caliphs' in Af-Pak areas outside the control of Islamabad and Kabul will not rest until they 'liberate' Xinjiang. China cannot remain aloof from the world's most dangerous battle zone.

India and China can find common cause because both are impelled by national security. There is no reason more powerful than this. I do not know if Beijing has given any consideration to such cooperation; or whether it still believes that relations with Pakistan are worth more than this threat to China's geographical integrity. Some in Beijing will argue that Pakistan can become an ally in this war, but if anyone wants to understand Islamabad's limitations they can put a phone call through to Washington. The Pakistan establishment is beset by too many contradictions for it to be a reliable friend, even if its intentions are honest.

The Chinese, psychologically, may believe in a wall. But no one can be secure behind a wall in an age of communications technology, and militias that dismiss borders as a farce. If we do not move forward, we will be driven back.

FIRST PERSON

Such is the uncertainty of our times that astrologers are searching for politicians almost as fervently as politicians are looking for astrologers.

JINNAH BEFORE 1937

History might be better understood if we did not treat it as a heroes-and-villians movie

12 June 2005

'Well, young man. I will have nothing to do with this pseudo-religious approach to politics. I part company with Congress and Gandhi. I do not believe in working up mob hysteria.'

The young man was a journalist, Durga Das. The older man was Muhammad Ali Jinnah. The reference is from Durga Das's classic book, *India from Curzon to Nehru and After*. Jinnah said this after the 1920 Nagpur session, where Gandhi's non-cooperation resolution was passed almost unanimously.

On 1 October 1906, 35 Muslims of 'noble birth, wealth and power' called on the fourth Earl of Minto, Curzon's successor as Viceroy of India. They were led by the Aga Khan and used for the first time a phrase that would dominate the history of the subcontinent in the 20th century: the 'national interests' of Indian Muslims. They wanted help against an 'unsympathetic' Hindu majority. They asked, very politely, for proportional representation in jobs and separate seats in councils, municipalities, university syndicates and high court benches. Lord Minto was happy to oblige. The Muslim League was born in

December that year at Dhaka, chaired by Nawab Salimullah Khan, who had been too ill to join the 35 in October. The Aga Khan was its first president.

The Aga Khan wrote later that it was 'freakishly ironic' that 'our doughtiest opponent in 1906' was Jinnah, who 'came out in bitter hostility toward all that I and my friends had done . . . He was the only well-known Muslim to take this attitude . . . He said that our principle of separate electorates was dividing the nation against itself.'

On precisely the same dates that the League was formed in Dhaka, Jinnah was in nearby Calcutta with 44 other Muslims and roughly 1,500 Hindus, Christians and Parsis, serving as secretary to Dadabhai Naoroji, president of the Indian National Congress. Dadabhai was too ill to give his address, which had been partially drafted by Jinnah and was read out by Gopal Krishna Gokhale.

Sarojini Naidu, who met the 30-year-old Jinnah for the first time here, remembered him as a symbol of 'virile patriotism'. Her description is arguably the best there is: "Tall and stately, but thin to the point of emaciation, languid and luxurious of habit, Mohammad Ali Jinnah's attenuated form is a deceptive sheath of a spirit of exceptional vitality and endurance. Somewhat formal and fastidious, and a little aloof and imperious of manner, the calm hauteur of his accustomed reserve but masks, for those who know him, a naïve and eager humanity, an intuition quick and tender as a woman's, a humour gay and winning as a child's . . . a shy and splendid idealism which is of the very essence of the man.'

Jinnah entered the Central Legislative Council in Calcutta (then capital of British India) on 25 January 1910, along with Gokhale, Surendranath Banerjea and Motilal Nehru. Lord Minto expected the council to rubber stamp 'any measures we may deem right to introduce'. Jinnah's maiden speech shattered such assumptions. He rose to defend another Gujarati working for his people in another colony across the seas, Mohandas Karamchand Gandhi. Jinnah expressed 'the highest pitch of indignation and horror at the harsh and cruel treatment that is meted out to Indians in South Africa'. Minto objected to a term such as 'cruel treatment'. Jinnah responded at once: 'My Lord! I should feel much inclined to use much stronger language.' Lord Minto kept quiet.

On 7 March 1911 Jinnah introduced what was to become the first non-official act in British Indian history, the Wakf Validating Bill, reversing an 1894 decision on waqf gifts. Muslims across the Indian empire were grateful.

Jinnah attended his first meeting of the League in Bankipur in 1912, but did not become a member. He had come to Bankipur to attend the Congress session. When he went to Lucknow a few months later as a special guest of the League (it was not an annual session), Sarojini Naidu was on the platform with him. Dr M.A. Ansari, Maulana Azad and Hakim Ajmal Khan attended the League session of 1914, and in 1915, the League tent had a guest list that included: Madan Mohan Malaviya, Surendranath Banerjea, Annie Besant, B.G. Horniman, Sarojini Naidu and Mahatma Gandhi. When Jinnah did join the League in 1913, he insisted on a condition, set out in immaculate English, that his 'loyalty to the Muslim League and the Muslim interest would in no way and at no time imply even the shadow of disloyalty to the larger national cause to which his life was dedicated' (*Jinnah: His Speeches and Writings, 1912–1917*, edited by Sarojini Naidu). Gokhale that year honoured Jinnah with a phrase that has travelled through time: it is 'freedom from all sectarian prejudice which will make him [Jinnah] the best ambassador of Hindu–Muslim unity'. In the spring of 1914 Jinnah chaired a Congress delegation to London to lobby Whitehall on a proposed Council of India Bill.

When Gandhi landed in India in 1915, Jinnah, as president of the Gujarat Society (the mahatmas of both India and Pakistan were Gujaratis), spoke at a garden party to welcome the hero of South Africa. Jinnah was the star of 1915. At the Congress and League sessions, held in Mumbai at the same time, he worked tirelessly with Congress president Satyendra Sinha and Mazharul Haque (a Congressman who presided over the Muslim League that year) for a joint platform of resolutions. Haque and Jinnah were heckled so badly at the League session by mullahs that the meeting had to be adjourned. It reconvened the next day in the safer milieu of the Taj Mahal Hotel. The next year Jinnah became president of the League for the first time, at Lucknow.

Motilal Nehru, in the meantime, worked closely with Jinnah in the council. When the munificent Motilal convened a meeting of fellow legislators at his handsome mansion in Allahabad in April, he considered Jinnah 'as keen a nationalist as any of us. He is showing his community the way to Hindu–Muslim unity.' It was from this meeting in Allahabad that Jinnah went for a vacation to Darjeeling and the summer home of his friend Sir Dinshaw Manockjee Petit (French merchants had nicknamed Dinshaw's small-built grandfather petit and it stuck) and met 16-year-old Ruttie. I suppose a glorious view of the Everest encouraged romance. When Ruttie became 18 she eloped and on 19 April 1918 they were married. The wedding ring was a gift from the Raja of Mahmudabad. Ruttie's Parsi family disowned her. The marriage, full of love, was also more intense than the temperament of either partner could bear beyond a point. They separated within a decade.

As president of the League Jinnah engineered the famous Lucknow Pact with Congress president A.C. Mazumdar. In his presidential speech Jinnah rejoiced that the new spirit of patriotism had 'brought Hindus and Muslims together . . . for the common cause'. Mazumdar announced that all differences had been settled, and Hindus and Muslims would make a 'joint demand for a Representative Government in India'.

Enter Gandhi, who had not got elected to any limited franchise legislature, and believed passionately that freedom could only be won by a non-violent struggle for which he would have to prepare the masses.

In 1915 Gokhale advised Gandhi to keep 'his ears open and his mouth shut' for a year, and see India. Gandhi went on a tour of the subcontinent. Gandhi stopped in Calcutta on his way to Rangoon and spoke to students. Politics, he said, should never be divorced from religion. The signal was picked by Muslims, ever ready to marry politics with religion in their first great campaign against the British empire, the Khilafat movement.

Over the next three years Gandhi prepared the ground for his version of the freedom struggle: a shift from the legislatures to the street; a deliberate use of religious imagery to inspire the illiterate masses through symbols most familiar to them (Ram Rajya for the Hindus, Khilafat for the Muslims); and an unwavering commitment to the impoverished peasantry, for whom Champaran became a political miracle. The massacre at Jallianwala Bagh in 1919 gave Indian anger critical mass. Gandhi led Congress into its first mass struggle, the Non-Cooperation Movement of 1921.

The constitutionalist in Jinnah found mass politics ambitious, and the liberal in him rejected the invasion of religion in politics. When he rose to speak at the Nagpur session in 1920, where Gandhi moved the non-cooperation resolution, Jinnah was the only important delegate to dissent among some 50,000 'surging' Hindus and Muslims. He had two principal objections. The resolution, he said, was a de facto declaration of swaraj, or complete independence, and although he agreed completely with Lala Lajpat Rai's indictment of the British government he did not think the Congress had, as yet, the means to achieve this end. As he put it, 'it is not the right step to take at this moment . . . you are committing the Indian National Congress to a programme which you will not be able to carry out'. (Gandhi, after promising swaraj within a year, withdrew the Non-Cooperation Movement in the wake of communal riots in Kerala and of course the famous Chauri Chaura incident in 1922. Congress formally adopted full independence as its goal only in 1931.) Jinnah's second objection was that non-violence would not succeed. In this Jinnah was wrong.

There is a remarkable subtext in this speech. When Jinnah first referred to Gandhi as 'Mr Gandhi', there were instant cries of 'Mahatma Gandhi'. Without a moment's hesitation, Jinnah switched to 'Mahatma Gandhi'. Later, he called Mohammad Ali, the more flamboyant of the two Ali brothers, as Mr, though the siblings were known popularly as 'Maulana'. There were angry cries of 'Maulana'. Jinnah ignored them. He referred at least five times more to Ali, but each time called him only Mr Mohammad Ali.

Let us leave the last word to Gandhi. Writing in the *Harijan* of 8 June 1940, Gandhi said, 'Quaid-e-Azam himself was a great Congressman. It was only after the non-cooperation that he, like many other Congressmen belonging to several communities, left. Their defection was purely political.' In other words, it was not communal.

History might be better understood if we did not treat it as a heroes-and-villains movie. The heroes of our national struggle sometimes changed with circumstances, when they felt compelled to change tactics. Non-violent Gandhi, who broke the empire three decades later, accepted a British honour, the Kaiser-i-Hind medal, on 3 June 1915 (Tagore was knighted the same day). Subhas Bose, ardently Gandhian in 1920, put on uniform and led the Indian National Army with support from Fascists. Jinnah, the ambassador of unity, became a partitionist.

Maulana Abul Kalam Azad, who opposed to partition even after Nehru and Patel had accepted it as inevitable in 1947, points one finger at the failed negotiations in United Provinces after the 1936-37 elections, and a second at the collapse of the Cabinet Mission Plan of 1946 which would have kept India united.

A deeply saddened Gandhi spurned 15 August 1947 as a false dawn (to quote Faiz). He spent the day not in celebrations in Delhi but in fasting at Calcutta. Thanks to Gandhi—and H.S. Suhrawardy—there were no communal riots in Calcutta in 1947.

THE MAO OF GUJARAT

Students do better than journalists at a Q&A, as Rahul Gandhi discovers

28 November 2010

The unnamed young students of Ahmedabad who had a question or two for Rahul Gandhi this week were pertinent, not pert. They also offered evidence that students are doing the job that many journalists either cannot, or will not, do; which is, ask relevant questions. In this case, media was prevented from reporting the event, so journalists can't be faulted, and we know what happened thanks only to an enterprising reporter from the *Times of India* who had a source inside the hall.

The students wanted to know why they should vote for Congress when Narendra Modi had developed Gujarat so much. One answer given by Rahul Gandhi was odd, to say the very least. Mao Zedong, said Rahul Gandhi, also developed China but 'he caused destruction to the country, too'. I am not too sure whether Narendra Modi would mind being compared to one of the great figures of the twentieth century. Rahul Gandhi probably gets his views on history from some briefing by a young and possibly naive associate, but he could have checked with the Chinese. They have moved on from Mao, just as India and the Congress have moved on from Mahatma Gandhi, but

China still reveres the leader of the Long March as the genius who laid the foundations of China's economic miracle. Mao's portrait dominates Tiananmen Square as well as the nation's banknotes. If Modi can become the second Gujarati to have his picture on the Indian rupee, he will consider his life well spent. Chairman Modi has quite a nice ring to it as well, although Modi would be going too far if he published a little red book packed with his quotable quotes and asked millions of young people to wave it in unison during a cultural revolution.

A young girl was sharper in her question. She asked which Congress leaders could measure up to Modi on the development matrix. Rahul Gandhi had four names on the tip of his tongue: Manmohan Singh, P. Chidambaram, Jairam Ramesh and A.K. Antony. It is interesting that three of the four did not contest the Lok Sabha elections, and the voters in Chidambaram's own constituency had such a poor view of his development capabilities that he was declared defeated before he was declared elected in the 2009 general elections. It would be interesting if Jairam Ramesh could find a constituency from where he could get elected on a development platform, but his ministry does take its priorities from Rahul Gandhi's travel plans. What is definitely interesting is that the finance minister of India, Pranab Mukherjee, does not figure in Rahul Gandhi's list of heroes, either in development or honesty. Rahul thought that the three most incorruptible ministers were the PM, Antony and Chidambaram. He did not, however, consider Jairam Ramesh worthy of a position in this honest brigade. Poor Jairam. Or, one wonders, is it more appropriate to say, rich Jairam?

The Ahmedabad students pressed on about Modi. Why was Rahul denying Modi credit for Gujarat's development? He had caused 'some issues' replied Rahul Gandhi. At this point the story takes a curious turn. This was where Rahul Gandhi could have become forthright. Instead, 'the Congress leader refused to engage further and walked out saying he was getting late'. Perhaps he was only getting restive. Rahul Gandhi had discovered that it is perhaps easier to field questions from journalists than students.

Those who take the young for granted do not understand the young. The young don't mind cosmetics, but they never confuse make-up with reality.

SMILE OF THE ANNA

Simplicity is not a compliment in power-obsessed Delhi

24 April 2011

Does one have to be as old as Anna Hazare to remember India's freedom struggle?

We were sitting in the shade of a magnificent banyan, a marvel that dominated the single-storey brick structures and temple that constitute his work complex in the village Ralegan Siddhi, some 90 minutes by car from Pune. So often during our conversation he addressed this question, sometimes to me and sometimes it seemed to himself: what was that marathon, non-violent war against British Raj all about? Had all we managed to do was replace white colonists with those of a darker hue?

We ate a simple lunch of local corn, yogurt and roti, brought by an enthusiastic well-wisher, in a small slap-up building consisting of a claustrophobic living room stuffed with sofas, a dining room barely larger than the dining table, and a comparatively spacious washroom, a few minutes' drive away. This was not built by the Anna trust, but by the Maharashtra government. The amenities were not meant for Anna, but for His Excellent Excellency the Governor, who had decided to bestow personal benediction upon Maharashtra's most famous village.

Apparently, the Governor's majestic office decided that a plastic chair, or a coir charpoy, would be too uncomfortable for the Governor's buttocks, and so constructed this house for the two hours that His Notably Notable Honour would spend in the village. The shock at waste lingers in Anna's voice as he repeats this anecdote. When he asked officials why they were wasting people's money, they offered protocol as the excuse. Such protocol, said Anna, might have been considered necessary during British rule, but why was it still in place in free India?

There was a moment when he was young, said Anna, when he seriously contemplated suicide because he could not find a purpose to life. Then he chanced upon a book by Swami Vivekananda at a railway bookstall, and found his raison d'être: service.

Quaint? Naïve? A bit too pious for a world consumed in the terrifying struggle for the next promotion, the next holiday, the next slippery road to some extra income (source irrelevant)?

His smile is the antidote of cynicism, which is probably why Delhi—where most smiles are dipped in grease—dismisses him as either a sanctimonious humbug or, at best, 'simple'. The second is the verdict of friends. Simplicity, it needs to be noted, is not a compliment in power-obsessed Delhi. In Ralegan Siddhi, where emotions are untouched by mercenary need, Anna is loved precisely because he is without guile. His first name is not 'Anna'. This appellation, meaning elder brother, is an amalgam of the respect and affection that captures the essence of his character.

This essence sparked some long-awaited fire in the young of urban India when Anna went on a fast, because they understood, instinctively and instantly, that Anna's reward lay in what he could give, not in what he could take away.

The band on his wagon is of course another story. There is no point in translating the Hindi phrase 'Shivji's *baraat*' as 'Lord Shiva's wedding' because the cultural chasm between the two is simply too wide. Suffice it to say that, along with the sincere, caring and honest, every hustler is also out with his trumpet, and every peacock and peahen has arrived to join the dance. One senses that Hazare is possibly less dangerous to the government than to the NGO industry, because so many do-gooders turn up with excess baggage, much of it slipped through the rules. When the rules fight back, self-appointed guardians of morality use the classic weapon of a hustle: drown out the alternative narrative by screaming at the top of your voice.

The hospital of politics can be very inhospitable. It was a politician who raised an acute debate in this raging debate about honesty in public life. Is the Indian corrupt or is the Indian Constitution corrupt? Why should we destroy the great edifice of our Constitution merely because those in power have lost their respect for it? Throw out the mucky bathwater, Anna, but please hold on to the baby.

WHY WAS BOSE DIMINISHED ON REPUBLIC DAY?

Bose's contribution to the formation of the Republic of India was no less than that of the very greatest of our founding fathers

27 January 2013

We measure power through size. Check any political poster. The boss gets the biggest face presence. Others in the pecking order descend till the miniature at the end.

Why was Subhas Chandra Bose struggling among the also-rans in the Bengal Republic Day tableau? Swami Vivekananda, understandably, had pride of place. But it might have been better to keep Bose out of the jumble rather than literally reduce his stature. If Bengal forgets, how long will India remember the only Indian to head an independent government of united India?

Bose declared independence before the British gave it in 1947. His government-in-exile did not have Gandhi's sanction. It fought on the wrong side of the Second World War, but it was a proud and free government whose contribution to our freedom has been reduced by the domestic political forces he challenged.

Bose is an embarrassment to the Congress because he challenged Gandhi, and was a powerful parallel icon to Nehru. Bose asked Indians to give him their blood, and he would give them freedom. Gandhi promised freedom without violence. Gandhi refused to join the British war effort in 1939; but Bose went a step further, and mobilised Indian troops on behalf of the Germany–Italy–Japan axis. However, their horizon, freedom, was the same.

More than six decades later the argument might seem pedantic, and yet India's experience in the two World Wars of the 20th century is worth revisiting. Britain used invaluable Indian blood and treasure to win the First World War. After victory, Britain reneged on its commitment to Indian self-rule without batting an eyelid. In 1919, instead of dominion status, Indians got vicious brutality at Jallianwala Bagh and the pernicious Rowlatt Act.

It is not generally known that Gandhi was not a pacifist during wartime; he served on British frontlines in the Boer and Zulu wars in South Africa, and was very eager to lead a medical unit to the killing fields of France in 1914. In 1918 Gandhi worked so hard as a recruiting agent for the British army, urging Gujaratis to prove they were not 'effeminate' by picking up a gun, that he almost died of exhaustion. Farewell bhajans began to be sung before he recovered. Gandhi lost hope in Britain only when he felt betrayed.

Britain had as much to protect in 1945 as in 1918. London knew that its empire would unravel at the point where it had begun, in India, if India became independent. What pushed Britain towards the exit gate in 1947? Of course there was the irresistible momentum of Gandhi's nationwide struggle. But the British had faced this challenge before, in the Non-Cooperation Movement twenty-five years earlier. The significant difference was the nationalist sentiment unleashed by Bose among Indians in uniform. Bose's Indian National Army (INA) showed them where their national loyalties should lie. Bose's war also inspired the young to surge beyond the confines of the Congress.

Even Gandhi, who only had faint praise for Bose in a 1945 obituary ('Subhas Bose has died well. He was undoubtedly a patriot though misguided'), had to admit in an article published on 15 February 1946, 'The hypnotism of the Indian National Army has cast its spell on us . . . [Netaji's] patriotism is second to none . . . He aimed high but failed.

Who has not failed? . . . The lesson that Netaji and his army brings to us is one of self-sacrifice, unity irrespective of class and community, and discipline . . .' When the British put three INA officers—Shah Nawaz, a Muslim, Sahgal, a Hindu, and Dhillon, a Sikh—on trial for sedition, India exploded in wrath. Nehru said on 24 December 1945, 'The INA trial has created a mass upheaval.'

Bose broke the backbone of British rule when he destroyed trust between the British Raj and Indians in its armed forces. The eminently sensible Sir Claude Auchinleck, commander in chief, accepted that any extreme punishment for INA officers would make governance impossible, because Indians adored them as national heroes. This, he said, was the 'general opinion held in India, not only by the public, but . . . by quite a considerable part of the Indian Army as well'.

Subhas Bose's contribution to the formation of the Republic of India was no less than that of the very greatest of our founding fathers. Bose proved in practice what an Indian secular state would be. At a time when the Muslim League was in the ascendant, he had the love and trust of Muslims. He lived his dream of gender equality when he set up the Rani of Jhansi regiment, under the fiery and beautiful Lakshmi Swaminathan. When Bose told the Japanese he was setting up a women-only force, they thought he was joking.

Perhaps India can survive without Bose. But such amnesia will only diminish India.

MAHATMA GANDHI WAS A HINDU NATIONALIST

Gandhi was the father of an ideology that knit the groundwork of modern India

21 July 2013

When logic snaps, rational discourse stumbles. Why is it perfectly acceptable to applaud a Muslim nationalist, but denigrate a Hindu nationalist? Either both terms are right, or both wrong.

Mahatma Gandhi gave 'Muslim nationalism' institutional credibility when, in the fractured decade after the Khilafat movement, Muslims who believed in him formed the All India Nationalist Muslim Party on 27 and 28 July 1929, with M.A. Ansari at the helm. Our present Vice-President, Hamid Ansari, belongs to this family.

Gandhi was the father of an ideology that knit the groundwork of modern India. His moral compass was set on a firm axis: politics without religion was immoral. Among the first to be impressed by this proposition were the maulvis who later banded under Jamaat-e-Ulema-e-Hind; their alliance would flower during the non-cooperation struggle. Hindu and Muslim are birth identities; they do not change, unless one converts or becomes an atheist. But nationalism, a political concept, can vary. Gandhi believed that India must be a land where all faiths coexist as equals, guided by *sarvadharmasambhava*. Gandhi's nationalism was the antithesis of communalism. He was distressed to the point of agony by the slow drift within the Muslim elite towards separatism. This culminated in Partition when Jinnah reduced 'Muslim nationalism' to 'Muslim nation'. It was a visible reduction, philosophically, intellectually and, finally, geographically. Gandhi promised Muslims honour and equality in a nation from Khyber to Chittagong; Jinnah's prescription eventually reduced Pakistan to a sliver of land on either side of the Indus, wracked by fundamentalism and riven by insecurity.

The difference between 'Hindu nationalism' and 'Hindu nation' is equally uncomplicated. If anyone wants to be a Hindu nationalist, offer a warm welcome; if the call is for a Hindu nation, point out that religion is ineffective as a basis for nationhood. Pakistan is a good example. Indeed, if religion was sufficient as a glue for nationalism, why on earth would there be 22 Arab nations? Hindu extremism existed in Gandhi's time, but it never got much traction beyond the fringe; and it could not, ipso facto, seek secession.

Gandhi would have been puzzled by any suggestion that Hinduism was an obstacle to secularism; his Hinduism was an inexhaustible well of brotherhood, just as his colleague Maulana Azad offered Islam as a superb rationale for inter-faith harmony. Both used a faith-influenced dialectic almost unconsciously. Hindu-majority India is not secular because Gandhi was secular; Gandhi was secular because India is secular.

Gandhi was proud to be a Hindu. He promised Ram Rajya, not some variation of a fashionable Western dictum, whether Marxist or Fabian. Ram Rajya was a metaphor for prosperity and equality, not subjugation. Gandhi did not shy away from caste. His tongue only partly in cheek, he told the Shafi faction of the Muslim League on 22 February 1931: 'Brethren, I am a bania, and there is no limit to my greed. It had always been my dream and my heart's desire to speak not only for 21 crores but for 30 crores of Indians.' He was answering the charge that he spoke only for Hindus.

Nor did Gandhi's disciple and heir, Jawaharlal Nehru, think that the prefix 'Pandit' would stain his status as a secular icon. Privately, Nehru was more agnostic than believer, but learnt from Gandhi that he could not sneer at, let alone abandon, his Brahmin identity. India is a land of the faithful. Those who today feel 'Pandit' might be an embarrassment have not seen Durga Puja in secular Calcutta.

Strangely, those Muslim League stalwarts who were determined to parade every mark of their religious identity as a fundamental right, spread the canard that Gandhi's Ram Rajya would enslave Muslims. We see variations all the time, among far lesser beings, as vocal networks control debate, and stoke a fear psychosis that suits those who think the Muslim vote is better sought through fear than development.

The insidious power of hysteria sent Indian Muslims en masse towards the separatist Muslim League in the 1946 elections. Gandhi was reviled and taunted along the way. An important caveat is necessary, however. The 1946 franchise was restricted; only about 11 per cent had the right to vote: landowners, rate-payers, graduates; the elite. How would elections have gone if Gandhi's masses, the poor—who often have better political judgement than those better off—had voted?

Faith does not make us communal, human nature does. A politician has as much right to be a Hindu, Muslim, Sikh or Christian as any other citizen. Any doubt about an aspirant to power can be cleared by a simple question: is he committed to *sarvadharmasambhava* or not? If the answer is unclear, vote for someone else.

Let those Indians who want to pray, do so; let those who want to watch television instead, switch on. Faith is a freedom. Let us celebrate this freedom with a smile, not a snarl.

DISCIPLES OF A DEEPER FAITH

Nelson Mandela passed away on 5 December 2013

8 December 2013

Is Britain's Prime Minister David Cameron an unabashed hypocrite, or is he merely another Conservative politician? His tribute to Nelson Mandela, delivered before cameras perched outside his famous address 10 Downing Street, was fulsome. But Cameron forgot to mention that when he was at university, he kept a 'Hang Mandela' poster in his rooms.

Cameron and his Tory circle still revere Mrs Margaret Thatcher, who was instrumental in propping up South Africa's apartheid structure long after America and most of the West understood that there could be no justification for its racist cruelty, and that support for such barbaric injustice undermined the claims of democratic nations to represent the best of modern civilisation. The British Conservative school of thought, which included its share of much-promoted historians, was the last hold-out. It remained insistent that colonisation and such evil variations as apartheid were good for 'natives' who had been 'blessed' by European intervention in their histories. Admittedly, the British Raj was far less malevolent than apartheid, but explain that to the millions of Indians who died in famines and Chinese who became slaves to opium.

It is entirely consistent that two of the three greatest visionaries of the 20th century emerged from the horrors of South Africa (and one, Martin Luther King, from the long shadow of slavery in the United States). Perhaps it requires the worst levels of degradation to inspire the genius of a Mandela or a Mahatma Gandhi. You have to experience hell in order to understand that the alternative cannot be revenge, which would only create another hell with a different power structure. As Gandhi used to say often enough, if we take an eye for an eye very soon the whole world will become blind.

We should never underestimate the rage that a Gandhi or a Mandela experienced when they set out to challenge systems that, according to prevalent wisdom, would survive for centuries. But they understood that the secret of oppression lies less in the strength of the master and more in the weakness of the slave. Their challenge was similar. They had to liberate their own people from fear if they wanted to destroy the dictatorships which had usurped their nations. Their own lives, their exemplary courage and unsurpassed sacrifice, became beacons that rescued helpless and hopeless generations from the vicious grip of tyranny.

Never, never, never, said Mandela, as he took the oath of office after 27 years of youth lost in an island prison, would South Africa see the return of brutal subjugation. And in 1947, once Gandhi had broken the shackles, the great European project of Afro-Asian colonisation crumbled like a palace built on sand. But what is truly astonishing is that, unlike Communists who killed their Tsars with a manic glee, Gandhi and Mandela understood that the future would be best protected by assimilation instead of civil or uncivil war.

The easy thing to do with great men is to remove them from our lives and stick them on to the insipid pages of clichéd textbooks. We ordinary mortals do not possess the character to emulate a Gandhi or a Mandela, who chose the abstemious culture of an ashram or suffered the loneliness of prison when surrender would have restored the comforts of existence. We do not have the inner power to place the turmoil of our hidden, weak, frail and contradictory selves for inspection on public display, as Gandhi did in his autobiography. But we can learn something from their extraordinary philosophy of compassion. Gandhi and Mandela were disciples of a deeper faith: they turned the other cheek—and did so before merciless enemies who had the temerity to call themselves Christian. They believed that the meek must inherit the earth. They loved their neighbours as themselves, particularly if the neighbour was a Muslim when they were Hindu, or white when they were black.

They were not perfect. They laughed if anyone suggested such nonsense. Heroes do not need sycophants; only petty adventurers seek flattery. They were not saints. They were not so naïve as to believe that the ideal could always become the practical; they absorbed and tried to deflect that vanity and puffery that was strewn within the political milieu that they served, protected and helped prosper. But they were wise enough to understand that without idealism on the horizon, the politics of any society or nation gets lost in a maze that quickly degenerates into a fetid prison of the mind.

They both believed in God. They did not get a chance to converse in this life, but perhaps their souls will meet in Heaven. As they look down they cannot be entirely content with the deviations and corruption of their inheritors. But I am sure they will both be pleased with Cameron's honest and heartfelt tribute, for that represents their ultimate triumph. The heir of Winston Churchill and Margaret Thatcher knows that the half-naked fakir and the black young man prevailed in the long war because they believed in peace.

AATISH-E-CHINAR (FIRE OF THE CHINAR)

The fulcrum of Sheikh Abdullah's faith was that poverty had no religion

Sheikh Muhammad Abdullah's life evolved into a stream of consciousness, one half lava, one half love. His politics was anchored in poetry, for it was born in the heart before it reached voice through a meditative brain. As he often said, a lover and a soldier led the same life; the crusader in his soul was sustained by a romantic sensibility. This could sometimes confuse the high and mighty who had to deal with him; being gentle of manner did not mean he was weak.

History did not offer Sheikh Abdullah the power of armies; if he did climb the pinnacles of public life it was only because he believed intensely in the power of the people. That was the soil on which his idealism found root, and then flourished with a strength that has inspired the unqualified admiration of contemporary and future generations. He wanted power, for that was the purpose of politics; and power had its privileges. The highest honour was to do something, however little it might seem, but to do it every day, to improve the lives of powerless people.

He was drawn into politics by the wretched poverty in princely Kashmir, and the arrogant suppression that kept people in a permanent state of terror. Sheikh Abdullah was outraged by injustice, but he rarely permitted himself the luxury of anger. He was a proud man, but could easily sublimate his ego, for his cause was always much more important to him than his self.

If he seemed intolerant of anything, then it was the hypocrisy and flagrant self-indulgence of a minute ruling elite, which had converted Kashmir into personal property and wasted its resources with an extravagance that seemed even beyond the imagination of Europe's lurid tabloid journalists. Sheikh Abdullah had to define the purpose of his own life; he could have joined this elite very easily, but he chose the dark, harsh silence of prison and exile as he stood by his people, confident that their will would change their destiny. During solitary confinement, Sheikh Abdullah made friends with birds, and learnt their beautiful ways; he spent time spinning the charkha and reading Maulana Azad's *Tarjuman ul Quran*, and marvelled at the intellect of his great contemporary, through which 'my nationalist convictions were further strengthened'. And he never lost faith in God, in Kashmir, and in himself.

The principal challenge of the coming age, he knew, was poverty, and poverty had no religion; this was the fulcrum of his political faith. This was why in 1938 and 1939 Sheikh Abdullah converted the Muslim Conference into the National Conference, a decision which shaped the future of this subcontinent. He wanted freedom as much as any other Indian, or later Pakistani. But there was always a supplementary: freedom for what? If freedom could not ensure land reform, what was it worth? If freedom did not ensure the liberation of women from gender oppression, then it had failed. Clause 12 of his New Kashmir Plan of 1944 said, 'Women citizens shall be accorded equal rights with men in all fields of national life: economic, cultural, political, and in the state services.' The state was important, but the individual was supreme. Sheikh Abdullah recalls Ghalib as he describes this momentous event: the strictures of a ghazal's form have become too narrow for my thoughts; give me more breathing space.

He was a believer, so he could not be a cynic. Sheikh Abdullah drew his strength and philosophy from the Holy Quran, where Allah is called 'Rabb-ul aalimeen', the God of all humanity, and not just 'Rabb-ul Muslimeen'; Allah sent us to this world to live with other human beings, who are also His creation, in peace. His nationalist convictions also came from a reading of the Holy Book. Few heroes are so fortunate as to lead a people at the crossroads of history, as occurred in 1947; but it takes more than fortune to take the high road less travelled, and reject the seduction of a communal concept. Sheikh Abdullah had deep resources of idealism and conviction. He was never a man who would flinch before a foe; alas, he could always be defeated by a friend. He was bitter in 1953 when he felt betrayed by his comrade, but two decades later he did reconcile with Nehru's daughter Indira Gandhi.

It is entirely logical that this translation into English is a labour of love; there could be no other route to commitment. The facts of Sheikh Sahib's life are well known; and they would have been even more detailed if, in 1953, a callous Indian police had not destroyed so many of Sheikh Abdullah's personal documents. The secrets revealed in this book are what no one could have seized: the compulsions and demands that led to great decisions. Sheikh Abdullah's 'romantic sensibility' gives this memoir a surcharged passion that can never be captured in a biography. This is rare in this genre; most politicians use deceit to improve their reputation for historians. But *Aatish-e-Chinar* is a mirror of an inner self untroubled by temptations of compromise in the pursuit of desire. It is pertinent that on the opening page of his narrative Sheikh Abdullah remembers the story of the ascetic Kashmiri saint Hazrat Sheikh Nuruddin Wali, whose envious enemies tried to destroy his meditation by sending Yawan Machi, the proverbial siren. The infuriated saint's gaze turned her instantly into an aged, grey-haired woman. Yawan Machi became a disciple. Sheikh Abdullah also turned temptations into disciples.

Sheikh Abdullah says, in a sparkle of wit that brought back memories of his gentle and slightly mischievous smile, that this book began when the soldier and the lover in him came closer to each other. There is both the discipline of a battlefield and the freedom of romance in this mesmerising account of a life that towered across India's 20th century. Sheikh Abdullah's dilemma is familiar to all those who believe in him:

'Zahid-e-tangnazar ne mujhe kaafir jana
Aur kaafir yeh samajhta hai ki Musalman hun main.'

On the day Sheikh Abdullah anointed his son Farooq as heir at a public meeting in Srinagar, he recited a couplet that also summed up his own life:

'Auron ka hai payam aur, mera payam aur hai
Ishq ke dardaman ka tarz-e-kalam aur hai.'

THE BOOK OF REVELATIONS

Why was Mrs Sonia Gandhi so furious with Natwar Singh?

2 August 2014

Why write a fat book when a single sentence might suffice?

There are many excellent reasons why Mrs Sonia Gandhi should pen a memoir, but Kunwar Natwar Singh's autobiography, *One Life Is Not Enough*, is not one of them. Once her 'closest friend' and now nemesis, Natwar Singh has raised some important questions about Sonia Gandhi's character and use, or misuse, of power during the UPA decade between 2004 and 2014. His revelations and remarks have got traction in media and among the people because they seem credible. Mrs Gandhi has to answer them now, not a few years later.

The central question is: Does Mrs Sonia Gandhi have something to hide. A simple, single word, 'yes' or 'no', would do.

If Mrs Sonia Gandhi has nothing to hide, why did she and her daughter Priyanka call on Natwar Singh in May this year to plead that he should delete certain portions from this book?

If Mrs Sonia Gandhi believes that her erstwhile colleague, advisor and friend is indulging in fabrication, she has an effective recourse: she can sue author and publisher for libel and collect handsome damages if she wins. She has enough lawyers in the party baggage who will appear for her pro bono. A legal notice can be sent within an hour.

So far, the Congress response has veered between a private squirm and a public shout. Hapless spokespersons on television have resorted to high-pitched diversion: when asked about Delhi they launch into a vigorous assault on Mumbai. Ask if Mrs Gandhi refused to become Prime Minister in 2004 because of her widely-advertised conscience, or her son's fears, and you get some sustained invective against the author rather than a direct answer. In any case this pales before the charge that official files were being shown to Mrs Gandhi by a bureaucrat, Pulak Chatterjee. It is not illegal to be afraid, but it is illegal to violate the Official Secrets Act. Dr Manmohan Singh has said, rather blandly, that he was not aware of any files being sent to Mrs Gandhi, but he would say that, wouldn't he? Otherwise he would be guilty as well.

Natwar Singh claims that he was dropped from high office and driven out from Congress in 2005, after being named among the 'non-contractual beneficiaries' of Saddam Hussein's oil-for-food programme, because Mrs Sonia Gandhi needed a scapegoat. Note, however, that the term is plural: beneficiaries. Among them was 'AICC'. Mrs Gandhi certainly led the assault against Natwar Singh with a fury that she never displayed towards anyone else in AICC; nor was any effort made by her or Congress to discover who precisely in 'AICC' was in play. Nor did Mrs Gandhi later show any such vehemence against corruption when the telecom or coal mine scandals broke, or indeed when her son-in-law Robert Vadra became wealthy in quantum leaps.

Natwar Singh values his honour. He had a distinguished career in diplomacy. He is erudite. He was very close to three generations of Mrs Sonia Gandhi's family. Mrs Sonia Gandhi told her daughter Priyanka in his presence, at the meeting in May, that he was privy to information that she could not confide even in her children. Mrs Gandhi and Congress might now try and portray him as bitter or false, but the basic question will not go away: would Mrs Gandhi have made that enormous psychological effort to go to his home and plead if she believed that his book was only a load of bunkum?

Natwar Singh was obviously devastated in 2005 when his integrity was minced and he was flayed by a ruthless political machine. Philosophy cannot hide such scars, nor reason erase them. But he did do Mrs

Gandhi and Congress one enormous favour: he did not permit publication before the general elections, when it could have done even more damage.

If Mrs Sonia Gandhi is not just buying time, and does actually want to write her version then one presumes she will lend her name to a book, rather than a pamphlet. Emperors of yore employed the finest minds in court to set down their official story. The lords, ladies and knights of the British Raj, who ruled India after the Mughals, were prolific memoirists. It was an obligatory rite of passage between retirement and the last goodbye. Their heirs after 1947, the 'English Indians', have not done too badly either in the genre. It is a grand tradition.

Those who have tasted power know that their historic value will be measured by memory. In 1945, in the closing phase of the Second World War, Franklin Roosevelt, Joseph Stalin and Winston Churchill were relaxing after a day of hard negotiations at the Yalta conference. Roosevelt wondered how history would treat them. Roosevelt was pessimistic, Stalin was enigmatic, but Churchill was perky. History, said Churchill, would be kind to him, because he would write it.

Amen to that.

FIRST A DEMOCRAT, THEN A SOCIALIST

What would Nehru have done if he were alive today, amidst the war between modernity and religiosity?

14 November 2014

How relevant is Mao Zedong to contemporary China? That is as good a starting point as any for an appraisal of Jawaharlal Nehru's place in the continuing project called Modern India.

Mao's portrait still dominates the iconic Tiananmen Square in Beijing, and his enigmatic half-smile stares warily from Chinese currency notes. But would Mao smile or rage at the China refashioned by his steely successor Deng Xiaoping's famous prescription for national revival from the doldrums of economic stagnation and political instability? Deng did not care what the colour of the cat was as long as it caught mice.

Mao, conversely, was ideologically fixated on red, both on his flag and in policies washed by shades of blood, a price he considered well worth paying for in the pursuit of his ideas. Mao saw human beings through the cold eye of statistics; individual life was worthless before common interest, except of course his own. Would Comrade Xi Jinping, president of China today, consider writing a little red book of his own and launch a hundred million purges in a 21st century Cultural Revolution? No. China is ruled now by victims of that misbegotten hysterical outburst sponsored by Mao and a coterie around him commanded by his wife.

The interesting aspect is that Chinese Communism has survived and indeed flourished precisely because it reinvented a creed that demanded devotion to the point of rigidity. The only constant in democracy, by contrast, is change. Governments change and bring with them fresh eyes and minds that can recognise when an idea, however sacrosanct at birth, has outlived its utility.

Nehru has more streets and spaces named after him than you could count through a lazy weekend, and long may they last. But how valid, in the 21st century, are his two most famous and self-perpetuating doctrines: a socialist economy and non-alignment?

Nehru was a democrat first and socialist second. His thinking was a product of egalitarian objectives. He was a child of luxury, but once he entered public life he could see the physical and emotional devastation caused by hunger and terrifying famine. Famine was not a curse of nature but of a colonial government that placed British interests above that of the people. In his intellectual and living experience, capitalism was the avaricious handmaiden of colonialism, selling the guns for gunboat diplomacy and reaping the rewards of protected trade and commerce.

His socialism was an antidote more than original thought. His logic suggested that an elected government of an independent India would perforce be pro-people, and hence the legitimate custodian of its economy. He proudly handed the commanding heights of a flat economy to the state and set up a Planning Commission to drive the decision forward.

By the time Nehru died in 1964, it was obvious to any objective analyst that those alleged heights were little more than bumps; and that planning had lost its way. But foundational myths are hugely resistant to reality. It took Congress more than fifteen years after 1964 to recognise that quasi-socialism, now blanketed by Mrs Indira Gandhi's flea-bitten political slogans, had become seriously counter-productive.

For understandable reasons, Congress could not find the will to officially abandon its inheritance, but the price of uncertainty and compromise has been heavy, both for India and for Congress. India will recover, because democracy has created an alternative. We shall have to wait and see what happens to Congress. It is clear, though, that the party cannot resurrect without a new clarity in its economic framework. That is the crux; the rest is semantics.

Nehru's unswerving faith in democracy should never be underestimated, let alone taken for granted. He became prime minister at a time when France had not given women the vote. Universal adult franchise was not considered such a good idea by many of Nehru's most famous contemporaries: Mao, from one side of spectrum, sneered, and Winston Churchill, from the other, waited for uppity India to sink into chaos. The environment was deeply troubled by post-colonial partitions even as the fog of a Cold War engulfed continents. America had no time for the shaded nuances of democratic opinion when it strode across like white knight chasing fire-breathing red dragons.

The story from the newly-independent nations was not encouraging either. Almost all the great figures of what came to be known, inelegantly, as the Third World, quickly used the pretext of problems to set themselves up as dictators, and despots, for life. When wasteful royals became unacceptable, or irresponsible legislatures could not function, generals stepped in to 'save the nation'. Nehru was aware of the temptations of Ceasardom long before he became prime minister. In a well-known short essay he mocked himself for entertaining pretensions, even if only in his imagination.

If we want to understand how easily he might have slipped, all we have to do is note that just a decade after his death his daughter Indira Gandhi imposed dictatorship upon India through an Emergency. And if she had continued to be guided by her son Sanjay, instead of recalling the spirit of her father, India might have been under dictators for another two decades with who knows what implications. Of course the Indian people saved democracy when the crisis came, but Nehru understood the power of practice and precedence. He set the patterns, and strengthened the institutions—not least of them being media—

that would keep democracy alive through faltering democratic governance. It has taken 30 years for Indian democracy to re-elect a stable government, but at no point in this difficult period was democracy ever under question.

What is under question, and probably deserves a quiet burial, is the other pillar of Nehruvianism: non-alignment. Nehru's mind was, obviously, shaped by the horrors of the 1940s, an age when nations committed genocide and fought wars with a barbaric ferocity that is both inconceivable and incomprehensible. India compounded this with partition. When everything turned into ash, Nehru found himself in charge of the ash-heap. The great driving force behind his commitment to non-alignment was the desire to protect India from war. But he was so fixated by the prospect of war between nuclear superpowers that he quite forgot that wars have more than one dimension. This is surprising, given the fact that Pakistan's very first decision as an independent state was to launch a war to seize Kashmir, which quickly expanded into a war against India. Nehru was so determined to find peace that he dismissed Pakistan's invasion as a seasonal aberration. And he dismissed any possibility of a war with China, in the curious conviction that such a conflict would lead to a world war, which China would never risk.

Non-alignment failed India even at the height of its glory days. No non-aligned country stirred when Chinese troops broke through the Himalayas. It was left to a supremely aligned United States to come to India's rescue. Mao's forces withdrew to a line that they still hold across 4,000 kilometres.

India, in a display of collective inertia, remained loyal to non-alignment even when Pakistan repeated its invasion, in 1965. It was a close run. But for a bold decision taken by Prime Minister Lal Bahadur Shastri to defend Kashmir through a counter-offensive in Punjab, India's external boundaries and internal stability might have been shattered. But the great betrayal was not the predictable behaviour of Pakistan. A large number of non-aligned countries abandoned any pretence of neutrality and gave Pakistan material and moral support during the fighting. Once again, India was isolated. What was our generic response once the dust had settled with the Tashkent agreement in January 1966? Our foreign policy mandarins began to prepare for the next non-aligned conference.

Mao, perhaps because he had a better understading of strategic dangers, protected China with a true leap forward when he triangulated the fixed lines of Communist alliance and reached out to America. China is still reaping the advantages of that historic move. What did we do? We clung to a straw floating on international affairs in the hope that it would save us from drowning. Indira Gandhi corrected this illusion with the Indo-Soviet treaty in 1971. And yet, such is our ability to fool ourselves, we still pretended that there was some merit left in a theory that had become as moribund as a swamp.

Another complex war is raging through large parts of Asia and Africa. It is an ideological war between democrats and theocrats; between nations that seek modernity and militias determined to impose deadwood religiosity upon their polity. The Islamic Jihad, which in fact is not very Islamic and certainly not Jihad in its original sense, has laid waste a stretch of the globe from the borders of India to north Africa. India is not without options. We need alliances for prosperity with those nations who recognise the chaos that threatens, and have the will to sacrifice blood and treasure in this epochal challenge.

What would Jawaharlal Nehru have done if he were alive today? To claim that he would have stuck to an idea that served the purpose of the 1950s is to condemn Nehru as a leader with a dead mind. That is an injustice to his memory.

BAHADUR SHAH ZAFAR: THE DEATH OF HOPE

The last Mughal emperor ran for safety to a tomb

When did the Mughal Empire die? In March 1707, with the death of Aurangzeb in Ahmadnagar? Or 1717, when a Mughal firman waived all customs duties for inland trade in salt, saltpeter (needed for gunpowder), betel nut, opium and tobacco, creating the first generation of East India Company 'Nabobs' who gave a new meaning to wealth when they returned home, when Farrukhsiyar's court became better known for its sher-i-kalin, lions of the carpet, rather than mard-i-maidan, warriors of the field?

When Muhammad Shah, who sat on a disintegrating throne for 29 years, turned into 'Rangila', the colourful? When Major Hector Munro defeated the large but ragged forces of Shah Alam, Shuja-ud-Dawlah and Mir Qasim at Buxar on 23 October 1764, breaking the back of the old nobility? On 12 August 1765, when Robert Clive accepted the cherished Bengal Diwani at Allahabad from a chastened Shah Alam, by which the East India Company acquired the rights to all the land revenue from a vast portion of eastern India in return for an annual payment of £325,000 to Delhi (the Company bought London's acquiescence by offering another £ 400,000 per year to Parliament). It was a decision with extraordinary consequences: in London, a bull run on the company's shares followed by a crash that stoked an international credit crisis and drove the East India Company to the edge of bankruptcy. And in Bengal, five years of unprecedented misery culminating in the great famine of 1770. In those five years, one third of Bengal's population died of hunger or disease as the new masters squeezed revenue relentlessly out of destitution. Horace Walpole was moved to write that 'the oppressions of India and even of the English settled there under the rapine and cruelties of the servants of the Company had now reached England and created general clamour here . . . To such monopolies were imputed the late famine in Bengal and the loss of three million of the inhabitants. A tithe of these crimes was sufficient to inspire horror'.

Or should we mark the demise to August 1789, when the insatiable, bloodthirsty Rohilla, Ghulam Qadir, sat on the old man and, using his own dagger, gouged out the eyes of Shah Alam—those eyes, cried the emperor piteously rather than piously, that had been employed for sixty years in reading the Holy Quran? Perhaps the true obituary moment is December 1803, when General Gerard Lake, following up Arthur Wellesley's September success against the Scindias at Assaye (during which campaign the Company took the great Maratha fort of Asirgarh simply by paying the garrison salary arrears of Rs 7 lakh), entered Delhi and the Sahiban-i-Inglishiya became the protector of a blind man in an empty palace. Was the empire already in a coffin when, in 1813, Lord Minto, governor general in Calcutta, refused the offer of the khillat, brought from Delhi as a symbol of Mughal sovereignty? Perhaps 1816, when Lord Hastings abolished the Mughal mint and made the British rupee the true coin of the realm?

By the second decade of the 19th century, the empire of Akbar and Aurangzeb had been reduced to a parcel of land on the banks of the Jamuna, held in trust by the British. The descendant of Babur had become a beggar, sending pathetic petitions for an increase in his stipend to maintain a family that sustained itself on fantasy. There is nothing called a free stipend. In 1833 the British offered to increase the dole from Rs 12 to Rs 15 lakh, on condition that the Mughals waived their claim on governance. They refused, but it was irrelevant. In 1843, Lord Ellenborough ended the emperor's right to award khillat, and offered as compensation an appalling additional Rs 883 a month. It was accepted. The barter of Mughal honour for British pittance was complete.

The rights of succession were usurped and the British suggested that the next pretender might be more comfortable in a few houses off the Qutab rather than the Red Fort in Shahjahanabad, the residence of emperors since Shah Jehan. They wanted to turn the fort into an arsenal. When the heir presumptive, Fakhruddin, died in 1856, the British decided that the next claimant would not be dignified with the title of king.

The Mughal Empire did not die in 1857. What died in that pendulum year was hope. It was a powerful hope. Two centuries of prosperous stability ensured that the Mughal Empire would survive for another hundred years on its deathbed despite being struck with that most debilitating of all illnesses, impotence. It lasted not on the strength of governors, nawabs and rajas, who had parcelled out Hindustan between them within two decades of the death of Aurangzeb, but on popular mystique. The strife-torn decay of the 18th century, and the extortionist greed of East India Company rule, surely increased the nostalgia for the stability and prosperity of the 16th and 17th centuries.

The arrival of empire might be fortuitous, but its survival never is. A powerful military machine, a network of royal alliances, an administrative code imbued by the spirit of justice, and respect for local custom were the pillars of Mughal governance. According to the first chronicle of Akbar's reign, *Tarikhi-i-Akbari*, a slightly breathless, anecdotal account by Muhammad Arif Qandhari, the imperial stables maintained 5,000 select elephants and spent over a lakh of rupees a day (or five million dam) on animal warriors. The number is confirmed by other historians of the time.

Wars were fought, but were not the only option. When a courtier urged Akbar to destroy all before him, the emperor replied, archly, that in his estimation there were 320 *rajas* in Hindustan with strong or massive forts. It took him between six months and a year to subjugate a fort. He would, at that rate, need about 230 years to conquer Hindustan. Instead, he offered protection and continuity to the established nobility if they accepted a place in his expanding empire.

The Sackler edition of the official history of his son, Jahangirnama, has a very unflattering illustration on the opening pages, a miniature that depicts Jahangir, resplendent in his halo, surrounded by angels (the Jesuit influence is visible), killing an ugly old man with an arrow to the head. Heroes do not kill helpless old men, however horrid their looks might be. The caption explains the mystery: the Emperor is destroying poverty. In 1704, three years before his death, Aurangzeb, not famous for his love of infidels, suspended the jiziya, the poll tax on Hindus that he had imposed, against Mughal tradition, in Maratha country because famine had compounded the misery of Hindu peasants during the Maratha wars. One of the titles of the Mughal emperor was 'Nourisher of the poor'. Successful kings knew that their power rested on such a responsibility.

Fray Manrique, the Portuguese traveller who visited Dhaka in 1640, narrates an example of Mughal justice. A Qazi punished a Muslim who had killed two peacocks for meat in a Hindu village. The judge explained that he was implementing Akbar's promise made to Bengali when the province was conquered in 1575, that local laws would honour local custom and culture.

The Jahangir commitment did not eliminate poverty, but it did ensure food security. Nick Robins compares Mughal and British policies during famine in *The Corporation That Changed the World* (Pluto Press, London): 'Famine had been an established part of India's social reality for thousands of years, and was only truly defeated following independence in 1947. Early English travellers had commented with horror on the scale of the terrible famine of 1631, which had severely disrupted normal trade. Yet, the incidence of famine expanded dramatically, first under Company and then under the British Crown. In fact, British control of India started with a famine in Bengal in 1770 and ended in a famine—again in Bengal—in 1943. Working in the midst of the terrible 1887 famine that he estimated had cost another 10 million lives, Cornelius Watford calculated that in the 120 years of British rule there had been 34 famines in India, compared with only 17 recorded famines in the entire previous two millennia.'

Mughals could not prevent monsoon failure, but they knew what Amartya Sen has confirmed: that famine is largely man-made.

'One of the factors that explained the divergence was the Company's abandonment of the Mughal system of public regulation and investment,' writes Robins. Just old-fashioned good governance. 'Not only did the Mughals use tax revenues to finance water conservation, thus boosting food production, but when famine struck they imposed 'embargoes on food exports, anti-speculative price regulation, tax relief and distribution of free food'.'

And this is the bit I particularly like.

'More brutally, if merchants were found to have short-changed peasants during famines, an equivalent weight in human flesh would be taken from them in exchange.'

Why did millions of Bengalis die in 1770?

'Like previous failures of the natural cycle, the inadequate monsoon of 1769 in Bengal could have been managed without great loss of life. But the Company had significantly increased Bengal's vulnerability to natural disaster. Bengal had been picked clean by the Company and its executives in the preceding decade. Revenue collection had increased dramatically from just £ 606,000 the year before the Company took over the diwani to a peak of £ 2,500,000 two years later . . . By 1769, Richard Becher, the Company's Resident at Murshidabad, admitted with some shame that "the condition of the people of this country has been worse than it was before", arguing that "this fine country, which flourished under the most despotic and arbitrary government, is verging towards its ruin while the English have so great a share in the Administration".'

There lies the rub. Shah Alam had clearly settled for an annual income of £ 325,000 on the assumption that this would be roughly half the revenue. The East India Company ravaged the land to multiply the average figure by more than four times.

It is relevant to indicate how prosperous Bengal and India were before British rule. By the middle of the 18th century, manufactures from India and China accounted for two-thirds of the world's trade on the high seas. When Clive entered the capital of Bengal, Murshidabad, after his victory at Plassey on 23 June 1757, he marvelled at what he saw: 'The city of Murshidabad is as extensive, populous and rich as the city of London, with this difference that there are individuals in the first possessing infinitely greater property than any in the last city.'

After he retired, Clive was widely suspected of being the wealthiest man in the kingdom: riches had never been more nouveau or riche. (The Portuguese had also found Calicut, the port city of Kerala, far wealthier than Lisbon.) In 1769, while Bengal was in despair, Clive told Parliament that the British had become 'sovereigns of a rich, populous, fruitful country in extent beyond France and Spain united; they are in possession of the labour, industry, and manufactures of twenty millions of subjects; they are in actual receipt of between five and six millions a year'. And then there is his famous description of the riches that he had moderately decided not to acquire. Defending himself against charges of corruption in 1772, he told the House: 'A great prince was dependent on my pleasure, an opulent city lay at my mercy; its richest bankers bid against each other for my smiles; I walked through vaults which were thrown open to me alone, piled on either hand with gold and jewels! Mr Chairman, at this moment I stand astonished at my own moderation.' A chart in Paul Kennedy's *The Rise and Fall of the Great Powers* lists the facts. In 1750, seven years before Plassey, India produced 24.5 per cent of the world's manufacturing output, against 23.2 per cent for the whole of Europe and 1.9 per cent for the United Kingdom. To complete the perspective, China had 32.8 per cent, Japan 3.8 per cent, Russia 5 per cent, France 4 per cent and the Hapsburg empire 2.9 per cent. By 1900, the switch was statistically near-perfect: United Kingdom had 18.5 per cent of world manufacturing output and India had slipped down to 1.7 per cent.

It is possible that the British had succeeded too well in the hundred years between Plassey in 1757 and Delhi in 1857. No matter how lopsided the balance between the opposing armies, it was the Company line that stood and the Indian standard that eventually fell. A major challenge to British ambitions ended when Arthur Wellesley, later to become Duke of Wellington, defeated Mysore's Tipu Sultan at the battle of Seringapatnam in 1798. After reaching Delhi in 1803, the Company's armies dealt with the Gurkhas in 1814-16, ended any hopes of a Maratha revival by 1818, took Sind in 1843 and annexed Punjab's great Sikh empire after the close wars of 1848-49. The British had met every regional or rising power, and won every battle, either on the field or by intrigue. The latter may have been more impressive than regimental discipline, for intrigue was supposed to be the forte of 'Asiatic forms of government'. With a little more regional cooperation, both Mysore and the Marathas might have kept even the genius of Wellesley in check, but the one thing that the British could count on was Indian disunity. It did not require religion to disperse Indians into warring camps; ego and greed were just as effective. Mirza Abu Zafar, son of Akbar Shah the Second, was born in 1775, and called himself 'Abul Muzaffar Sirajuddin Muhammad Bahadur Shah Badshah Ghazi' upon succeeding to the throne in 1837. It was an adventurous claim for a supine man. Bahadur Shah Zafar would have been remembered as a minor, if moving, poet had he not been the last Mughal dynast. He had neither courage, nor conviction, nor craft to be a leader of men. He was certainly not, as the war of 1857 was to prove, a holy warrior, which is what 'Ghazi' means.

British contempt for the later Mughal kings was punctuated by surprise at such decay of a lineage they had once held in awe: could such men have the blood of Timurids running in their veins? In fact, there was little impressive about the multi-ethnic elite that the British encountered on their long march from Calcutta to Delhi. The ease with which they had co-opted landlords, after Lord Cornwallis' Permanent Settlement in 1793, into the economic exploitation of fellow-Indians; the manner in which the dazzling Nawabs of Bengal and Awadh were shorn of their luster; the effortless manipulation of the Marathas; and finally the invariable success in the final test, the battlefield, were not designed to heighten respect.

But contempt is only a few steps away from complacency, and so the British did not hear what the bazaar knew at least six weeks before the rebels from Meerut knocked on the palace doors of the Red Fort at eight in the morning of 11 May. There was loud bragging at gossip centres like Chandni Chowk that the Russians and Persians were coming to help the Mughals. In 1856, the Persians had tried to get a foot through the subcontinent's door by occupying Herat, just across the border in Afghanistan, but the British bombed the port of Muhammarrah to pressure Persia to withdraw. The Great Game was in the air. The trial summary records:

The following facts were ultimately established by these proceedings: First, that the intended revolt was known to, and encouraged by, the Shah of Persia, who at the request of the king, promised money and troops to ensure its success; his proclamation to that effect being posted upon the gate of the Jumma Masjid, from whence it was taken down by order of Sir Theophilus Metcalfe, who himself was informed by a Christian Ressaldar very popular with the natives, that he had been warned to fly, as the Persians were coming, and the Mussalmans were exceedingly excited. Unfortunately Sir Theophilus considered the information from such a quarter of no importance. Secondly, it was proved that a paper was addressed to, and received by, the late Mr Colvin (Lieutenant Governor of the North West Provinces), by Mr Mohamed Dervish, revealing the whole plot six weeks before the rebellion actually broke out and this warning also was considered so unimportant that it was neither acted upon by the party to whom it was given, nor reported by him for the consideration of the supreme government: and, thirdly, that the murder of Europeans in Delhi was committed by order of the king, in the presence of his sons and other persons connected with the royal family, and by means of the Khassburdars, his special bodyguard.

In the event, the Tsars remained in St Petersburg and the Shahs stayed in Tehran. The man who arrived at the door was Bakht Khan, a subedar in the 8th Foot Artillery at Bareilly who had served his British masters well for four decades and was now 60, fat and leader of the rebels. He had 'a large stomach', the records note without comment. As the political mercury rose that summer, visions of glory flowered in more than one heart.

A certain Jumuna Das, 'resident of Muttra', wrote that he had 2,000 men at his command, promised to pay Rs 10 lakh to the treasury, and wanted artillery, infantry and cavalry along with ammunition and a seal of authority. That promise of money was a mistake. Zafar asked his son, Mirza Mughal, who had been appointed commander-in-chief of the army, 'Does this man propose to dig up a buried treasure of ten lacs of rupees, or does he know of any treasury where this money is deposited, or does he intend to plunder anyone for it?' Amir Ali Khan, Nawab of Khurajpura, did not promise hard cash, just a lofty goal. He petitioned on 12 July that if he was put in charge of the war, he would 'in three days totally exterminate these people with white skins and dark fortunes'.

What is impressive is how quickly the Mughal court became the natural centre of administration, as if one stroke of the sword in a battle that had not ended had restored the past. The petitions and orders that began to arrive and depart from the Red Fort were to become evidence at the trial. The paperwork was proof that, for a hundred and thirty days, the Mughal seal had regained some authority. It also exposed the weakness of a storm that was chaotic at its centre: there was no forethought, no strategy, no money, and no means. What they did possess was erratic bravery and perhaps excessive conviction.

The minutiae of administration tell an evocative story. On 27 May, orders were given to provide Chuni Lal, the superintendent of the Jamuna bridge, with two iron hatchets, two adzes, two saws, two chisels and a hundred nails to strengthen the structure. On 29 May, James Skinner's Delhi house had been handed over to the principal subordinate office for the collection of land revenue. On 5 June, three pipes of spirits, taken in plunder, were passed on to the 'writers of the Kayastha caste, old servants of the King'. But by 18 June, the early optimism had begun to fade, as the soldiers began to show signs of serious indiscipline. Zafar wrote to Mirza Mughal: 'It is the business of the Army to protect, and not to desolate or plunder. The officers of the Army will, therefore, immediately restrain their men from the commission of these improprieties, and further, as the intelligence of the approach of the enemies' troops was false, these lawless soldiery should not be kept in the old Fort but, on the contrary, entrenchments should be constructed for them, at a distance of five or six miles, and they should be stationed there . . .'

One of the earliest petitions, of 18 May, from Maulvi Muhammad Zohur Ali, police officer at Najagarh, identified the problem: he respectfully wanted funds to maintain law and order in his jurisdiction. There was nothing to send.

Decisions that involved no expenditure were easier to take. On 24 June, Zafar gave permission to Jumma ud Din Khan to start a newspaper, but to 'observe great care, that false intelligence, or that statements by which the characters of respectable individuals, or of the residents of the city, may be aspersed, directly or by implication, be not inserted'. As a measure against libel, the language was impeccable. During Bakrid that year, Zafar prohibited cow slaughter in order to maintain harmony between Hindus and Muslims at a time when agent provocateurs were active. And of course, Zafar refused to see any difference between Muslims and Hindus in matters of state: this was Mughal policy clearly established by Akbar, and followed, the occasional breach notwithstanding, by almost every Mughal ruler.

There was good news for the army on 27 June, when Sheo Das Pathak and Narayan Singh, sepoys of the 46th Regiment Native Infantry, brought in 162 sheep and goats. They claimed that five European soldiers had been killed in the process. But it was the home front, rather than the battlefront, which was the problem.

On 19 June, Chand Khan and Gulab Khan, residents of Jysinghpur and Shahganj, complained that the troops were 'oppressing the shopkeepers, forcibly taking away their wares, without the payment of prices, and also entering the dwelling houses of the destitute and the indigent, [to] forcibly carry away all such articles, as beds, woods [sic], vessels, etc., that they can lay their hands on, and wound with firearms and swords, those who may supplicate their forbearance'.

Very soon the royal princes were in on the looting as well. A joint petition of Jogal Kishwar and Sheoprashad, merchants, accused some of the princes of plundering their homes. 'If the Princes Royal, delegated to protect the subjects of the State and the poor, begin themselves to plunder and oppress, where then can there be safety for the subject?' They even named the princes: Mirza Mughal, Mirza Khair, et al. On 4 July, Ahsan ul Hak complained that Mirza Abulbakr Sahib, another son of the King, 'has lately been in the habit, with unrestrained licence and recklessness, of visiting for evil purposes the house of Princess Farkhunda Zamani . . . and indulging in the practice of all those acts which may be expected to result from drunkenness'. When Hak objected, he was robbed: he lost a prayer rug worth two rupees, a Benaras scarf worth seven rupees, a horse worth two hundred rupees, a pair of bullocks worth a hundred rupees and a sword worth fifteen rupees. By 17 July, mobs were looting the shops around Kashmere Gate every day.

There was anarchy by the end of August. Nabi Baksh, representing the distress of merchants, petitioned: 'That in the present anarchy, your slaves have suffered heavy and ruinous losses inasmuch as whatever commerce we carried on, whether at Calcutta, or Benaras, or Cawnpore, or Delhi, or Umballah, or Lahore, has been ruined, and all our mercantile stores have been plundered and devastated, while the burden of our former debts still lies on our shoulders, and we are now without even the means of meeting the daily expenses necessary for the subsistence of ourselves and our families . . . Mirza Mughal Sahib now demands 50,000 rupees from us. Whence can we produce the same?' The next document is from Mirza Mughal, who says without fuss that 'the Army having been reduced to starvation in consequence of not being paid their daily allowances' there was an urgent need to raise a loan. There was no loan, and soon there would be no army.

It is not a particularly long story, and certainly not an edifying one. Long before he lost the war to the British, Bahadur Shah Zafar had lost credibility at home. In August, Urdu newspapers were fantasizing about the imminent arrival of the King of Persia via Attock, although the *Urdu News* preferred to be more circumspect: 'Local News. Persia. Some people now again say that the Persian army has come through the Bolan and Bibi Narri passes, and that the Amir Dost Muhammad Khan cheerfully gave them a free passage through his dominions; but according to the common Indian adage that "a Brahman believes in the promise of a feast only when he gets it", the people of India will believe this matter only when they have some ocular proof; but from certain signs nevertheless we cannot help allowing credence to some extent.' The troops, more realistic, had begun to accuse the queen, Zinat Mahal, the physician Ahsanullah Khan, whose home was plundered, and the eunuch Mahbub Ali Khan, once the power behind a castrated throne, of conspiring with the British. There was a serious move by the army to depose Zafar and make his son, Mirza Mughal, king.

The British settled all pretensions by 20 September, when they captured the Red Fort. Zafar took shelter in Humayun's tomb: there is a metaphor in his decision to run for safety to a tomb. When he was discovered he did not have the self-respect to accept his fate with dignity. Despite being a frail 82, he begged for his life, even while the British killed his sons and hung their bodies from a tree.

According to legend, Mirza Mughal had a more illustrious end: before he was killed, he asked Hindus and Muslims to remember what they could achieve with unity. All Zafar could think of was his own skin. Having drawn his life out, the British promised him his skin.

Bahadur Shah was found guilty as charged on all four counts: assumption of independent sovereignty, levying war against the British, ordering the massacre of 49 British women and children and abetting Bakht Khan in the rebellion. His trial, which began on 27 January 1858 and lasted for 21 days, was an obituary of a great empire, and could have been a noble moment, a strirring testimony and final tribute to an extraordinary heritage. Instead it was a weasel's lament. The only respectable thing Zafar did at his trial was to take an occasional nap.

He may, or may not, have been entirely honest when he protested that he knew nothing about the drama that was to descend upon his feeble life, but the lies begin to cascade soon after. He had no compunctions about calling the soldiers who fought the British 'traitors', and calmly passed on the blame for the slaughter of Europeans to his own sons! He says, in his defence, '. . . they may have made use of my name'. There is no mention of the daisy-chain of orders he issued each day as 'The King! Shelter of the World!' It was 'dread', he pleads, that forced him to appoint Mirza Mughal commander-in-chief. The one occasion on which he seems genuinely honest is when he suggests a weariness and a desire to adopt the mendicant's habit and leave for pilgrimage to Qutub, Ajmer and Mecca—'but the Army would not allow me'.

Major F.J.Harriott, deputy judge advocate-general and prosecutor for the government, summed up his case with skill. His numerous forensic feints need not detain us, but there is one telling argument. Hindus and Muslims, who had rebelled against the Raj because of pork or beef grease on their cartridges, seemed to have no problems when serving both meats to their British Sahibs at table. Touche. Neither Hindu nor Muslim had any problem about using the same cartridge when they were aiming their guns at the British. If their religious sentiments were genuinely so outraged, why didn't they consider a far simpler alternative to rebellion, an application for discharge. So what was it, if it wasn't grease? Major Harriott told European Military Commission that tried the prisoners, '. . . after pondering in every way in which my reason has presented it to me, I am obliged to infer that something deeper and more powerful than the use of greased cartridges has been resorted to . . . (the) vibrations felt almost at one and the same moment from one end of India to the other . . . in many of the places where the native troops have risen against their European officers, there was no pretext even in reference to cartridges at all . . . Does it appear consistent with the natural order of events, that such intense malignity should start into existence on one single provocation?'

Spot on, Major Harriott. Grease was the apparent reason. The real reason lay hidden in the tumult. Was it Indian nationalism by any chance? 'In October 1858, accompanied by Zinat Mahal and Jiwan Bakht, the last of the Timurids departed from Delhi. On reaching Calcutta the party were at once placed on board a warship and conveyed to Rangoon where the ex-king finally ended his days in 1862 at the age of 87.'

Seven years after Bahadur Shah Zafar died, having destroyed the hopes of his age, on 2 October 1869, in the city of Porbandar, Mohandas Karamchand Gandhi was born.

THANK YOU, JEEVES AND PATAUDI

Every dreamland is anchored in a main street borrowed from reality.

MELODY NEEDED POETRY, SOUND NEEDS PHONETICS

Pity those who have not discovered Rafi and Kishore Kumar

17 August 2008

A child born in the year that Kishore Kumar died would be 21 years in the first week of August, out of college and already well into the most movie-and-music intense phase of his life. And if he had been born on 31 July 1980, the day Mohammad Rafi died, he would most likely be sharing baby duties with his wife. Would either be aware of the age of melody that they had missed?

Temperamentally, Rafi and Kishore were as far apart as men can be, and I am not talking geography, although one came from Lahore and the other from Khandwa. Kishore Kumar came to Bombay to sing, but could not get work because he had not been trained in classical music. His elder brother, Ashok Kumar, already a hit star, advised him to make a bit of money by acting. It would be safe to say that every film Kishore made was an autobiography. He was as mad off-screen as he was zany onscreen. He couldn't keep his limbs still, and his first songs were commissioned as part of patter-and-song comedy. He was the first and only Hindi film singer with the ability to yodel, but of course yodelling was considered outrageously hilarious in the mores of those times. But the extraordinary timbre of his voice seeped silkily through the false-front of '*Ina-mina-dika*' nonsense-verse. It was only a matter of time before Dev Anand picked him up, and although *Teen Deviyan*, in which Dev woos three highly forgettable ladies, was a flop, its music was a singular success with the Kishore croon in full flow. (Raj Kapoor owned Mukesh; Dilip Kumar had first rights over Rafi; Dev floated.) Even when he sang in B-grade films like *Mr X in Bombay* Kishore could lift the music above the movie. When he made *Door Gagan Ki Chaon Mein*, whose music was a superhit, Kishore proved that his range could match that of Rafi. His one song in *Guide* was incomparable.

Rafi was the gentlest, most respectable person you could meet in Bombay, an artiste of the highest quality without a trace of the airs and arrogance that trail stars. He was grounded in classical music; he could not have sung the superb bhajan, '*Hari Om*' otherwise. The repertoire was unmatched, from '*O duniya ke rakhwale*' to '*Apni to har aah ik toofan hai*' to '*Yeh duniya agar mil bhi jaaye to kya hai*' to '*Chu lene do naazuk hoton ko kuch aur nahin hain jaam hain yeh*' to '*Chahe koi mujhe junglee kahe*' to a thousand I could name and still feel that I had not done justice to Rafi.

Kishore Kumar made his first film, *Chalti Ka Naam Gaadi*, for the oddest of reasons in an industry driven by greed and commerce. He hoped that it would flop and he would lose all his money. His logic went thus. He had reached the top income tax bracket and hated the thought of handing out money coldly to a Delhi bureaucrat. He decided that he might as well have fun wasting it on a movie. Unfortunately, the film—starring all three Kumar brothers, Ashok, Kishore and Anup—became a breathtaking superhit. Kishore Kumar was so upset that he gave all the rights of the film to his secretary.

The story has to be true. No one could have made it up, except possibly Kishore Kumar—but why make up something you can do? As it turned out, Kishore Kumar fell in love with the leading lady of his film, the glorious Madhubala, and married her, which turned out to be an expensive proposition as well. Poor rich chap.

Kishore would have been 79 today if he had been alive, about the average age for a top politician, and far better value for Indians. Rafi died of that typical Lahori–Punjabi weakness, good, rich food. Melody ebbed with them, leaving space for the emergence of the age of sound.

I do not mean to disparage contemporary music; some of it is quite attractive, and even good for health, sometimes inducing the only form of exercise I get. And who can ignore the fact that India's growth rate was 3 per cent in the age of melody and is 9 per cent in the age of sound? Dare sniff at that, if you can. It is simply that the two worlds are not only in different time zones, but set against cultural horizons that would not recognise each other. The pecking order of the senses has changed along with sensibilities. The ear has surrendered to the foot. You cannot really sing along with most modern Hindi film songs, but you can dance. The shift began with the arrival of the discotheque as a quasi-sexual subculture. It has been raised into a highly lucrative stratosphere by television. The passé singing contest, *Antakshari*, is dowdy and very Doordarshanish compared to the sexy dance contests on television that are now a staple of small-town and middle India. Nautch, a professional art, was once the privilege of the racier section of the elite. Sexy gyrations, meant for display before millions, are now the fantasy of possessive sari-clad middle-class mothers for their middle-class daughters.

Melody needed poetry; sound needs phonetics. Sahir Ludhianvi, Majrooh Sultanpuri, Shailendra, Hasrat Jaipuri, Neeraj: it is good that you died natural deaths. These days you would have starved to death before Mumbai cinema commissioned your poetry.

The greats of the Old World are, ladies first, Lata Mangeshkar, Geeta Dutt, Asha Bhonsle, Mohammad Rafi, Mukesh, Manna Dey, Hemant Mukherjee and Kishore Kumar. Mukesh and Hemant sang within a much narrower focus than the others on the list, but they were yet superior to the current stars, exceptions apart, who tend to repeat the same song with marginal variations in beat and accompaniment. The difference is between type and stereotype. One has to admit, though, that stereotypes end up with a much larger bank balance.

Perhaps the most authentic indicator is the average life of a hit song. Popular music of the 1960s and '70s still packs the shelves of shops, and even the '50s get a healthy look-in. Current hits are like floodtides.

They swamp the market and then disappear. They are suddenly everywhere, and suddenly nowhere. How many songs can you remember from the last 21 years? How many songs can you forget from the 21 years previous to Rafi's death? Hamburger versus biryani: if you don't know the difference, you'll never get it.

Is nostalgia the last temptation of the bore? It isn't as if the thought hasn't crossed my mind while I was writing this column. And yet, and yet. Permit me the luxury of pity—pity for those who were born two and three decades ago and have not discovered Rafi and Kishore. They have one advantage though: they still have time.

BITING THE BBC BULLET

Common sense, anyone?

21 December 2008

The butler who calmed his feudal lord by noting that the uproar was a mere revolt and not a revolution had a point. A revolution needs the brains of a Gandhi or a Lenin, not to mention a replacement for the object of destruction. I would be loath to replace the BBC. I would not even dignify my little protest with the label of 'revolt'. Moreover, it was Gandhian, which makes it even less glamorous. Perhaps the only relevant part of my response was non-cooperation.

During the sixty hours of unabated terrorism in Mumbai, the one group that was almost as much in demand as security forces was journalists. With the media desperate to fill space or time, a journalist could pass off any amount of gibberish as on-the-spot wisdom. Many international radio and television stations did not even demand, or perhaps expect, correct grammar: mangled phrases and minced diction can sound quaintly ethnic.

It was after the last terrorist had been shot in the Taj that something snapped within me during a telephone conversation with an extremely polite news anchor from the BBC in London. I refused. I said that I would not cooperate with the BBC as long as it described the murderers of Mumbai as 'gunmen' rather than calling them what they were: terrorists.

The BBC is full of friends, with whom one has had a happy and fulfilling professional relationship since the 1970s. I am privileged to consider the father of the BBC in India, Mark Tully, as a friend. Rita Payne, who headed the South Asia service for television till recently, is another. It was suggested that I might consider writing to Richard Porter, head of BBC World News Content. Perhaps my language was angry, but it only reflected the rage one felt: 'I am appalled, astonished, livid at your inability to describe the events in Mumbai as the work of terrorists. You have called them "gunmen", as if they were hired security guards on a night out. When Britain finds a group of men plotting in a home laboratory your government has no hesitation in creating an international storm, and the BBC has no hesitation in calling them terrorists. When nearly two hundred Indian lives are lost, you cannot find a word in your dictionary more persuasive than "gunmen". You are not only pathetic, but you have become utterly biased in your reporting . . . Shame on you and your kind.'

Mr Porter's reply was worded in far more courteous language. 'The BBC's policies on the use of the word "terrorist" have long been a subject of public discussion. The guidelines we issue to staff are very clear—we do not ban the use of the word terrorist, but our preference is to use an alternative form of words. There is a judgment inherent in the use of the word, which is not there when we are more precise with our language. "Gunman", or "killer", or "bomber", is an accurate description which does not come with any form of judgment.'

Mr Porter said that BBC policy, of 'accuracy and fairness', helped 'audiences to understand the world we live in. I believe those audiences can make their own mind up about the people who carried out the attacks in Mumbai and don't need us to give them any label to reach that judgment'. This seemed a curious claim. Isn't there judgement in the use of the word 'killer'? It can hardly be considered a term of endearment. If the BBC called you a 'killer' or a 'gunman' or a 'bomber' you would tend to sue, would you not?

But there is a subtler point here, which, at least in my view, acts as implicit protection for terrorism.

There is a clear distinction between gunmen and terrorists. Criminals use guns, and can be called gunmen; they do it for a purpose, to steal or kidnap or loot. Terrorists use guns and bombs in the random killing of innocents in pursuit of a political or personal agenda. The killers at Chhatrapati Shivaji railway terminus, Taj, Oberoi and a home where Jewish people lived did not come to steal art, or money, or railway property. I put this point as forcefully as I could to Mr Porter: 'It is a shame that the BBC cannot see the difference between a criminal and a terrorist, and chooses in fact to protect the terrorist by giving him the camouflage of a criminal. This is not a matter of semantics. Terrorists are always happy to fudge the definition.'

In response Mr Porter, once again with the maximum courtesy, urged me to read the Editorial Policy guidelines of the BBC, disputed the use of 'camouflage' and argued that 'our reporting from Mumbai was extremely effective in putting across the full horror of what happened even within the constraints of our policy. And to repeat what I said before, we do not ban the use of the word, and it has been used many times on our output in relation to Mumbai.'

Yes, used by Indians, and by British commentators I am sure, but not by the BBC.

It is possible that Mr Porter's eyebrow shot up in hurt surprise when he discovered that a story on this protest had appeared on an Indian website. He wrote, 'I must therefore assume that everything I say to you will be published, although I did not know that was your original intention.' Actually it was not. I merely did not think that an individual's reaction would be considered important enough to become a story. But that did not mean that this exchange was in private space. I had no knowledge of Mr Porter's existence before this correspondence, and am equally certain he had none of mine. Why would I endeavour to enter into a private correspondence with the BBC? The BBC's policy is a public fact, not a private one, and affects the public discourse, not a private chat. One would also assume that there is nothing that Mr Porter would say privately on his corporation's policy that he would not be prepared to air publicly.

Institutions do not change their convictions on the basis of a single protest. But media giants need to remember that while the common viewer may not have the sophistication of their committees, or the acumen of their lawyers, or the weight of their power, he does have common sense. Common sense defines the difference between the criminal and the terrorist.

It would be interesting to find out if the BBC called the destruction of the twin towers of New York the work of 'gunmen' or 'killers' or 'airplane bombers', or whether it called them terrorists. Did the BBC consider the men who killed innocents on London's trains and buses 'bombers' in search of a little private excitement? I am not sure about the nature of the coverage.

What I am sure about is that to describe the terrorists of Mumbai as mere 'gunmen' is mealy-mouthed, weak-kneed and just plain offensive.

HOW DO YOU CENSOR A TEASHOP?

Social media is the largest teashop in human history

11 December 2011

Spokesmen do not speak for themselves; they are their masters' voices, or they don't remain the voice for very long. Ministers, similarly, do not propose dramatic, or drastic, policy options without implicit clearance from their boss. This is standard practice. Kapil Sibal is not solely responsible for the proposed censorship of social media, currently the most effective communication system on the net. He is only the official advocate.

Censorship is generally the last temptation of self-delusional governments who want to console themselves with the illusion that their problem is not misrule but vilification. The alibi for censorship is always national interest, of course. During the Emergency the government promoted whispers that the CIA had bought out those journalists who did not crawl at its command. Now that the KGB has died along with the Soviet Union, and the CIA has become a bit of an ally, such insinuations do not wash. These days, the government charges opponents with communalism.

Delhi's present rulers have become more clever, if not wiser. They think they can get away with surrogate censorship. The stick is in one hand, a carrot in the other. Ministers work to punish puralist, who are not pliant, and inflate both the ego and bank accounts of the pliable. Sometimes journalists are pressurised through instruments of investigation in order to silence criticism. Owners of media feel the icy hand of power on their neck, often disguised as a pat on the back. There are rewards for being faithful, from baubles to material benefits, although the number of reward points required for pay-off does tend to keep rising. Media managers and writers know this. Those who can't stand the heat get out of the kitchen—and walk straight into the air-controlled comfort of the politician's drawing room. Others, who honour the dharma of journalism, do not make a fuss about discomforts or denial. Ministers can get addicted to bullying even when the environment is peaceful. When the weather becomes turbulent they slip into a war mentality.

William Westmoreland, the only American general to have lost a foreign war comprehensively, consoled himself with the explanation that Vietnam was the first war in modern times fought without censorship. He told the *Washington Post* that 'Without censorship, things can get terribly confused in the public mind.' This is what worries the powerful most, that people can get 'confused' by the truth. They want to eliminate debate, questions and consequent accountability because their greed for office is limitless. They sanitise media under their control, like Doordarshan and All India Radio, thus castrating its credibility. Then the scissors come out for media they do not control.

If censorship of the net was nothing more than a technicality—switching off the servers, for instance—it would have already happened. A democratic government does not, however, have the arbitrary authority of a puffed-up dictator, or the anonymous muscle of a Chinese Communist Party. But the Government of India will soon discover that the net does not bend as easily as some of its collaborators in private sector communication. The miracle of social media is its unique combination of individual voice and mass audience. It is a conversation with millions. How do you censor a teashop? In 1975 Mrs Indira Gandhi could imprison the Opposition and pockmark a newspaper's front page with blank space, but she could not lock up every teashop. Social media is the largest teashop in human history.

There remains the vital question. Kapil Sibal is the spokesman; who is the master? Somehow Dr Manmohan Singh's name does not seem to be the answer. He would not recognise an emoticon.

A pattern can be observed. The Congress is concentrating all its efforts on the coming UP Assembly elections, which have become Rahul Gandhi's pole for a vault into the PM's chair. Serious political decisions are being made to improve Congress fortunes. Ajit Singh would never have had any chance of joining the Cabinet had it not been for the possibility of an electoral alliance in western UP. Rahul Gandhi is aware that the Anna Hazare movement has made brilliant use of social media to spread its anti-establishment message. Hazare has publicly blamed Rahul Gandhi for weakening the proposed Lokpal legislation. The government can do nothing about Hazare. Is it trying to censor the internet that carries Hazare's message?

If this is the logic behind Kapil Sibal's idea, then here is some breaking news. Get real. This teashop has no walls.

THE MAHARAJA'S WIVES

Buy nothing. Save 100 per cent

26 February 2012

There is only one rational response to the classic airport offer: buy one, save 10 per cent; buy two, save 20 per cent; buy three, save 40 per cent.

Buy nothing, save 100 per cent.

Cities once had airports. The same airport now has every city. An airport once smelt of local history, or was perfumed by its culture. Stressed tourists began their tryst with Hawaii through military crates sitting around the tarmac since the Second World War. The tiled roofs and open walls of Denpasar offered the languorous smile of Bali. The gridlock of Tokyo began at Narita. The sly excitement of Frankfurt was contained in the surreptitious enclosure of its sex shop, the symbol of free Europe sitting at its gateway. Delhi offered sufficient evidence that the Third World still had some way to go before it reached the Second; its airport was a punishment posting for professionals and a trial for visitors.

Every airport now is the same mall playing cheap tricks on those trapped within its monotonous glass and chrome. The predictable brands that define modern merchandise occupy stalls in curved rows, offering leftovers at false prices. The fast food is neither particularly fast nor really food, just churn from a giant machine. Even the colourful bazaar of Istanbul airport, once redolent with the chatter and spice of the 13th century at the foot of the Blue Mosque, is now an antiseptic, amorphous collection of trinkets produced by some politically correct junk manual. I don't particularly mind being cheated during my spare hour at an airport, but would someone please cheat me with some grace?

The one islet of relief is the bookshop, a treasure trove of the noble art of raw invention. Exaggeration is an author's privilege, but these shelves heave with imagination exonerated from any relationship to reality. I write this in utter admiration: never has poetic licence been less poetic and more licensed, with every genre crossed with the agility of a fawn released from responsibility.

I would never have bought *Maharani* without the prospect of a transcontinental flight interrupted by a long layover. Its cover said the author was Diwan Jarmani Dass; inside, a second Dass was given equal mention. The uncertainty is exhilarating, and is indeed the theme and purpose of the book. But it is reasonably certain that there was once a Diwan Jarmani Dass, born in 1895, who served the Maharaja of Kapurthala, and during the audacity of retirement wrote a book about maharajas who were all conveniently deceased and therefore unable to engage the services of a libel lawyer. No harm done. A brand is all about life after death. I occasionally wished the publishers had greater familiarity with the English language, but that is a minor crib on this magnificent tour of early 20th century gossip.

The diwan is nostalgic about the golden age of Punjabi princes when 'the woman was shared by the husband and his brothers', but is outraged by modern times in which a wife sleeps with friends, or, heaven forbid, joint secretaries of the Government of India. The author opens his narrative with a wink. He was a stripling of 30 when His Highness the Aga Khan told him, 'Jarmani, if you are successful with women, you are successful in life.' He had just danced a tango with the French consort of the Aga Khan, and knew instinctively what the great Groucho Marx was to make more familiar: that dancing is a vertical expression of a horizontal desire. Jarmani had a good life, with a choice from 20 to 25 women each night when abroad and more frugal but regal options at home.

It was all great fun, except when it wasn't. Nawab Hamidullah Khan, ruler of the seaside state of Sachin (Sachin?) wanted Rs 25 crore to build a local version of Monte Carlo or Las Vegas, and didn't much care whether his favourite, Begum Naseem, nicknamed C in some mysterious alphabetical order, slept with diwans or financiers. The nawab went off to sleep after a champagne dinner, and the begum entertained who she pleased till dawn, when she slipped into burqa.

The wives of one maharaja were no less capricious than their master, which was one reason for the proliferation of tall, handsome Sikh aides. His European wife, illegitimate daughter of a Hungarian count, would faint each time the maharaja approached her for sex—not at the prospect of his virility but in terror at his impotence. Maharaja Jagatjit Singh became besotted with a certain Arlette Serry (the publishers don't have a spellcheck on the office computer), who took the sensible precaution of keeping a journalist lover on the side. She reserved Fridays for the maharaja. His Highness knelt before the scriptures and prayed fervently for an erection before he entered her bedroom. When the Lord answered his prayers, gifts as generous as 10,000 francs were offered to each minister in his entourage. But the treasury was safe: this happened only twice or thrice a year. Then there was the occasion in London when Jinnah pleaded on behalf of an abandoned mistress while the diwan . . .

What happened next? I don't know. We landed in Sydney and I threw the book away.

THANK YOU, JEEVES

The true master of innocence is P.G. Wodehouse

Every dreamland is anchored in a main street borrowed from reality. It may be a romantic ideal, but is nonetheless real for that. The English romantic poets, notably Wordsworth, developed the theory, or conceit, that we are purest at birth—presumably having landed from heaven or wherever that miracle called a baby comes from—and that age is a process of regressive distance from that glorious innocence.

But occasionally there comes along a literary genius who can freeze that moment of innocence, and nourish that magical cocoon in which we can find sustenance outside the boring daily menu of greed, envy, ambition and failure that mark the milestones of life. Lewis Carroll comes to mind. Alice. A sleepy afternoon. A rabbit hole. Wonderland. But however helplessly you taste the delicious cake that demands to be eaten, there is just that veneer of adult satire hovering over *Alice in Wonderland*, an extra laugh tucked away in the contours, a metaphor for a more 'serious' habitat. A Peter Pan seems less encumbered by duality, but it is a one-off, not an oeuvre.

The true master of innocence is P.G. Wodehouse. It helps, of course, that he is a wizard of the English language. As an eminent British author remarked, anyone who can create five original similes on a page has to be beyond the reach of mortal pen-pushers. But English has found its magicians before and will find them again. It seems impossible that there will be another Lord of a Garden of Eden who has banished the snake, or, if the snake persists in hanging around, paints a large moustache on its upper lip. Blandings Castle, the idyllic playing ground of lords, ladies and lovers, is Paradise disturbed mainly by stern arguments between an earl and his gardener over the proper preservation of flowers. The periodic forays that its inhabitants, led by the inimitable Lord Emsworth, make to London are journeys within the same universe. And if a pseudo-fascist like Roderick Spode does turn up to reflect something as silly as politics, his stern jaw is soon muddied by the nether contents of a flung flowerpot. What price stern ideology if it slips before slugs and beetles in Emsworth's immaculately preserved flower gardens?

In Wodehouse's most famous series, Bertie Wooster's flat and Drones Club were built by the same architect, as playgrounds for frolic, where the true crisis might be an excess of aunts or the provocative colour of a cravat. Every Wodehouse book has a happy beginning, a happy middle and a happy ending. The blips of narrative tension, largely conflicts between penurious young love and censorious old authority, teeter between misunderstanding and petulance, variations on a joyous rhapsody. There is no class division between master and valet, for Jeeves, Bertie's gentleman's gentleman, is in a class by himself. Downstairs spends all its time upstairs. Jeeves is indispensable, while the privileged are chumps.

Wodehouse spent half his life in America, but he never lives abroad; he simply carries his England along with him, to show his irascible cousins across the Atlantic, ruined by rough prosperity, what they missed by declaring independence.

Pelham Grenville Wodehouse, Plum to his friends and anyone else who chose to call him so, was born in 1882 and wrote 98 books of what is loosely described as fiction. There was one collection of poetry (*The Parrot and other Poems*, which I have not read but am desperate to find), a compendium of letters and three memoirs. A few pompous asses have remarked that he wrote the same book over and over again. Silly goats. He wrote only about the same azure, breeze-scented, self-contained, world over and over again, much as the gloomy Russian novelists wrote repeatedly of war, suicide, crime, punishment and adultery. There was barely an adult in Wodehouse, how could there be adultery? Wooster's dilemmas could be fiendishly varied. To test Jeeves' ingenuity they had to be complicated, at the very least. And when you evolve to Mr Mulliner's tales told from a perch in the bar of the golf club, then they get distinctly complex.

Since anyone with a claim to literacy must surely have read every single Wodehouse available at the better kind of airport, may I suggest that you stroll towards your nearest bookshop and order *P.G. Wodehouse: A Life in Letters*, edited by Sophie Ratcliffe, a brilliant compilation of the great writer's correspondence. I hesitate to bracket labour and love, for if it is love then it cannot be labour. But Ratcliffe curates this collection with a fond disciple's devotion and an academic's attention to notes, all available thankfully at the bottom of the page.

I refuse to offer any glimpse of the enormous treasure that glitters inside. For that you need to pay the bookseller. There is nothing called a free book, which is why every borrowed book is lost. The lender does not care sufficiently about the book to be rude, and the borrower does not care at all. But a teaser, nevertheless. In 1921, Wodehouse writes to his stepdaughter Leonara about his arrival in New York. Immigration was tardy, but photographers buzzed around who 'took all sorts of pictures including some movies. The only trouble is that I can't find that any paper has printed them.'

Anyone who laughs must first learn to laugh at himself.

And the Wodehouses kept open house for all stray dogs in their New York neighbourhood. There is no better description of a heart of gold.

IN PRAISE OF LALIT MODI

The IPL is a harvest of bounty

22 April 2012

A question has left me wondering: how incendiary is the combination of great ideas with great luck? History must be full of sensational ideas that withered because they did not possess the luck that attracts capital, or find the right moment when they could flower. Lalit Modi, the genius who invented the Indian Premier League at some eureka point in his mind, might have easily failed if he had found a patron ten years before he did. If IPL was only about cricket, it would have been a pallid addition to the genre, and not that original either. It is spectacular because it merges game and spectator in a seamless knit through the elastic morality and entertainment needs of a new, young and successful India.

It can be argued that you cannot have economic reforms without social reforms, or perhaps the other way around; in any case, India has both. IPL laced a six with sexual frisson. The cheerleaders with bikini pants, jiggling their bosoms behind the lame excuse of dance, and stories of sex-fuelled after-game parties, are as essential to the total experience as 22 players engaged in a contest. Sport was once called war by other means. IPL is a one-night stand by other means. No one really cares who wins or who loses. Everyone cares about tension and excitement that must ideally culminate in an orgiastic final over. As in sex, both sides win.

Mass entertainment is the sum of individual sensibilities. The Indian sexual revolution, like all upheavals, has been building and bubbling below the surface for two decades at the very least. As usual, Mumbai-led commercial cinema, which survives by selling tickets to the street, and therefore must, ipso facto, recognise the onset of change and then help it forward in order to thrive, was the first mirror. Helen, the iconic film dancer, who began her career in a 1950s' skirt and ended with an 1980s' cling-semi-see-through, already belongs to a forgotten age. Today's item numbers leave neither the body nor its possibilities to imagination; and imagination has travelled long beyond the missionary position. For environmental evidence all you have to do is get details of the sex scandals that filter through even the tightly protected political class into the news. The contemporary Indian campus is another story altogether.

Cinema was limited largely to the controlled space of a hall, and social censorship was possible through the rating system as well as the obvious option that you did not have to buy a ticket. Television, particularly through item song-heavy music channels, has converted this revolution into a drawing room phenomenon. Print, inevitably, followed. The pressure from the market was too strong.

The new morality has not abandoned religion. We may no longer hear the old warble of supplication towards the Almighty ('*Bhagwan . . . o duniya ke rakhwale sun dard bhare mere naalein*') or the challenge to God ('*Bhagwan kabhi do gharhi insaan ban ke dekh, Dharti pe chaar din kabhi mehmaan ban ke dekh*'), but narratives from religious epics still dominate the screen and a faith-inspired qawwali is as popular as ever. The appeal of religion continues to be non-denominational. But morality is no longer just a middle-class bedroom virtue. Its larger role has shifted to accountability in governance. The rage against corruption tells its own story and the media, in all its manifestations, must make it the lead. Lifestyle can coexist but on the back pages.

Lalit Modi's luck ran out because he forgot that financial transparency is now a non-negotiable requirement in public life. And yet we must recognise the impact his IPL has made. The supplementary benefits have been breathtaking. It is my conviction that the IPL has revived cricket in the West Indies. There is now an unprecedented financial reward for quality and genius. Sir Garfield Sobers would have been as rich as Sachin Tendulkar if he were playing today, and deservedly so: knighthood is nice, but it does not pay the bills beyond a limited point. A generation of West Indian kids must be dreaming about becoming Chris Gayle. Can you imagine the crowds that would have come for Viv Richards? Batting, bowling and fielding techniques have taken a radical turn for the better. Since the market pays the price, a dropped catch is not just letting the side down, it means letting your own bank balance down as well. Fewer catches are dropped.

The IPL has rescued Indian cricket from the stranglehold of that secret society called selectors. There was never much light between cricketers who flourished in the limelight and those hidden in anonymity. Today, the public sees tomorrow's talent on the field, and knows the choice that is available. Prejudice in selection might still be possible, but it is no longer easy.

The IPL is now part of the all-year seasons of cricket. Every season is not equal, but we celebrate a harvest with joy. The IPL is a harvest of bounty.

CATS, WHISKERS AND DIFFERENT KINDS OF MICE

The watchful media

13 May 2012

. . . The Media, alas, is only a cat in the corner. It spends most of its life doing very little except licking its own face, and purring contentedly at its own brilliance. Narcissism and journalists are pen pals. But it does have one advantage. Unlike Narcissus, who kept staring at his reflection, this cat keeps its eyes open and records, to the extent it can, every brawl that takes place in the privacy of the home or a street alley. It is the cat you notice occasionally, but it watches you all the time.

SHAH RUKH KHAN: THE LIMITS OF DESTINY

Shah Rukh Khan should live in memory as a symbol of joy, not anger

20 May 2012

Money is a strange aphrodisiac. It stiffens obstinacy and softens the brain, when the reverse might be far more useful. Add a bit of face recognition, which celebrities crave and idol worshippers offer, and the cocktail becomes so heady it takes only a moment to explode in your face. Petulance is but a step away, since celebrities consider it injurious to their health to admit guilt. Not every superstar becomes a victim of this syndrome, but few escape an occasional attack of mania.

I have met Shah Rukh Khan twice, once recently; and perhaps fleetingly on a third occasion. That is certainly not evidence of proximity, let alone acquaintance. But the little I know confirms the first impression. He is an extremely likeable and intelligent person. His finest quality is a gentle sense of humour punctuated by sharp, even caustic observation. He could laugh at the world without injuring relationships because he included himself in that laughter. He had neither the manner nor the conversation of a cloud-dweller; and if he sat on a pedestal, he made sure that his feet touched the ground from that lofty perch to which he had risen from obscurity.

There will be many explanations as to why he lost his temper at the Wankhede stadium. An important one could be stress. He is not young any more; his first song on the screen was sung a quarter-century ago, as any music channel on television will tell you—those songs now appear among the oldies. Age is the abyss of dread for any actor who has promised the elixir of youth to his worshippers. The excruciating gymnastics required to hide age from the telltale muscle tone are precisely that, excruciating.

To camouflage age is a punishing business, and torture does not become any less searing merely because it is self-imposed. You have to whip your body to deny it its natural gravitational pull towards flab. When medieval Catholic monks flagellated themselves, they had at least the comfort of doing so in the cause of God. I cannot believe that money would mean anything any more to a middle-class boy who has earned as much as Shah Rukh did when he became a man; so the provocation can only be the ego, and that insane desire to remain atop a summit that is not merely above, but beyond, competition. Ambition is a legitimate virtue; without it, we would not have much progress. But when you are your own product, and when the measure of your worth is controlled by an image that cannot be protected from decay, wisdom demands recognition of limits. That, alas, is easier written than done.

The hero of imagined space wafts on the cherubic celebration of adulation, even as he contends with private demons that become monstrous in those hours when an individual must remain with himself. Guilt has many dimensions. Those who survive on the admiration of others bear the cross of how much love they have given to others, including their children. Both you and your children grow older at the same time; and at some point the intersection must come, when children depart to have their own children. Time shortens on both sides of the equation. The sceptical question in your child's eyes reduces the glories of the world to an ephemeral mirage; and perhaps the temptation to win the child by an expression of power over a fawning world becomes irresistible.

Shah Rukh's great predecessors searched for notional alchemists who could deliver them from demons. Sometimes the night passed in stupor, and the day in self-deception. Raj Kapoor, an authentic genius, danced brilliantly while singing '*Suno ji suno, hamari bhi suno*' with Waheeda Rehman, but the puff around the cheeks had changed the face that had mesmerised both Nadira and India in *Shree 420*. Dilip Kumar had generations at his command, but could not resist continuing long after he peaked in *Mughal-e-Azam* and *Gunga Jumna*. Dev Anand thought he could defeat time by hiding sagging skin with high collars and a scarf. Time had a harsh answer, mockery. Dev Anand should have treaded warily through the 1970s and never stepped into the 1980s, let alone the 21st century. There is nothing called evergreen. Wood merely takes a longer time to die.

The purpose of life must change for those who have crossed the middle of its finite span. Shah Rukh Khan should live in memory as a symbol of joy, not of anger. I cannot believe that he can succumb to the arrogance of wealth. That would be a disappointment too far. The human being is never master of all he surveys, but he has been given the intellect to recognise that destiny has to pause at some destination. Shah Rukh Khan invented a persona that has given us extraordinary delight. The moment has come for him to reinvent himself.

AS A MATTER OF FACT

The fault line of democracy is that it cannot guarantee equality in practice

22 June 2012

Facts come in every shape, size, variety. Their survival is determined not by value but by how inexplicable they are. The human being has 23,000 genes, only 'half as many as a tomato', I am told. But humbling as this formative fact of life might be, it does not quite catch the imagination as much as the perplexity called death, particularly when death escapes the boundaries of reason: a plague decimates a continent, war murders a generation, or an evil maniac orders a genocide. Statistics distil facts to stark simplicity. Between September 1939 and August 1945, the period of the Second World War, 27,000 people were killed each day. (This figure does not include war-related casualties like the three million-odd Bengalis who died of a famine that was a direct consequence of British war policy.)

There is always enough to be learnt from war, its machines and its machinations. Guess who is the largest buyer of oil in the world? If you thought it was a country, wrong. The Pentagon. America's military consumes more oil each year than the whole of Africa. And yet, when you think about it, is this very startling? The armies of the British

Empire surely drank up more oil than all the colonies they ruled. None of us were there to count, and contemporary historians had more delicious details to record, but you can safely bet that Rome alone had more chariots than the rest of the Roman Empire. It has always been thus. To the victor go not only the spoils of war but also the far more substantial rewards of its blanket peace: a Pax Romana then, a Pax Americana now.

So what's the story? The privileges of power have not changed, but the world has.

If the ascent of America begins with victory in the First World War; its supremacy after the Second; and domination after the Third (also known as the Cold) War, then many of today's contradictions also lie in the liberal ideas that America encouraged as a template for the future it hoped to control. America sought the rights of power without the problems or obvious injustice of foreign rule. It tried to fashion, particularly after 1992, what might be called the Good Empire as distinct from the Evil Empire (Ronald Reagan's description of the Soviet Union). The thesis, broadly, was this: all nations would be equal; post-colonial nations would be formed on the basis of public will, with claims being resolved by plebiscite; the world as well as its parts would be governed by the broad principles of democracy.

Confusion is the bridesmaid of change, so after the applause died down there was achievement, failure and bewilderment in roughly equal measure. The fault line of democracy is that while it offers equal rights in theory, it does not guarantee equality in practice. Every vote has the same weight, but every voter does not possess equal weightage, whether in a municipality or the United Nations. Wealth feeds power and power reinforces wealth, both at the macro and micro levels.

In countries like India, the coexistence of democracy with degrading poverty cannot be easily justified, by either idealism or intellect. But poverty is both absolute and comparative. America's poor, famously, are better off than the middle class in most of the world. However, they do not compare themselves to sub-Saharan Africa, thank God for their good fortune, and live happily ever after. They get angry with their President when their comfort zone is threatened. No child suffers the anguish of malnutrition in Greece, and yet Greek rage at loss of standards of living has boiled over into a volatile crisis.

The battles being fought across the world are over inequity, a perception of injustice. Democracy does not, unlike socialism, offer economic equality, which is impossible; but its spirit does insist on economic equity. When disparity between the top 5 per cent and bottom 50 per cent becomes obscene, the deprived do not remain silent forever. The establishment's traditional response has been to blame the victim. But democracy permits a victim to scream, and the Greeks are doing so pretty loudly. Europe and America are rushing to its help, as they should if they want to.

It does seem odd, though, that India, where fifty times the population of Greece lives below the poverty line, should gift $10 billion to help resolve a problem it did not cause. Till two decades ago, rich nations still felt some mild moral obligation to reduce poverty through aid. They now expect aid from the poor. Miraculously, they get it. Delhi cannot find Rs 20,000 crore for Bengal, but hands over Rs 56,000 crore for Greece. Bengal's poor can shout as much as the Greeks.

Will India ever get this money back? Fact from history: Greece is still waiting for Germany to pay what it claimed as reparations after the Second World War.

MEN ARE THE WEAKER SEX

Women's cricket is one of the many reflections of the changing status of women

3 February 2013

The one certain fact about this uncertain business called advertising is that you can't do without it. Such compulsion does not mean this hit-and-run affair necessarily works. It is difficult to predict when a campaign will be a hit, and when the agency has managed to lubricate its salary sheet.

The worst spiel in recent times was surely the advertising of a brief, and eminently forgettable, India–Pakistan cricket encounter last December. The agency was not promoting sport between traditional antagonists; it was announcing the consequences of an existentialist war with all the finesse of the massacre-friendly Nadir Shah on a Delhi weekend in 1739. Conversely, the best campaign I have seen in a long while has been the television advertisements which raised the curtain on the women's cricket tournament: wry, tongue very much in cheek, and emasculating men with a pleasing insouciance.

There is no mystery about why. Women's cricket went well because the agency believed in it. It represents something far more than fund-raising for an already bloated game.

Women's cricket has been around for a long while, scratching at the turnstiles, seeking attention and the legitimacy of public support. At long last, it is an idea whose time has come. It now represents the third great revolution in a sport that has long been a mirror of social mores.

The first liberation came when 'professionals' in Britain won equal terms with 'amateurs'. Professional is a term that carries so much pride now that we quite forget that once it was synonymous with something as 'grubby' as earning money for talent in sports. It took a world war, the second of the 20th century, to destroy the stupid pretensions of aristocrats who forced their working-class 'professionals' to use a separate entrance to a cricket field. The nobles wore silk scarves and gloried in the vanity that they were, literally, a class apart because they did not have to actually do anything for a living. They were lords of the manor, and hence lords of the field. Today, mercifully, merit rules. Commerce bows only before success, and success is not a genetic entitlement.

The second revolution matured in India and Pakistan, when merit took cricket away from the confines of the middle class, and into the small towns or city bylanes where a new India and Pakistan were being incubated. The urban middle class shares at least one trait with the white or brown aristocracy: it has many alternative routes to achievement. Cricket was a pleasure, even when exacting, but it was not quite a hunger. The gnawing desperation to beat the odds of life through excellence in a game whose financial value exploded beyond the dreams of avarice created a new base for triumphant upward mobility. If any astrologer had told 10-year-old M.S. Dhoni's parents that he would one day become as wealthy as he is now, they would have given him a nice cup of tea and told him to go tease someone else. It is the same with many dozens of other achievers; and Dhoni was financially far better off at birth than Yusuf or Irfan Pathan.

Women's cricket is one of the many reflections of the changing status of women. Women were once taunted by men as the weaker sex only because they could not compete with the brutal violence of males. In truth, you need a much tougher body and spirit for childbirth; men, by comparison, are sissies. They simply have more powerful muscles. Women have a far stronger mind.

But this assertion is only a part of the emerging story. Men have punished women through the ages with segregation, and then attached a false morality to their subjugation. Sport is freedom from segregation. We might not notice this in India, where trousers and jeans have become the preferred wear of women. But the fact that Pakistan's women wear trousers when they go to bat and field will be a huge spur to a society that is still controlled too often by men who have not left the 19th century. There was a time, during the regime of General Zia-ul-Haq, when some Pakistani fundamentalists wanted television coverage of cricket banned because women at home would be able to see the alluring Imran Khan rub a red cricket ball down the front of his trousers, and therefore near his crotch. It has been a long journey since then. We should celebrate this journey. Cricket will do a hundred times more for gender equality in Pakistan than a thousand speeches by well-meaning liberals.

There are countries which do not send women to the Olympics for 'moral' reasons; or, more accurately, because they believe that the sight of women will encourage immorality. I cannot imagine anything more stupid. To display one's face and ability is not nudity, neither among men nor women. Why shouldn't women be allowed to behave as normally as men?

One thing is clear. It is men who are the weaker sex.

ON THE SPECIAL JOYS OF AIRPORT TRASH

The latest Dan Brown

23 June 2013

The joys of an airport book may not quite meet the escalating demands of an upwardly liberal sensibility, but who can deny it is liberating? Environment is the daddy of content. You won't get many books at an airport store on the vagaries of civilisation, but you will discover a hundred ways in which to turn your boss into a vegetable, and yourself into a sex symbol. But the best trash is not about changing the world; it is about saving it from dark satanic forces controlled by a mastermind. Nothing has changed since Superman, except that Superman now reads Dante instead of the Daily Plonk. Dan Brown is back at the airport with a thud that can be heard at the cash register.

I discovered Dan Brown when I joined the long line of suckers who made him a billionaire, and realised why precisely it was such a long line. *The Da Vinci Code* was an exotic tale of a power-thirsty Catholic cult which wanted to destroy something or the other before it was stopped in the nick of time by Brown's alter ego, a Harvard professor who, naturally, did not waste too much of his time on teaching. The hallucinations worked well through my pliant brain about a decade ago. I am pleased to inform you that both the Vatican and the world survived Dan Brown's assault. It is, however, a tribute to this master chef of potboilers that he did, for a brief while, make the Vatican wince.

The trick is to perfume rubbish with a bottle of incense hidden beneath the pile. Brown's bottle is artfully shaped, with secret sub-containers for clues and questions that persuade you to suspend rational judgement. But, contrarily, this would not work without a writing technique that is so stupid it can only be described as courageous. The latest Dan Brown, *Inferno*, exhausts the reader with some serious heavy breathing in punctuation. There are more dots separating words with simulated tension than in an optical illusion graphic. Words appear in bursts within sentences; sentences stutter through paragraphs as short as summer underwear. Chapters are as flimsy as a negligee. We are playing peekaboo with destiny, so why not?

But recognise the paradox: the tension must be both real and fake, for we know that while everyone from a slick lone ranger working for a deadly consortium to the whole of the Italian police is trying to kill the hero from the opening page, the hero cannot die, for that would effectively end the book. This is therefore precisely the opposite of crime mystery, where anyone can die. If you think it is difficult to read such deathless, breathless prose, consider how difficult it must be to write it. Events must consistently outpace credibility. But that's okay. Dan Brown wants readers, not the Nobel Prize. The Nobel fetches far less money.

The problem may be that Brown has run out of incense, and is now using the kind of cheap deodorant advertised on music channels. Our Harvard Hero's mission this time is to stop a dead genius from killing one-third of the world's population through some kind of plague, which is about as original a thought as the Son of King Kong. Most of the action takes place in Florence, but the dramatic revelations can be picked up from any good city guidebook. Maybe that is why tourists like the stuff. Why bother to stretch facts when it is so much more lucrative to stretch the imagination?

The inducement to buy the book is born of a genetic fascination for the pleasure of prurience during the idle wasteland of an airplane trip. A holiday gives the body a rest; Brown gives the mind a rest. Junk is only as good as it is bad. I fear, however, that Brown may be in some danger of taking himself seriously, which would be fatal to his craft. Every once in a while, possibly tortured by the need for self-respect, he introduces some inexplicable word into the text. Do you know the meaning of 'chthonic'? I didn't. Do you care? I don't. But just in case you want to word-drop, the 'ch' is silent.

Here is a tip from a concerned if occasional reader. Brown should never leave London out of his books. The British Museum is a treasure house of clues from here to eternity. Take, for instance, the stark Egyptian black slab with a hollowed square at the centre, with ten lines stretching away like rays from a little child's sun? It was probably done by a pharaoh's imbecile toddler, but who is to stop a Harvard professor from calling it the first instance of modern art laden with the deep warning that neurons would destroy matter ten centuries after the 8000 BC. Whoa . . . wait a minute . . . THAT MEANS NOW!

Maybe Dan Brown has reserved this symbol for his next book, Deferno.

A HISTORY OF THE FUTURE

A cathartic film

14 July 2013

Life's most traumatic cemetery is surely the memory of pain, for it is buried but not dead. Neither amnesia nor vengeance is a solution, although the timid find solace in the first and the violent seek options in the second. Individuals, communities, nations have to find the spirit that can liberate them from the bonds of past anguish, to discover a future in a new perspective that is something far more than a distorted reflection of fear.

It is not often that a Bollywood film can lay claim to that cleansing experience called catharsis, but *Bhaag Milkha Bhaag* is a film made by Indians inspired by a vision of the future from the countless narratives of that terrible past called Partition. They recognise the great dangers in single-tunnel truth, for it can so easily turn a script into a game of vindictive flames. But *Milkha* is not just another Friday release; its bleak landscape blossoms with many shades of subtlety woven into events and characterisation.

The box office is always tempted by simplicity. Good and evil must be caricatures. The formula is uncomplicated. Laugh in the beginning, cry in the middle, find relief at the end, go home happy. But this is a film about reality, not exaggerations. Nothing is overdrawn, nothing is underwritten.

Milkha's childhood is destroyed by the slaughter of most of his family in the Punjab that went to Pakistan. Out of this holocaust emerge real people, not saints and sinners. Milkha runs, reaches a refugee camp in Delhi and finds his way through loneliness, despair and a lost first love, before discovering that unfathomable elixir of indomitable spirit that turns a child who might have become a hardened criminal into an international athletic superstar. His best childhood friend, a Hindu boy who trudged to a maulvi's school with him, finds survival through another process, and who can say that this was less agony? The Hindu lives through 1947 by converting. The point is made simply, without fuss, without accusation or praise, as a choice human beings make when torn between life and death. One of the great tragedies is that nearly seven decades later, the few Hindus left in Pakistan are still sometimes forced into such an awful debate with their conscience.

There is no difference between Indians and Pakistanis; we are the same people, with the same weaknesses and strengths. If the two partitioned neighbours have evolved differently, it is because they are influenced by their root ideology. The ideologues who inflict violence within Pakistan have not understood a very simple truth: if your mission is to search for someone to hate, you will continue to find them. Yesterday they were Sikhs and Hindus, today they might be Shias or Barelvis or whoever interferes with some fantasy of an artificial purity.

Filmmaker Rakeysh Omprakash Mehra's sensitivity and genius is at its nuanced best when, almost surreptitiously, he depicts violence in all its myriad evil, including the many forms which we compartmentalise into 'lesser' categories. The tight, ringing slap of a husband across the face of a wife who did not respond to a demand for instant sex in a refugee camp is also madness mixed with hatred. Milkha's girlfriend is dragged, screaming, into an arranged marriage while he is away, trying to prove that he can succeed in something more than petty crime. When he discovers his loss, his old friend from the mohalla puts it plainly: you know how we Indians treat women. Sonam Kapur, in the role of the girlfriend, appears briefly, perhaps spanning fifteen minutes of a film that exceeds 180. Any commercial movie which stars a missing heroine is blessed with calm self-assurance. I will not mention the denouement, except to indicate that it will surprise those who enter the theatre with preconceived notions.

Those who believe are all, in a sense, convicts of their conviction. The ideology of a humane spirit, soaring towards the unbelievable, is also infectious, and it lifts every aspect of this film. Farhan Akhtar has put in a performance that is beyond mere awards. The lyrics of Prasoon Joshi, the music of Ehsan–Loy are transformative. Both might work better in the film than outside, in cafés or radio, but that is an asset, not a liability.

Mahatma Gandhi is mentioned once, as a reason for a holiday. Perhaps this is deliberate, because Gandhi has now become synonymous with preachy, and no one has time for sermons. But Gandhi left us with a lesson that saved India in 1947 and the years beyond; and is now resonating through the world. Violence destroys both perpetrator and victim. Violence sucks compassion out of our heart, and turns it into a barren desert enveloped by the mirage of rage. Even violence in the cause of justice, which is necessary for order and civilisation, can devastate beyond its purpose, as the final metaphor of Mahabharata tells us with unambiguous pain.

Gandhi wrote the history of the future, not a history of the past.

MONEY SHOUTS, CONSCIENCE MERELY MURMURS

Honour on the cricket field

21 July 2013

Would you walk?

Think about it. You have time, which Stuart Broad did not, when he was batting for England on the third day of the first Ashes Test in a fierce game which was certain to produce a result, and where, therefore, every single run counted in double digits. Stuart Broad had to choose between honesty and expediency in those instinctive seconds between a vociferous appeal and the umpire's decision after he nicked a ball to first slip. He realised what everyone saw, except for the umpire who, being eyeless, shall be left nameless. Broad knew he was out. Honour demanded voluntary departure from the crease; he chose to wait for the jury to make a mistake even when he knew he was guilty.

For you, lolling on a sofa, or, if a cricket junkie, watching the match on television, any debate with conscience may seem merely theoretical. But is it any the less important? For the debate is about values. Is honesty dispensable? Are survival and success the only priorities in life?

Cricket, like existence, is not always black and white. There are situations in which a batsman has every right to hold his ground against a chorus of theatrical appeals, because he is genuinely uncertain, most often in a leg-before-wicket decision, or when a catch has not gone cleanly to hand. Innovations like the technology-driven third umpire have been created to find light through grey space. But Stuart Broad's case is worth mention precisely because there was huge daylight between black and white. He was out. Everyone on the field, and millions outside, knew the truth.

Honour was once essential to the spirit of cricket. Bad behaviour, caused by temperament or the pressures of sport, was a discrepancy. No one has ever wanted to fail through the long history of human endeavour, and yet cricket looked down upon success without honour. In the larger field of life, honour bred the honours system, which was society's way of recognising merit. You could, of course, occasionally buy your way to a gong, for money always talks. But money used to speak in a whisper. Today it shouts. The little murmur of conscience is lost in such noise.

Cricket was always proud to place itself on a pedestal, even when inconsistencies existed lower down. Till the 1950s, there was obnoxious class distinction, in which the amateur entered the field through the club gate, and professionals used a turnstile. A gentleman considered payment beneath his dignity, largely because he had enough money. The professional, from the working class, could not afford to take a week off from his job. But during the game honesty was not divisible by class.

We claim to live in a more egalitarian age, but we have turned 'professional' into a synonym for amorality. Broad was exonerated because of his 'professional' approach, as if honour is now a derisory hobby of the parson or a preacher.

In 1980 India and England played a Test in Mumbai to commemorate the jubilee of the BCCI. India's captain was the courteous, gentlemanly G.R. Viswanath. England was led by the gentlemanly analyst Mike Brearley. At a turning point in the match, England wicketkeeper Bob Taylor was given out leg before. Visibly upset, he hung around in obvious protest. But there was obviously no review system. Viswanath, to everyone's surprise, overturned the bemused umpire and asked

Taylor to play on. He did, and helped England win the Test. Was that the holy moment when the world of cricket saw the light? No. Since then, it is the tough school of thought which has taken over the game. Some cricketers still at the crease have resisted the trend. Australian Adam Gilchrist famously walked against Sri Lanka in 2003, and South African Hashim Amla does not linger if he knows he is out. But both have an old-fashioned look about them.

So would you walk? The question is larger than cricket. Ministers, ordinary, extraordinary, chief or prime, do not walk when exposed as corrupt, or when atrocious administration kills children after a mid-day meal. Do those on lower rungs of power, whether secretary presiding over a department, or clerk guarding a file, walk away from a bribe? Do business executives walk away from offering one? What prevails in the constant battle between commerce and conscience? If we all walked away from temptation, wouldn't the world be a nice little Utopia?

The first commandment of contemporary religion is unambiguous: Thou shalt win. Everyone, as the saying goes, loves a winner. There is a second commandment: Thou shalt not be so stupid as to get caught. There is no third commandment. If Stuart Broad were only a cog in a game it might not matter, but he is also a role model for millions of young people. If survival by any means can guarantee heroism, then surely plain old morality sucks.

Enjoy the delicious fruits of survival. Don't walk.

THE MEDIA MENU OF A LAST SUPPER

Credibility, not ownership, is key to a media house's success

18 August 2013

'Newspapers are owned and published by rich men. Rich men all belong to the same club. Sure, there's competition—hard, tough competition for circulation, for newsbeats, for exclusive stories. Just so long as it doesn't damage the prestige and privilege and position of the owners. If it does, down comes the lid.'

This is not from any book of quotations. But it does suggest that truth finds a better home in fiction than anthology. The author is Raymond Chandler, an authentic master of modern fiction who created the shabby and sharp private detective Philip Marlowe. Marlowe—and Chandler—lived amid the shadows that enveloped wealth and crime in mid-20th century Los Angeles; they knew that the difference was marginal and the price was high if you talked too much. Marlowe talked too much. He did something even more risky. He spoke the truth.

Newspapers in his time made the rich richer with their explosive mix of political influence and advertising monopoly. A British Prime Minister of the 1930s famously charged newspapers with enjoying the privilege of a harlot, exercising power without responsibility. But this was a self-serving taunt. Media barons can give prime ministers advice from a pillow, but it is prime ministers who let them into the bedroom. Be that as it may, money has always chased power through the media, and every democracy has provided this incestuous opportunity.

Transition destabilises any industry, and this is happening with newspapers. At least some of the rich are becoming poorer, thanks to newspapers they own. The most dramatic illustration has been the sale of the *Washington Post* by the Graham family to Jeff Bezos, owner of Amazon. This transfer does not suggest, as many have moaned, that news is going out of business; at worst, it could suggest that paper is going out of business. Bezos bought the *Post* with spare change in a forgotten trouser pocket, but he rose from denim to riches through the information trade. Newspapers will be reshaped, as they should be from time to time, but this does not change the fundamental need for an information carrier.

It is a car with two drivers. Owners step into journalist space through a conundrum called 'publisher'. Editors comfort themselves with the romance of independence, and perhaps there is the occasional powerful personality who dominates a newsroom at the expense of the shareholder. But that is the exception. Editorial decisions are a shared enterprise. The *Washington Post* became an indelible chapter in media history when its series of reports, familiar to us as the Watergate exposé, brought down Richard Nixon just after he had won a landslide endorsement from the people. But the decision to run the investigation was made as much by Katherine Graham, the owner, as by Ben Bradlee, the editor.

Bezos is a wise chap. He has appointed Bob Woodward, one of the stars of Watergate, as managing editor. The key to media does not lie in ownership, but in credibility. Without credibility, a newspaper is just wrapping for fish and chips if not a rag for rubbish. Credibility makes journalists indispensable to publishers.

Are publishers indispensable to journalists? Yes. Journalists may be know-alls, but the one thing they do not know is how to run a business. The newspaper industry is also an industry. It is not an accident that owners of an old Indian media conglomerate like the *Times of India* and a new one like Zee have a very healthy respect for profits. They understand what journalists should acknowledge, that a newspaper or television channel cannot stand up against any government without a healthy bottom line. They do not have to look over their shoulder if they want to break stories at the cost of a ruling family's displeasure.

A media house fails when it forgets that both credibility and cash flow are important. The list of Indian media companies that have forgotten this basic rule is long and growing. Behind very thin curtains, big names are crumbling. The cost of plaster being applied to disguise this collapse is the transfer of shares and control. We will not find out the full truth till the end arrives, suddenly, and not without a residual whiff of bitterness, as in the case of the *Washington Post*.

But the media will survive, whether in America or India, even if owners do not. Information is not an aggregate of everything on the highway. It is a cull of that which is relevant. Of course, there are interests, as the cynic Raymond Chandler noted, with his usual caustic flourish. But even the super rich cannot hold on to these laser scalpels called newspapers if they do not understand that while their personal interests may occasionally dent the integrity of a product, they should never damage it.

A good newspaper proprietor feeds the goose that lays golden eggs. He does not put it on the menu of a last supper.

PERCHANCE TO DREAM, IN FABLED INDIA

A frenetic, foolish search for gold

20 October 2013

Why has horror fiction never taken off as a genre in popular Indian literature? There is simply too much competition from newspapers. Which bizarre author's imagination could ever compete with the day's news in the wild and improbable? You do not need Bram Stoker, and blood being sucked from a woman's neck with the pearly fangs of a Dracula, in an India replete with the leech habits of some rascals who sell themselves as godmen. The devotees of such frauds run into millions. Their usurped land extends across thousands of acres. How stupid can Indians get?

As it turns out, very stupid indeed. In the long and complicated story of herd madness, very little beats the frenetic search for a thousand tonnes of gold at a place called Daundia Khera in Uttar Pradesh because a certain Swami Shobhan Sarkar recently dreamt it was buried there more than 150 years ago by a Raja Ram Baksh. No one had heard of this raja until the Swami's dream turned him into a potential hero of a Bollywood film. But apparently this princeling buried this vast treasure before 1857 so that the victorious British would not be able to lay their hands on Indian gold.

Don't blame the masses for frothing at the mouth. Even the august mandarins from the Ministry of Culture and the Archaeological Survey of India are licking their lips. And our very modern, computer-savvy Chief Minister Akhilesh Yadav has apparently sent an emissary to the venerable Swami to check whether the man of god will permit the man of the people to use this gold for the state's development. Of course, this magic gold, if ever found, will probably be used for the welfare of politicians in power rather than a populace in distress, but that is another story.

Personally, I hope they find this gold, even though I am unlikely to get permission to even sniff at it, let alone be able to slip an ounce in a back pocket. Akhilesh Yadav might then be able to pay up for the computers he has bought to gift away, which is good news for multinationals. But silly questions keep wandering around in my vacant mind, and will not shift to better breeding space.

The pointy-heads of Government of India have explained that they are digging for this gold because they have 'scientific evidence' of its existence. Interesting. This is not a rich seam of gold in the bowels of mother earth that we are talking about. This is gold stored in clay or iron pots, depending on the advice that the old Raja Ram Baksh got from his mandarins. How do you get scientific evidence about pots and pans? Did some clever laser beam actually see an underground glitter, and conclude that all that glitters is in fact gold? Gold, to the best of my limited knowledge, does not get musty or rot; so they probably did not smell its existence. Or would it be fair to suggest that a few babus in Delhi have been reading *Treasure Island* during their festival holidays?

An early victim of insanity is common sense. How rich was Raja Ram Baksh? He was not the Nawab of Awadh, or the Peshwa of the Marathas, or Raja of Benares or the Rani of Jhansi, or we might have heard a bit about him in our school textbooks. He did exist, certainly. But if he was not in the big league, how did he amass a thousand tonnes of gold? Even the East India Company, the richest merchant of the age, could not claim possession of such a hoard. The Mughals of Delhi might have, but Nadir Shah emptied their vaults in 1739, and that alas was that.

How do you bury so much gold at a time when the heaviest equipment for digging is a spade? With lots of labour, one presumes. All those peasants must be the most honest Indians of the last two hundred years. India is a land of worst-kept secrets, not best-kept ones. It is a miracle that no one returned to the site in 1867 or 1877 or even 1887. And no one snitched to the British either.

In any conflict between superstition and sense, superstition wins hands down in India. The baba had a dream, and no one dare argue with the mysteries of nightfall. Psychoanalysis, and its interpretation of dreams, would never have survived if Sigmund Freud had visited India.

Is India a land where dreams come true? Judging by everything from poverty to the manner in which road hogs drive in Delhi, the answer is clearly no. But if the manufacture of dreams were ever added to the Gross Domestic Production, we would have a GDP that surpassed the rest of Asia combined. Make no mistake. Those in charge of this production line make a neat profit. It is only suckers who invest in such dreams who return empty.

LET THE MEMORIES BEGIN

Every viewer is his own Neville Cardus when watching Sachin Tendulkar

24 November 2013

Sachin Tendulkar was ten years old when in 1983 Indian cricket suddenly, even inexplicably, turned into a sky-bound butterfly from the plodding caterpillar it had been since the British began to play with bat, ball and umpire. There was nothing exceptional about the team that Kapil Dev took to the World Cup tournament in England that year, except perhaps Kapil himself. He was the most remarkable of the cricketers peeping out from a new India rediscovering its confidence. Kapil shrugged off his limited English with a laugh that was neither silly-aggressive nor cringe-inducing inferiority complex. Kapil spoke with both bat and ball till the world understood his language.

A prophet should not be born before his time. The World Cup victory of 1983 was the launching pad of a mission to supremacy. Sachin entered his teens at precisely the moment when Indian cricket began to zoom towards a stratosphere of ability and wealth that would have been dismissed as absurd even in an anthology of fairy tales.

Before India lifted the 1983 Cup by defeating a jaw-frozen West Indies, international cricket was run along sniffy caste lines. The

Brahmins, England, and Thakurs, Australia, dominated the game. The West Indies claimed headlines sometimes with meteoric dazzle—who can forget Garfield Sobers, Rohan Kanhai, Wes Hall, Charlie Griffith?—but remained 11 players until Clive Lloyd knitted a team. The underclass consisted of old colonies, India, Pakistan and New Zealand, with South Africa as the ghost at dinner (heard on radio but never seen).

If Sunil Gavaskar was the outstanding talent of the old world, then Sachin was pilot of the ship that discovered and conquered an array of unknown continents. The audience explosion could be heard in cash registers. His first advertising contract was the kind of figure considered sufficient as seed money for heavy industry. The brave Mark Mascarenhas, who signed that extraordinary commitment, never doubted that it made perfect business sense. Neither did young Sachin have any doubts.

Cricket had its genius galaxy before Sachin came; it will have even more talent after he has retired. But it is given to only one man in a century to change the content, culture, horizon and history of his craft. Sachin Tendulkar is that architect who saw barren land dotted with a few oasis spots, and turned it into a megapolis of the Indian imagination, a vast boundless city of green stadium and television set that thrives in both reality and virtual reality.

I shall not dwell upon Sachin's mesmerising grace which reduces his bat to a scalpel one moment, a jeweller's tool in another, and the Nordic god Thor's hammer when he gets into a thunderous mood. We live in an age of permanent television with its audio-visual banquet. Every viewer is his own Neville Cardus when watching Sachin. Description seems an intrusion upon the magic bond between Sachin and each of his starlit fans in a unique universe. This is adoration, mind, not mere admiration. Sachin has given at least two generations a memory of greatness that will feed their conversations till they stumble into their graves.

The talk around him is over. The talk about him has only begun. Two decades later memory will do what it always does, exaggerate, but only because people never know how precisely to recall a wondrous dream that they have been privileged to witness in the space beyond life's cage of the mundane. When Sachin is 60 he just might recognise himself in the stories that will lift many an evening around a bar or drawing room. But he must never intervene to infect that stardust with the sprinkle of statistics, or even perhaps facts.

Sachin Tendulkar is a legend not in his lifetime, but in our lives. His life belongs to him. His memory belongs to us.

GOOD RIDDANCE, 2013.
LONG LIVE 2014!

Too often the state exploits secrecy to bury mistakes

29 December 2013

The sense of an ending—a phrase borrowed from the title of Julian Barnes' moving book—inevitably breeds nostalgia for a year that has just passed. Fortunately nostalgia does not regress into the welter of headlines that claimed daily attention, a toxic porridge of conceits, hypocrisy and lynch mob hysteria that often sought relevance in the name of virtue. There were more illuminating moments in solitude.

One of the great pleasures of 2013 is recent: the just-concluded first Test between India and South Africa, which I watched from the comparative isolation of a holiday resort in Kerala. This was an absorbing Test of skill and character by two teams determined to win, and if they could not, then deny victory to the opponent. The last day was a magnum opus thriller, brilliant spurts of lightning across large patches of steady play: to watch India slip was agony, but to turn off the television was impossible.

Defeat is easy to accept. We do it every day of our normal lives. But defeat so close to victory is another story. The biggest reason for defeat is not the strength of a victor but the complacency of a loser. If you take anything for granted, the prize will slip away before your troubled eyes. I don't know if art imitates life any more; one suspects not. But sport certainly does. Nothing is certain until that final bell rings and the umpire—or indeed the Chief Election Commissioner—announces close of play.

The best books I read this year were both from America. *The Blood Telegram: India's Secret War in East Pakistan* by Gary Bass is less on the secret war conducted by Delhi and far more on Washington's secret policy of indifference towards the Pakistan Army's genocide in what was then East Pakistan during the fateful year of 1971, which ended in a war that created a new nation, Bangladesh. The second great read was *The Brothers: John Foster Dulles, Allen Dulles, and Their Secret World War* by Stephen Kinzer, which graphs the lives of the two brothers, one a secretary of state and the other a CIA chief. They controlled American foreign policy during the Eisenhower administration between 1952 and 1960.

If you think there are too many secrets on the cover, rest assured this is no exaggeration judging by what is revealed between the covers. If you want to revel in America-bashing, go ahead. There is enough to fuel a lifetime of fulminations. But I also marvelled at the unwritten subtext, which neither author chose to stress: how focused and unrelenting America, with its many leaderships, is when it comes to national interest.

National interest can become a moveable feast. This decade's convictions can be the next decade's disaster. There is probably some wrong in every right, even if the proposition does not work the other way around. But national policy is made by present vision, not hindsight. In the 1950s America believed it was fighting a cold war against world domination by Communists, and if morality became hostage to this conflict, so be it. That American and European generation of Eisenhower, Stalin and Churchill had just survived a war that could have shattered the West and the East completely (if, for instance, Germany had also been able to construct nuclear weapons by 1945). It did not need any lessons in cynicism, or worried too much about casualties.

In 1971 Richard Nixon and Henry Kissinger were focused on another great game that they knew would change the dynamics of international relations (as indeed it did) and impact world affairs for generations. Bangladesh was hardly on their radar; they were concentrating on how to sacrifice Chiang Kai-shek's Taiwan and correct an obvious anomaly by recognising Maoist China as the legitimate China. Russia and China had already begun to drift apart, pulled in separate directions by national compulsions; the American intervention ended all hopes of Communist solidarity. The much-vaunted concept of a Communist International reassembled into Communist Nationals. A good theorist could trace a direct line from 1971 to 1991, when the Soviet Union fell apart and Russian communism disintegrated.

One wonders when India's foreign policy will be injected with a little more steel of self-interest, instead of being a charity shop of good intentions. It is good that Indian diplomats have stood up for one of their own* in America. But this is only evidence of what they can do, individually and collectively, if they are given the freedom to stand up for their country with equal backbone.

The remembrance of things past, to use another book title, can be a mixed joy. On balance, I am relieved that 2013 is over, never to return. Long live 2014!

*Devyani Khobragade, who was arrested despite diplomatic immunity.

INDIA'S COUCH FOOTBALL SYNDROME

Palliatives that work when you have no stars of your own

29 June 2014

Readers with an unpolluted, refined memory will recall a news story put out by the dregs of western media some months ago saying that the hallowed Kim Jong-un, Supreme Leader of the Blessed Earth of North Korea, had issued a democratic order to all patriotic youth to get a haircut in his style. This Kimcut is a sort of roundhead operation in which everything hirsute below eartop level at the minimum is sheared off. The story represented gross under reporting typical of jealousies inherent among those journalists who perform part time duties as running dogs of imperialism. Even a cursory examination of mops on display in the football fields of Brazil proves that the Kimcut has become an international cult.

You will, I hope, recognise the depths of the bias. If footballers at the 2014 World Cup had generally opted for the salt and pepper drizzle on Barack Obama's head, or the early 20th century slickback atop David Cameron or the lawnmower effect favoured by Vladimir Putin, media would have gone manic in giving credit for inspiration where it was due. But because it is Comrade Kim there is collective silence. I would definitely call this an international conspiracy.

One notes with regret that India also is not getting its due after the ingenious leadership it has displayed on how to handle the rigours of a World Cup. The All India Football Federation has discovered a brilliant and consistent solution to the problem of potential heartbreak, angst and anguish that has wrecked the soul of two proud nations like England and Spain, forced to fly back home after two straight and ignominious defeats. They should have learnt from India. Never be good enough to qualify and you will never have to face the humiliation of defeat.

England have had so much practice at being thrown out before the long whistle and yet they remain too proud to follow India's example. Their fans must be masochists. Who else would enjoy humiliation before hundreds of millions glued to TV sets, most of them jeering? If you don't lose, no one demands the resignation of your coach or captain or all players above the age of 75. Everyone is safe. Have you ever heard anyone demanding the head or neck of any Indian football official? Never. Things go on as usual. Every official can continue to do what he does best—work out creative schemes to maximise personal benefits from every junket to pious havens of moral rectitude like Monte Carlo or Rio de Janeiro.

Alas, the British football fan possesses more passion than prudence. I learn that hundreds of them were persuaded by smooth salesmen in old school ties to purchase land in deepest Amazon on the assumption that property prices would rocket up the moment England won the World Cup. They are searching for justice in law courts now, but that is naiveté. British fans must become like Indians. They must abandon hope the moment their players get on a football field.

Failure, particularly of the kind of epic scale indulged by India, has its creative side effects. It is good for both physical as well as mental health. There is never going to be the emotional strain which so many doctors believe is so terrible for the heart. See how the enormous struggle to win wrenches the gut of an Iranian or Ghana player. The Italian coach looked fit for a spell in hospital and the Spanish one for a psychiatric ward. But no one has ever seen even an eyebrow flutter on the face of an Indian official. They will live serenely till the blissful age of 100, confident that their jobs are eternal.

The only serious challenge before Indian officials is how to prepare a team for the World Cup of 2074, probably scheduled for indoor stadiums in the Arctic, the rest of the world having run out of venues by then.

The good news is that Indian fans do not much care any longer. They have acquired the best of both worlds. They can leave the actual running around to foreigners on television screens. And they can concentrate on the cerebral aspects of football, on theories of racing around in curves, arcs, spurts and swirling dotted lines which are in such evidence on drawing boards. If there was a proper examination with pen, paper and invigilator in a hall no one could defeat India in any World Cup theory contest. Others may consider football to be a game requiring the skills of a wrestler, morals of a dupe and luck of an opportunist. For Indians it is a symphony best heard from a couch conveniently near a bowl of potato chips.

Moreover, why should Indians waste precious loyalty on bowlegged domestic defenders and cross eyed strikers when TV globalisation offers a choice between two Manchesters, Liverpool, Arsenal, Barcelona and Madrid? Why waste time on Doldrum Baboos from Kolkata when Suarez can defeat England and then bite off more than he can chew?

True stars belong to the firmament. A sky can never belong to any nation.

This is the sort of noble thought that works beautifully when you have no stars of your own.

CURSE OF THE GAME

The historian as attorney

7 August 2014

Nazar Mohammad was the first Pakistani cricketer to score a Test century, in 1952, at Lucknow, but his brilliant promise was aborted by an arm injury in 1953. This could have been a heroic tale in the annals of cricket, if perhaps Nazar had been felled by a fearsome fast bowler like West Indians Hall or Griffith. Alas, the incident is merely tragicomic, the stuff of tired cartoons rather than epic poetry. Nazar broke his arm when he jumped out of his paramour's first floor bedroom window to escape the wrath of a jealous husband.

This exciting story appears in a footnote on page 24 of Peter Oborne's devoted history of Pakistan cricket, *Wounded Tiger*, and is reason for a complaint. Peter should have done a switch: turned his fabulous footnotes into treasure house chapters and shaved off a few stubbles in the body copy. But Peter, who ponders often in this fine book without becoming ponderous, has become an attorney instead of a historian. Since he cannot quite ignore anecdotes that have done so much to enliven the reputation of Pakistan's once-happy band of cricketers, he places scintillating stuff at the mercy of asterisks in small type. As the greatest of Pak legends, Imran Khan, once proudly announced on his T-shirt during a trip to Australia, 'Big Boys Play at Night.'

I know Peter Oborne, and while one cannot quite claim him as a close friend, he is certainly a luncheon companion during my infrequent visits to London if he is not trotting across distant corners of the globe in search of a story. Peter's bread comes from political reporting and columns; the butter is from excellent books like *Alastair Campbell: New Labour and the Rise of the Media Class*; *The Rise of Political Lying*; *The Triumph of the Political Class* and *Basil D'Oliveira: Cricket and Conspiracy: The Untold Story*. In *Wounded Tiger* Peter indulges his twin passions, politics and cricket. I wonder if he realised that expertise acquired in political commentary would work so seamlessly in *Wounded Tiger*: conspiracy, power politics, shifting class and cash relationships, intrusive media and nuanced lying by so many with a cause or career to promote through sport.

So much of Pak cricket is about different games, ruled by politicians and military dictators who thought they could win the affection of subjects through a surrogate triumph on a playing field. As hockey faded, cricket took over in both India and Pakistan, but Indian cricket reinvented itself through brilliant entrepreneurship which has created a template for the world. Since money keeps an open-door policy for talent, there will be plenty of both in India during the foreseeable future. Pak cricketers, sadly, have not found an economy that can pay for their abilities or meet their aspirations. Too many of them, therefore, have been mesmerized by an alternative sub-plot, illegal betting. Throw in terrorism and ethnic violence, and Pakistan cricket has become a refugee searching for temporary habitation where it can play a Test series. If it were not real it would be too weird to contemplate. This is no fault of the cricketers. They are simply young men trapped in the wrong place at the wrong time.

Peter is accurate enough about his wounded tigers, but he seems almost reluctant to note that these wounds are self-inflicted. This is understandable. He is in love with his subject (at least until the next infatuation and another book come along), and every lover manages to convince himself that the hairy wart on the beloved's moon-face is actually a pretty little mole planted by an angel from Heaven's beauty parlour.

Investigative rigour, consequently, disappears even on so important a problem as the various forms of corruption: spot-fixing, match-fixing, umpire-fixing, and even organiser-fixing in at least one infamous arid venue. Peter may have every humane reason to be kind to the young Mohammad Amir who, along with Salman Butt and Mohammad Asif, was caught spot-fixing, and pillory him for naiveté rather than condemn him for crime, but why does he abandon basic journalist demands when it comes to men at the centre of this fix, the bookies? He refers, for instance, to 'a bookmaker named Ali, who tried to induce him [Amir] to cheat'. Any newspaper editor would have placed queries on the side: Surname? Details? Where does Ali operate from? Et al. Ali was no stranger to the players; they would have talked. But Oborne is reluctant to add flesh to bare bones.

In 1979, Pak captain Majid Khan voiced alarm when a 'big fat chap' sat regularly on the team bus, despite being a stranger. What is even more strange is that the fat chap remained on the bus. The captain never ordered him off. Would such an order have led to a revolt in the team? Oborne does not provide the name of this big fat chap when dozens would have disclosed his identity. He simply does not ask. Nor does he disclose the name of the bookie who greeted the Pak team at Delhi airport and then shadowed the team in an expensive BMW—a pretty rare car in those days on the subcontinent, and as sure a sign of flashy wealth as any.

Peter is in a hurry to run past discomfiture, although, to his credit, he never whitewashes dirt from the narrative. But he does fall into that old trap of seeking justification in equivalence. He fingers Asif Iqbal, who once told his surprised Indian counterpart G. Viswanath that the latter had won the toss. Peter adds, 'Besides it was openly alleged that Asif Iqbal had joined hands with the top Indian speculators and gamblers, and that some of his team-mates were found too weak to resist similar sort of temptation'. So that's all right then. Pakistanis can never do anything wrong without having Indians to blame.

It is perfectly true that Indian captain Mohammad Azharuddin and South Africa's Hansie Cronje's careers were ruined by similar scandals. (Cronje died a broken man and Azharuddin became a Congress MP.)

But South Africa and India never suffered the epidemic-level infection that wasted Pakistan's superb cricket talent. Not this incident from a New Zealand tour, where Salim Malik 'claimed to have won the toss in the first Test after making a call in Urdu. He then picked up the coin before the home captain, Ken Rutherford, had a chance to look at it, or ask for a translation'. That touch of Urdu is pure genius. You can't be a good crook without brains.

Only a thin crust of corruption has become public knowledge. As Imran Khan once pointed out, it takes collusion between five to seven players to fix a game. Even matches against sworn rivals India in the 1996 World Cup were not above suspicion. I quote: 'A rumour circulated [at Lahore's Gaddafi stadium] that Wasim's injury was spurious and that he had taken money from bookies to miss the match against India. He was forced into hiding as his effigy was burned and his home in Lahore was pelted with garbage by an angry mob. Wasim [Akram] denied the rumour at the Qayyum Commission, which acquitted him.' Memory has not acquitted Wasim, which is why this ghost flutters into the book.

Honest members of the Pak squad knew what was going on. In 1994 manager Intikhab Alam made his players swear on the holy Quran, but neither flag nor God could keep everyone clean. Surely the most interesting Test of that time would have been South Africa vs Pakistan in 1994, the former led by Cronje and the latter by Malik. Which captain made more money on the side? The joke that year was Pakistan's loss to Zimbabwe by an innings and 64 runs. Jackie Hendricks, the match referee, refused to accept Malik's claim that he had won the toss, and ordered a second flip of the coin. This time Zimbabwe won the toss.

There is similar eagerness to save Pakistan's reputation on that other massive bone of contention: umpires who got a stye in the eye at crucial moments of a match. Once upon a time long, long ago there was no television coverage, and nothing in the form of camera and computer-generated gymnastics that indicate where a ball would have travelled up to next Sunday. An umpire was God. Run-outs and leg-befores were the happy hunting ground of patriotism. Cooking up an elaborate defence, Peter makes an indigestive meal out of statistics, pointing out with slapdash enthusiasm that Pakistani umpires declared as many of their own players run out or lbw as they did Indians. Anyone with an ounce of cricket in his brain (and Peter has tons of it) knows that it is not quite the same thing giving Sunil Gavaskar out as sending Waqar Younis back to the dressing room when it doesn't matter.

Umpiring has caused such bad blood that it even infected the great goodwill series of 1978 between India and Pakistan, when play resumed after 17 years. The bonhomie, the graciousness of guest and host, the nostalgia, were exemplary. A fancy Mercedes was sent to the airport for that great son of Lahore Lala Amarnath when he went as a commentator. The manager of the Indian team, Maharaja of Baroda Fatehsinghrao Gaekwad, thought the limousine was for him, and was politely told to get into the team bus. (Since you ask, the Maharajah's full name was Lt. Col. Farzand-i-Daulat-Inglishia Shrimant Maharaja Fatehsinghrao Prataprao Gaeikwad, Sena Khas Khel Shamsher Bahadur.) But even this happy chapter ended on a bitter note when Indian captain Bishen Singh Bedi walked off from the field in the third one-dayer because Sarfraz Khan kept bowling bouncers beyond the reach of Indian batsmen without being called by Pakistani umpires.

In 1987 Tom Graveney said that Pakistan have been 'cheating for 37 years and it is getting worse and worse'. That might have been an exaggeration but indicates the simmering bitterness of all visitors. Ian Botham spoke for the tribe when he suggested that Pakistan was just the place to send your mother-in-law to. (History does not record what Botham's mother-in-law had to say on the subject.) Pakistanis themselves clearly had more fun when they were out of the fatherland.

In 1993, Wasim and three colleagues were caught in the West Indies by the police for possession of marijuana in the company of two British girls. More details, please, Peter, in the next edition. It is to Imran Khan's eternal credit that he recognized the damage to his country's reputation, and led a long campaign for neutral umpires. Imran Khan was the most honourable and honoured player in Pakistan's history, a class apart—literally. When Imran's father Ikramullah Khan Niazi returned in 1948 after doing a post-graduate course at Imperial College, half the town came to greet the 'England returned' at the railway station. Imran decided his future lay in cricket after he saw his cousin Javed Burki (also Oxbridge) score a century. By the time Imran joined the Lahore cricket team in 1968, the class character of Pakistani cricketers had already begun to change; he could barely communicate (as he notes in his autobiography) with some of his teammates, who were from largely Urdu-medium schools. You cannot ring-fence a game synonymous with such glamour. Imran evolved to absorb elements from both worlds he bridged, one of agnostic blue-blood west-oriented privilege and the other of values derived from his religion. He claims he was jolted by culture shock when he went up to Oxford in 1972 and encountered the anarchic, subversive, iconoclast humour of Monty Python on BBC. Imran complete trusted a clairvoyant named Mian Bashir, who predicted his future and told his wife Jemima, who came from a more cynical London elite, the three things she most wanted from life.

As an Indian who witnessed the emotional upheavals around the 1978 Karachi Test, as well as the delirious 2004 Lahore one-dayer, I wish there had been a little more about the complex interweave of sports, politics, culture and memory on the subcontinent. But that does not detract too much from a magisterial labour of love. My own encounter with cricket history came when a ragbag collection of Indian journalists were pitted against a local media side for an impromptu match on the rest day of the Karachi Test in 1978. To our shock and awe, the legendary Hanif Mohammad came to bat for the hosts. I was hiding somewhere on the field when a Hanif on-drive came straight towards me. With superb, youthful agility I jumped smartly to the side and let the ball carry on for a boundary rather than crack a finger trying to stop Hanif's drive.

There was applause from my fellow Indian hacks on the field, not all of it ironic.

TIGER, TIGER BURNING BRIGHT

The magic of Pataudi

25 September 2011

In the loneliness of the small town where I was born, and the shuttered years of boarding school, dream was a five-letter word called Tiger. Mansur Ali Khan's magic transcended the supreme piffle that passed for cricket commentary when radio, with a glowing green eye in the right-hand corner, was our primary passport to Test cricket. Secondary knowledge came from the grey photographs in black-and-white newspapers; but the red cherry seemed to blossom when it was smacked imperiously in an arc that began with the single eye of the master and traversed along the hooked nose that had been designed by God for aristocracy. The radio went into memory. The photograph was lovingly preserved in a scrapbook along with peers like Neil Harvey, Richie Benaud, Wes Hall, Garfield Sobers and Frank Worrell. I kept the unassuming Worrell in that illustrious company not because he could bat, but because he could lead.

Pataudi's inherited title was a bit of a two-way sniff. We certainly sensed if not heard his occasional sniff at the plebs; but the fun was that he heard our periodic snort at yesterday's elite as well. By the 1960s a nawab had already become an effete caricature, a piteous descent from the glory days of the 18th century, first reduced to a whining fawn of the British and then to a vainglorious hanger-on of post-Independence politicians. Even Hindi cinema had begun to laugh at the 'Chhote Nawab', unless it tipped towards lachrymose self-pity as Nawab Sahib auctioned off his precious heirlooms in *Mere Mehboob* to protect some immensely idle honour.

Then came Indira Gandhi. In 1969 she made titles like nawabs and rajas illegal, and stripped away their dole, called a privy purse. Their consequent fury was as silly as their impotence. They learnt how distant they had become from changing India when they tried to challenge Mrs Gandhi in the general elections of 1971. Mrs Gandhi won. The new Rani of India was Indira Gandhi, the Begum of Democracy.

Tiger was as upset as any of his brotherhood, but he disguised any personal trauma behind a finely chiselled sense of humour that combined the riot of practical jokes with the deadpan of a British mask. He was the perfect Indo-Anglian, as comfortable in stately sherwani as in a hunting jacket on Scottish moors. If he did not belong to any Drones club from the fiction of P.G. Wodehouse, it was only because he carried a bit of Drones inside him wherever he went. The strategy for his impish pranks was often perfected across a convivial bar, and secrets were carefully protected till long after the victims had been duped—harmlessly of course. It was tragic that the last incident in his life was a snub from the MCC, which refused to hand out the traditional Pataudi trophy at the end of an India–England series this summer.

The Indian prince was bound to English cricket by a silken bond. At one level it kept him on friendship terms with the contemporary ruling class, just as hunting had done in the Mughal days. It also became an appropriate theatre for the display of regal talent. It did not threaten the British, and it did not involve subservience. It would have been demeaning for Pataudi to become, for instance, a highly successful multinational executive: even a blue-chip private company was not blue enough for India's blue-blooded. The army was an honourable sanctuary but demanded too much discipline for too little reward. Politics was an option, but required rubbing shoulders with the serf.

Tiger had an equitable relationship with glamour. He was not a hypocrite, so he never disdained glamour. But he never fell in love with his mirror, either.

Many reasons have been cited to explain the comparative paucity of runs: he scored just six centuries. The popular theory is the tragic loss of an eye in a car accident when still at Oxford. I tend to believe that he just could not be bothered. Cricket was a game, not a religion. He did not sacrifice joy at the altar of statistics.

Pataudi became an acknowledged Tiger because of his sleek style, his calm demeanour at the crease until the moment came for the instinctive pounce. He also wore the smile of the Tiger, a quiver that only once in a while bubbled across his face. This Tiger had class: Royal Bengal, an epithet that Calcutta happily adopted when he married a Bengali, a brilliant daughter of the great Tagore family, Sharmila.

I wonder how Tiger would have reacted to the cant that has surfaced after his death. A shrug, a nod, a half-weary smile. He hated clichés, so could we please abandon rubbish like 'Cricket has become poorer', etc. Cricket has become infinitely richer in both cash and technique since Tiger last held a bat. But the world has certainly become poorer since his death.

GOODBYE, SIR!

In memory of Shammi Kapoor

19 August 2011

Every childhood hero takes away a little bit of one's life along with him when he dies. Shammi Kapoor filled those wondrously difficult years when laughter and optimism were the only pathfinders from an unknown jute-mill settlement in Bengal to an unwelcome Calcutta teeming with every variety of revolution. Shammi Kapoor was our torch, for he combined three essentials of teenage: he was mad; he got his girl on his own terms; and there was always a happy ending. He joined the dots between changing the world and dreaming of love.

Love, with all its hide-and-seek propensities, lurked in the shadows of real life: in street poetry at gas-lit mushairas; in the banter of conversation; and, not least, in the assembly-line production of babies that is a visible fact of small town joint families. Sex was more secretive, either as predecessor or successor of love.

Shammi lifted love from familiarity with an insouciant tug that hinted sharply at the excitement of sex. There was a safety clause in the contract, of course: frolic was only a symptom of a celluloid hero's utterly eternal true love. But even when Shammi Kapoor's heart broke, and the skies echoed with his lament, his saucy eyebrow never dropped.

Which saxophone has been more poignant in the service of its master than Shammi's in '*Hai duniya usiki zamana usi ka, Muhabbat mein jo ho gaya ho kisi ka*'. His fingers hammered at the piano as if it was personally responsible for Mumtaz's woes in *Brahmachari*. He acted in over a hundred films, but I don't think the sentimental Punjabi love epic *Heer-Ranjha* was part of that oeuvre. If Shammi had been Ranjha, he would have pounded a grand piano on the banks of the river Ravi and it would have been perfectly in character.

Forty years later it is easy to be dismissive about that yell which rose from the belly, filled the throat and then knocked your head off: Yaaaahoooo! For me, sitting in a bug-infested cinema hall called Swapna, that cry from *Junglee* was a roar of liberation from the silly boredom of convention. Suddenly, lovers did not weep, as Dilip Kumar did by the bucketful; or go perpendicular with patriotism, as Raj Kapoor considered necessary; or adopt a stomach-ache face, which was Rajendra Kumar's speciality. Shammi Kapoor told us, when I was all of ten and had just been sentenced to boarding school, to go find our own voice, even if that turned into the occasional scream. Be brilliant, if you could; be a fool, if you had to; but be authentic in either case. There was fun to be had in all avatars.

Shammi's singing voice was Mohammad Rafi. Between them seemed to traverse a range as wide as the Himalayas but, more accurately, moved from the sunshine of daybreak to the velvet of night through the smoke of evening. '*Sar par topi lal*' is only one of innumerable unforgettable numbers sparkling with sunshine. Dusk begins to gather when Shammi serenades Sadhana in '*Is rang badalti duniya mein insaan ki neeyat theek nahin, Nikla na karo tum sajh dhaj kar imaan ki neeyat theek nahin . . .*' The night is in its element when Rocky seizes the drums in *Teesri Manzil*, a brilliant foil to twirling Helen. What fun the gang of Shammi, Rafi, Shankar Jaikishan or O.P. Nayyar and poet Hasrat Jaipuri must have had as they matched the mischief of words to the curvature of music and then spiced it with the élan of Shammi Kapoor. Shammi admired the greats who made Bollywood music into a sublime art. When Talat Mahmood tried to become an acting star, Shammi gave him some sensible advice, 'Talat Sahib, you sing so well . . . why are you wasting your time acting?'

Only Rafi and Shammi could transform a boom from the high aristocracy of the British Empire into a gentle Indian croon, as they did with 'Tally ho' (reconfigured in Hindi to 'Taali ho'). 'Tally ho!' is the signature war cry of the British ruling class when hunting a fox across the country through the powder-sleet of winter, the talisman of aunts in any P.G. Wodehouse novel. Shammi and Rafi softened it to a treble variation, and infused it with musical magic that sways the mind and body as easily today as it did four decades ago. You listen to '*Baar baar dekho, hazaar baar dekho*' and you move. If you can sit through '*Kisi na kisi se kabhi na kabhi, kahin na kahin dil lagana padega*' without twitching, you were born without a soul.

We forgave Shammi his flab, his astonishing descent from a helicopter in a bathrobe flapping around a potbelly towards a svelte Sharmila skiing in a swimsuit like a nymph; his premature bloat and hamming, everything, because he taught us the one lesson we needed in those many battles with uncertainty: attitude. Goodbye, Sir! '*Tumne mujhko hansna sikhaya, roney kahogey ro lenge hum . . .*' You taught us to laugh. If you tell us to cry, we shall do that as well.

DEATH TAKES NO PRISONERS

Dev Anand had a motto: 'Never say die'

9 December 2011

Dev Anand hated death as intensely as he loathed the demands of time. Age itself became an unbearable coffin; and in some unfathomable way he believed that death could be postponed indefinitely. He thought of death as some kind of personal defeat, and defeat did not enter his vocabulary. He might falter, but never fail. For a six-decade superstar life does not imitate art so much as become an art form.

His movies always had a happy ending, and there was no way he was going to deny himself the same privilege off-screen. He was not quite a Peter Pan, the child who froze time, but he remained rooted in his twenties, unable or unwilling to step beyond a bracket that distilled the exuberance of existence into love, sex, success and adulation.

But a body does not have the flexibility of the imagination, and Dev Anand chose to wrap his neck in flowing scarves to curtain the telltale desolation of skin stretching away from flesh. He could hardly hide his face, but a miracle occurred each time I met him. The years visibly peeled off, through his eyes, driven out by the dazzle of his smile and the mystique of memory as conversation crept inevitably back into the past. There was nowhere else to go. The past was the only golden age, and if gold needed constant burnishing to glisten, it would get all the massage it required. In that exultant narrative, Dev Anand was both his name, a god of Joy, as well as Kama Dev, god of Love. The two were indistinguishable.

The one startling variation in a resplendent career was *Guide*. The film had very little to do with its origins in R.K. Narayan's book; Dev and his talented younger brother Vijay, who directed the best of Dev's oeuvre, threw it out of the window and made their own movie. *Guide*'s Rosie, played exquisitely by Waheeda Rehman, was not mere rebellion, but a revolution that injected gender independence into the consciousness of an India still wandering through the fog of conservative social norms in the 1960s.

Guide is also the only film in which Dev Anand dies. But this death was a strategic manoeuvre. He resurrects triumphantly as eternal truth, beyond the tragedy of time. No ghost has ever been so handsome.

While Dilip Kumar made a lachrymose fortune as part of his public persona obligations, and Raj Kapoor evolved from saving his trousers in *Awara* to saving the nation in *Jis Desh Mein Ganga Behti Hai*, Dev Anand stayed faithful to an insouciant street smile, whether in *Baazi*'s cheap gambling dens, or amid diamonds in *Jewel Thief*. He seemed ambivalent about smart theft; his loyalties were securely with law and order, but there was always a faint suggestion that his heart belonged to the panache of sophisticated crime.

Dev Anand was 42 when *Guide* was released in 1965. He solved his unacknowledged midlife crisis with style. He created the 1960s' look with a sequence of memorable hits: *Kala Bazar*, *Hum Dono*, *Bombai ka Baboo*, *Asli Naqli*, *Tere Ghar ke Saamne*, *Guide*, *Jewel Thief*, *Johny Mera Naam*, *Tere Mere Sapne* and *Hare Rama Hare Krishna*. He was the Sixties. His high-collar shirts, exotic hats and ankle-length corduroys ended the baggies era. His heroines were a cast from heaven: Waheeda Rehman, Nanda, Sadhana, Suchitra Sen, Nutan, Vyajayantimala, Hema Malini and finally the only woman who broke his heart because she shifted to Raj Kapoor in exchange for a role in *Satyam Shivam Sundaram*, Zeenat Aman. As he grew older, his girlfriends became younger. He had broken so many hearts it was but fair that someone should break his at least once.

When history is written, as it should be, the tipping point will be a subject of legitimate debate. When did Dev Anand's decline begin? His hand, it is true, began to go limp from the wrist in *Kala Bazar* (1960), but that remained no more than a personal oddity even when his pistol in *Jewel Thief* notoriously pointed 45 degrees south instead of straight at villains. The ebb began with *Gambler*, offered to a shocked public in 1971: Dev Anand had a straight handlebar moustache that Groucho Marx would have shunned. The icon of charisma had lost it. By the 1980s his films were nothing more than a tawdry list of embarrassments. But, to use a phrase that has never seemed more appropriate, it was 'Never say die'.

Dev Anand had the rare ability to make a stranger seem a friend, and a friend feel irreplaceable. Anyone who entered his aura returned with at least an anecdote. Alas, now that there is no one to contradict them, stories about personal encounters with Dev Anand will both magnify and multiply. But that is how a life becomes a legend.

A WORLD WHICH SPUN ON THE AXIS OF THE HEART

The chemistry between Suchitra Sen and Uttam Kumar went beyond science

12 January 2014

Nostalgia is not very good news for the nostalgic. The elegy of age lies a layer below the surface, trying hard but unable to hide. As the present hurries along towards the future at its usual frenetic pace, the draw of the past persuades one to pause in contemplation, unredeemed by any practical definition of utility. But nostalgia is not the sadness of an end; it is a search, melancholic maybe, for nuggets in the rubbish dump of time.

Suchitra Sen has entered the last days of her life, in some Calcutta hospital. This is no longer news. In the 1950s and 1960s there seemed to be no other news worth bothering about in Bengal except the enchanting Suchitra Sen, particularly when she appeared on screen with her great paramour and thespian partner Uttam Kumar. Suchitra Sen was married to someone. No one knew who, and no one cared: Suchitra and Uttam possessed chemistry beyond science. Marriage seemed irrelevant. Everyone was married, including all—unlike today, when the operative if ebbing word is most—parents. But how many gorgeous women and handsome men were in love that was both subversive and flagrant? The world spun on the axis of the heart.

I had not put razor to chin when I first saw them in a movie, in a cinema hall called Jyoti. The seats confirmed my knowledgeable view that bedbugs were misnamed; they had quite a life outside bed as well. We lived, or were locked, in a hamlet outside a jute mill on the banks of the meandering river Hoogly; but imagination always escaped into an interwoven collage of dreams unbridled by any boundary. Nothing set fantasy on fire more quickly than a Suchitra smile, subtle, mischievous, and in full command of the relationship. Uttam Kumar was happy to become an adult boy before the goddess.

I cannot recall the name of that film; perhaps *Saptapadi*, perhaps not. It would be easy to check through the smooth alleys of modern internet technology. But that is only as necessary as a shrug. It was a time of black and white. It was an age of grain and velvet, and the sheen of velvet became a separate colour. Memory is better served in diffusion than in the particular.

The 1960s were draped by a grainy peel of shifting dots: nothing was clear, not a job in sight, not a prospect in place, the economy as disconsolate as aspiration. Little wonder then that the decade was marked by insurrection and violence, some in a Maoist cause, others for ethnic or communal reasons. A large comfort zone was the company of Suchitra Sen—and, to be fair, Uttam Kumar.

It was not the only one, of course. Dev Anand's jaunt, his street-smart zigzag through petty crime (selling black market movie tickets, picking pockets, finding courage in a gambling den) as the only option for survival, was equally irresistible. I never understood why Suchitra Sen and Dev Anand looked so distant from each other in their one film, *Bombai ka Baboo*. Every part of the construct was separately perfect: hero and heroine at the top of their game; the music divine; the plot far better than the soporific nonsense that was the usual diet for scripts. There could be only one reason. Suchitra and Dev were cold. There was nothing personal. We who knew Bengali cinema felt relieved. It was Suchitra and Uttam or Suchitra or nothing. Suchitra and Uttam even did a Bengali rendition of *Othello* in one film, Uttam's face heavy with black boot polish. Through some human miracle, it worked.

Suchitra never adapted to Hindi cinema; and nor did Uttam. Suchitra succeeded only when she did not need a stand-in for Uttam, in films where she was stellar rather than co-star. If you have not seen her brilliant performance in *Mamta*, order a copy now. It is a moving story of love lost and life betrayed. Two songs are classics: Lata Mangeshkar's '*Rahte thhe kabhi jinke dil mein hum jaan se bhi pyaaron ki tarah, Baithey hain unhi ke mehfil mein hum aaj gunahgaaron ki tarah*' and Hemant Kumar's immortal '*Chupa lo yeh dil mein pyaar mera*'. The second success was *Aandhi*, where Suchitra portrayed a politician modelled on Mrs Indira Gandhi. Suchitra belonged to Bengal and Bengali.

Uttam Kumar died, suddenly, more than three decades ago. I was editor of the newsweekly *Sunday* then. The commemorative issue in his memory sold out the moment it reached the stands, and not just in Calcutta. His funeral had an element of insanity, as young crowds fought to touch their idol on his final trip through the city he loved. Suchitra is still with us*, and may the inevitable be delayed as much as a generous Providence can manage. But her memory will not die, as long as admiration is alive.

*This piece was written just before her death.

A SOFT TOUCH ON THE SHOULDER

The inimitable style of Khushwant Singh

10 August 2014

When a tyrant asked Plato for the Constitution of Athens, a proud democratic city-state five centuries before the Christian era, the philosopher sent him the plays of Aristophanes. Among them is The Clouds, which lampoons Socrates, father of Western philosophy and Plato's guru. The message was evident. In a free state, nothing is sacrosanct, neither the strut of a political peacock nor the heavy tread of an intellectual elephant.

If a contemporary dictator wants to know the Constitution of modern India, send him *99: Unforgettable fiction, non-fiction, poetry & humour*, a brilliant selection of Khushwant Singh's writing, compiled by his beloved granddaughter Mala Dayal, and David Davidar, the esteemed editor who once worked for him.

Laughter is the amazing grace of freedom. Khushwant loved, above all, to laugh. Did this make him a humorist? He enjoyed being provocative, particularly about the middle-class hypocrisy surrounding alcohol and sex. Did this make him a voyeur? He slipped easily into bawdy language. Did this make him a dirty old man? No. Khushwant Singh became India's most famous writer-historian because he possessed a deeply serious mind, a sensitive imagination, a perceptive eye and the heart of a humanist.

Like so many intelligent men, he could never suffer a fool, particularly a pompous one. Since the ranks of the mighty are littered with the delusional, he always had much to laugh about. But he pursued comedy with such chronic persistence that his public image was bound to morph into some sort of caricature. If you look at photographs of some dignitaries in his company, they seem to feel obliged to laugh even before he has said a word. They went away with a sense of disappointment if they did not hear anything salacious while conversing with him.

The beauty of Khushwant's style lay in the power of simplicity, backed by the eye of a social historian, and deep understanding of the multiple silken threads that link or fray in human relations. He could capture the whiff of an era in a sentence, the totality of experience in a startling image picked from the welter of facts. The opening piece in this collection is a powerful account of his last visit to the village where he was born, Hadali, now in the heart of Pakistan. Its caption, Village in the Desert, is as clean as the first sentence: 'It is safest to begin with the beginning.' By the time, six pages later, he has said his last, emotional farewell, your eyes brim with as many tears as his. In less than 3,000 words you have travelled through the warmth, tensions, tragedies and values of a united Punjab, shredded into fragments by a partition that no one fully understands.

That fraternity, even when under strain, began in the convivial games of children and sparkled in the songs of women, and stretched across a geography from the Indus to the Jamuna, from the lower Himalayas to the deserts of Sind and Rajasthan. That Punjab is irretrievable now; and even its memory has begun to weaken as the generation of Khushwant Singh leaves us. It will linger on in such prose, but literature is unfair compensation for a thousand years of living magic.

As the past withers with such formidable pain, Khushwant Singh repeatedly asks himself that question to which no one has found a satisfactory answer: what is death about?

Life had a powerful resonance for him. Did death mean anything more than its absence? Death did not even offer the satisfaction of being the opposite of life. It was nothing, an arid void, a disappearance after such exotic appearance. Khushwant Singh did not possess enough religion to find consolation in devout obedience to the script of any scripture. But he found the courage to make his peace with the unknowable. The thought of death taught him, obliquely, how to live. He went to Delhi's Nigambodh Ghat to watch funeral pyres, and found the experience cathartic. The finality of ash cured him of 'petty vanities and anxieties'.

Absence of faith did not mean absence of belief, however anachronistic that may sound. When his marriage was on the verge of breakdown, he spent the night at a gurdwara praying for resolution to this crisis.

The agnostic in Khushwant surrendered easily, and I think willingly, to the touch of the divine: 'Many a time in Tokyo, when I got up at three in the morning to work on the translations of the hymns of Guru Nanak, I felt the hand of the Guru on my shoulder. Though I knew it was make-believe, I found it comforting.'

Did he really consider it to be 'make-belief'? I doubt it. Khushwant Singh could have never found comfort in the false. He wanted his own end to be swift and painless, and that indeed is precisely how it came.

When the time came, the Guru took him with a soft touch on the shoulder.

GOOD MORNING, 2015

Finding temporary heaven, on a patch of earthly time

28 December 2014

We believe in God not because of but in spite of His magnificent creation, man. There is nothing much left to learn from the track record of a morally bipolar race. In a past age, the Sufi messenger of peace, Khwaja Muinuddin Chishti, came to India after the marauding Sultan Mahmud of Ghazni; in more contemporary times, the Gandhian Khan Abdul Ghaffar Khan preceded the murderous Taliban.

The analogy might suggest a false equivalence, as if good and evil exist on this tense spinning ball called Earth in a fifty-fifty trade-off. Most of our time is consumed either fending off or dealing with violence and its barbarous cousins. God is the stable ideal of all that we miss: love, security, justice in a world where pain is synonymous with life. Our need for justice is so desperate that we let our imagination get virulent in search of metaphors for hell.

Every faith sets aside a few days each year for a sort of temporary heaven on a patch of earthly time, where human beings discover goodwill to a choir of angels singing within a subconscious muzak. It is officially declared a season of peace and generosity.

Charity is a distraught term, with hints of snobbery. Islamic doctrine has a solution: charity should be anonymous, to eliminate the grating pride of ego. But if there is a proper way to give then there is also a suitable way to receive, none better than through the eyes and heart of a child. A child is wish-friendly but money-neutral. Value is judged by joy, not cost. A child, contrary to perception, is also a realist. While an adult, suborned by greed or ambition or upward mobility or downward depression, may demand a spacecraft where a balloon would serve, a child is happy to accept a balloon and turn it into a spacecraft. The finest gift for a child cannot be hung from any tree, or wrapped in a parcel: it is the gift of time.

A central question about Christmas, which marks the birth of Jesus Christ, and the nativity narrative, is rarely asked as psalms predict and song celebrates the adoration of kings of who lay gold, frankincense and myrrh at the feet of the lord. What did Mary, his mother, give her child? Time, from cradle to cross.

The offerings of three wise men, or kings, or Magi, are surely the most celebrated gifts of a cultural phenomenon that has long escaped the brackets of a single religion. As in all memory, there is more than one version. Saint Matthew's testament reports that the monarchs followed a star to their destination, Bethlehem. Scholars, ever anxious to convert belief into specific strands, suggest that the Magi were Parsis, guardians of the holy flame, masters of astronomy, astrology, medicine. They could have come from Persia or India, following the Silk Route, currently the passion of communist, God-less China. But all are agreed that they came from the Orient.

Christianity has become such a pervasive Western fact that we tend to forget its Asian origins. Early church iconography painted the first family of the faith, correctly, in shades of brown, not the degrees of white in post-renaissance portraiture. Mary's head was, and still is, draped in a modest chador, the custom of her age. As easily ignored is that Mary has a chapter in the Quran, and Muslims revere Jesus (called Isa) as one of their greatest prophets. The Quran blesses Isa as Ruhallah, or the spirit of Allah. Muslims do not accept that Jesus was crucified, but that he was saved, nursed back to health, and went east to continue preaching outside the Roman Empire.

Christmas, however, is not about disputes. Let us rejoice that Muslim Turkey continues to glory in one of its most famous ancestors, Santa Claus. The cherubic face of Christmas gifts is not a Nordic old man riding a sleigh. Saint Nicholas was born in 270 in southern Turkey, when the land was mainly Christian, and rose to become Bishop of Myra. Today the town is known as Demre; locals revere their hero as 'Noel Baba' and his church is a major tourist attraction. The Bishop was canonised soon after his death because he restored to life three sons, who had been butchered by their father; and, in another grim tale, rescued daughters on the point of being sold to slavery for lack of dowry. He brought a sackful of gold to their home and all was well.

For those interested in the piquant, St Nicholas never wore a red gown. That was the Coca Cola marketing department's contribution to pop culture.

As we wait for 2015, nervous as usual about the future, one wonders if goodwill is too much to ask for and peace too much to pray for. Perhaps I should, like a child, stick to only the possible. May there be peace in India, and goodwill between every Indian for the next 51 weeks. The 52nd should look after itself.

COPYRIGHT ACKNOWLEDGEMENTS

Many of the articles in this book first appeared in M.J. Akbar's weekly column in *The Sunday Guardian*. We are thankful to the following publications for permission to reproduce the articles mentioned alongside that were published by them:

The Times of India: A House of God in Telinipara (originally published as 'Deep inside India, Secularism Is a Way of Life'); GDP Down, Gross Domestic Bitterness Up; Mahatma Gandhi was a Hindu Nationalist

The Economic Times: Why I Joined the BJP

India Today: The Great Wall of Silence; As a Matter of Fact; Goodbye, Sir; Death Takes No Prisoners

The Asian Age: Eyeless in India; The Culture of Political Cash; Speechless; The Answer Is Gandhi; A Chance That Came, and Went; Outbreak of Peace; Jinnah before 1937

Open: First a Democrat, Then a Socialist; Curse of the Game

Foreign Affairs (New York): A Conditional Caliphate

'Four Poets: Chapter and Verse' has been adapted from M.J. Akbar's foreword to Rafiq Zakaria's *Indian Muslims: Where Have They Gone Wrong?* published by Popular Prakashan and Bharatiya Vidya Bhawan in 2004. '*Aatish-e-Chinar*' is his introduction to Mohammed Amin's translation of Sheikh Abdullah's autobiography, published in English as *The Blazing Chinar* by Pragun Publications in 2013. 'Bahadur Shah

Zafar: The Death of Hope' is his foreword to H.L.O. Garrett's *The Trial of Bahadur Shah Zafar*, published by Roli Books in 2007. 'The Fourth Great War, for Modernity' was written as a theme for discussion at the plenary of the Halifax International Security Forum, held between 21 and 23 November 2014. 'Thank you, Jeeves' was written for the Tollygunge Club magazine.

ABOUT THE AUTHOR

M.J. Akbar was born in 1951 and graduated with honours in English from Presidency College, Calcutta. He joined the *Times of India* as a trainee in 1971 before moving to the *Illustrated Weekly of India*, then India's largest-selling magazine, as sub-editor and feature writer. In 1973, he took over as editor of the news fortnightly *Onlooker*, owned by the Free Press Journal Group in Bombay.

In 1976, Akbar moved to Calcutta to join the Ananda Bazar Patrika Group as editor of *Sunday*, India's first genuine political weekly. The magazine took an uncompromising stand against the Emergency, and fought press censorship and dictatorship. *Sunday* not only established major trends in journalism but also spawned a new generation of journalists in the country. In 1982, he launched what would be called India's first modern newspaper, the *Telegraph*.

He left journalism for a brief stint in politics in 1989, contesting and winning the Kishanganj seat in Bihar on a Congress ticket in the general elections. He resigned from government in December 1992 and returned to journalism and full-time writing. He launched the *Asian Age* in February 1994 with editions in Delhi, Mumbai and London. During this period, he was also Editor-in-Chief of the *Deccan Chronicle*.

In September 2005, Akbar was invited by King Abdullah Bin Abdul Aziz Al Saud, Custodian of the Two Holy Mosques, to become a member of the Forum of Islamic Scholars and Intellectuals, held in Makkah al-Mukarammah, and to write an agenda for the next decade for Muslim nations. He joined the Brookings Institution, Washington, in 2006, as a Visiting Fellow in the Brookings Project on US Policy towards the Islamic World, and remained till 2013.

He launched the *Sunday Guardian*, Delhi's first Sunday newspaper, in January 2010. In September 2010, he joined *India Today* and *Headlines Today* as Editorial Director; he left in 2012.

Simultaneous with a full-time career in journalism, he has been a prolific and bestselling author of major political works that examine the conflicts and challenges of the last, disturbing century. His critically acclaimed books include *India: The Siege Within*; *Riot after Riot*; *Nehru: The Making of India*; *Kashmir: Behind the Vale*; *The Shade of Swords: Jihad and the Conflict between Islam and Christianity*; *Blood Brothers*, a novel; and *Tinderbox: The Past and Future of Pakistan.*

He is also Chairman of the Board of Trustees, Calcutta Muslim Orphanage.

In March 2014, he joined the BJP and was appointed its National Spokesman during the historic general elections that brought the party back to office after a fractured decade.